W9-AVQ-471

SUBJECT TO
HISTORY

WITHDRAWN

WSU VANCOUVER

SUBJECT TO HISTORY

IDEOLOGY, CLASS, GENDER

Edited by

DAVID SIMPSON

Cornell University Press

ITHACA AND LONDON

Copyright © 1991 by Cornell University

All rights reserved. Except for brief quotations in a review, this book,
or parts thereof, must not be reproduced in any form without
permission in writing from the publisher. For information, address
Cornell University Press, 124 Roberts Place, Ithaca, New York 14850.

First published 1991 by Cornell University Press.

International Standard Book Number 0-8014-2561-1 (cloth)
International Standard Book Number 0-8014-9791-4 (paper)
Library of Congress Catalog Card Number 91-13592

Printed in the United States of America

*Librarians: Library of Congress cataloging information
appears on the last page of the book.*

⊗ The paper in this book meets the minimum requirements of
the American National Standard for Information Sciences—Permanence
of Paper for Printed Library Materials, ANSI Z39.48-1984.

Contents

Acknowledgments   vii

Introduction: The Moment of Materialism   1
  David Simpson

1. The Revenge of the Author   34
   Colin MacCabe

2. The Bioeconomics of *Our Mutual Friend*   47
   Catherine Gallagher

3. Domesticity and Class Formation: Chadwick's 1842
   Sanitary Report   65
   Mary Poovey

4. Visualizing the Division of Labor: William Pyne's
   Microcosm   84
   John Barrell

5. Emerson's *Nature*: A Materialist Reading   119
   R. Jackson Wilson

6. Keats and His Readers: A Question of Taste   143
   Marjorie Levinson

7. Public Virtues, Private Vices: Reading between the
   Lines of Wordsworth's "Anecdote for Fathers"   163
   David Simpson

8. Lyric in the Culture of Capital   191
   Frank Lentricchia

   Contributors   217
   Index   219

Acknowledgments

Six of the following essays began or first came together as papers in a conference titled "Materialism and Criticism" at the University of Colorado, Boulder, in March–April 1988. I am most grateful to those who made that conference such a success. The first and most substantial financial support came from (then) Dean Everly Fleischer; without it, nothing else would have happened. Other essential resources came from the President's Fund for the Humanities; from the vice chancellor (James Corbridge); and from the (then) dean of the Graduate School (Bruce Ekstrand). I thank the conference speakers themselves, including those whose papers are not reproduced here: T. J. Clark, Fredric Jameson, and Jacqueline Rose. Marshall Brown, then director of the program in Comparative Literature, was a constant source of advice and support. Thanks to Sandy Spahn's efficiency and constant good humor, we avoided all the nonclimatological misfortunes. Among those who rallied to outwit the traditional conference blizzard, John Flynt deserves special thanks.

The final manuscript and, most of all, my own parts of it have been significantly improved by the generous attentions of two anonymous readers for the Press. Not the least of Bernhard Kendler's gifts was revealed in the discovery of these readers, and he has been instrumental in the successful production of the volume from start to finish.

DAVID SIMPSON

Boulder, Colorado

SUBJECT TO
HISTORY

Introduction:
The Moment of Materialism

David Simpson

Readers sensitive to the conventions of book titles will notice the statutory artfulness of this one. A dialectically alert opener, *Subject to History*, is followed by the no-nonsense punching out of a triad of the most emphatic concepts in the lexicon of state-of-the-art cultural criticism: *Ideology, Class, Gender.* The paradoxical and the plain-speaking are both divided and connected by the obligatory colon, as if the first entails or is at least illuminated by the second. This is of course a means of having things both ways, a way of signaling at once the seriousness of these essays—for what is more urgent to materialist criticism than ideology, class, and gender?—and the revisionary or at least skeptical intelligence they promise to focus upon these now canonical terms. And this clash of styles in title and subtitle is more than just a ploy, for nothing is now more urgently contested than the nominal exclusivity and apparent stability of these well-worked terms: ideology, class, and gender. Their pseudoparticularity has been widely interrogated, whether in the form of antagonism (so that, for example, class has been argued to be prior to gender and everything else) or in the form of synthesis (wherein no one of these terms can achieve articulation without embodying each of the others as already a part of what it describes).

The social historians and political theorists have traditionally been consulted as the providers of a stable concept of class and have been produced as the still points in an otherwise turning conceptual world. This tendency was probably always a reifying and reductive one, but it has become spectacularly so of late, as the social and political historians themselves turn, precisely, to poststructuralist literary criticism for a revivifying model of historical inquiry. As Lloyd Kramer has remarked, "The one truly distinguishing feature of the new cultural approach to history is the pervasive influence of recent literary criticism, which has taught historians to recognize the active role of language, texts, and narrative structures in the creation and description of historical reality."[1] To take but one example, Gareth Stedman Jones regards the very term *class* as a "congested point of intersection" among all sorts of methods and discourses, and he calls for an end to the "essentialist conception of class."[2] He thus imports into history the same problems and paradoxes that literary criticism had confronted in recognizing the "textuality" of various forms of knowledge. To his credit, he does so less by way of a "triumphant manifesto" than as a "response to the breakdown or impasse reached by previous interpretative frameworks" (p. 24).

With the bastion of *class* given up, there is even less hope of finding a point of origin in the term *ideology,* which has usually been theorized as in some sense deriving from class, and has itself always been subject to a range of rival formulations. Thus, for many liberals, Marxism is just another ideology, while for many Marxists it is the major principle in the critique of ideology. Within and around Marxism itself, there have been important disagreements over whether ideology is false consciousness, and thus only partial and open to rectification, or a neutral emanation of each particular class consciousness or an omnipotent paradigm inevitably governing all thoughts and acts at every point in history. (I will return to this debate in my own essay in this volume.)

Gender, in turn, seems even less available as a foundational term of analysis because it is now commonly posited as a function of other

    1. Lloyd S. Kramer, "Literature, Criticism, and Historical Imagination: The Literary Challenge of Hayden White and Dominick LaCapra," in *The New Cultural History,* ed. Lynn Hunt (Berkeley: University of California Press, 1989), pp. 97–98. Lynn Hunt's introductory essay (pp. 1–22) makes clear that this new cultural history is, like the new historicism, very fond of anthropological models and very reluctant to posit a history that is not articulated as discourse.
    2. Gareth Stedman Jones, *Languages of Class: Studies in English Working Class History, 1832–1982* (Cambridge: Cambridge University Press, 1983), pp. 2, 21.

determinations (such as class and ideology), which it may indeed reformulate or redirect but which it can never by definition create. This nonessential employment of the term *gender* has indeed made some activist feminists feel that the cause of women has not been much advanced by this version of gender studies, even though the possibility of an alliance politics with other marginalized groups must surely be the higher for it. Teresa de Lauretis has argued that gender is always and only "the representation of a relation" that it reflexively (re)constructs: it is *"both the product and the process of its relation."* The social subject is thus "constituted in gender, to be sure, though not by sexual difference alone, but rather across languages and cultural representations; a subject en-gendered in the experience of race and class, as well as sexual, relations; a subject, therefore, not uniform but rather multiple, and not so much divided as contradicted."[3] This situation is good for broadening the references of a practical politics, but it requires for its analysis (an analysis that most academics by no means deem sufficient to qualify as an effective "practical politics") a cautious epistemological skepticism and an open-mindedness about how to describe any particular instance of social subjectivity. Without these attitudes, models of multiplicity and contradiction risk becoming as abstract and a priori as the single-cause models of determination they are intended to replace.

So much, then, for any imaginary simplicity to the pseudodefinite terms of our subtitle: ideology, class, gender. For it is the main title, *Subject to History,* that can now be seen to express the dialectical spirit in which each of these terms, and others like them, must now be deployed. We do indeed bring back the subject, but it is by no means as the figure understood in traditional humanist criticism as "the author" and as such decisively demystified by Barthes and Foucault among others: it is not at all this "author" who gets his revenge in Colin MacCabe's essay following this Introduction. Rather, we see here the return of a subject that is enunciated within and interactive with a range of histories (among them those of ideology, class, and gender), as well as being a figure of the past-in-present perspective that is criticism. The exact profile of this subject (or subjects) is not to be anticipated by simple a priori paradigms, but these essays often show a predilection for a model of subjectivity that is neither the

3. Teresa de Lauretis, *Technologies of Gender: Essays on Theory, Film, and Fiction* (Bloomington: Indiana University Press, 1987), pp. 4–5, 2.

old humanist agent of free will and free expression nor the late-Foucauldian conglomerate of totally preconstructed expressivities.[4] They suggest, thereby, that the debate about agency and subjectivity is no longer usefully kept going by embracing either extreme of the spectrum from total self-empowerment to total determination but must engage more and more with the difficult and perhaps even indecisive registers of the middle range, where theorists have all too often foundered in the face of evidence for the varieties and degrees of determination and opportunity (a better word for being metaphysically unencumbered, I think, than "freedom").

Another term now mandatory in this debate does not figure in the title to this volume: *discourse*, perhaps the most confused and confusing word of all. Here, let me simply point to an apparent ambiguity in its most famous exposition in the writings of Michel Foucault. In *The Order of Things*, Foucault tends to employ *discourse* to describe the nature and power of the classical episteme and its claim to total perspicuity.[5] For Foucault, the classical episteme was the expression of the most efficient functioning of discourse, where "being and representation found their common locus" in the paradigm of a complete taxonomical language (p. 312). The heyday of discourse was, in other words, prior to the emergence of "man" as Foucault described him, thus prior to the problems of reflexivity and disorigination that he sees as constitutive of the modern condition of knowing. This emphasis tends to give the impression of discourse as a totally determining power-in-practice, and it is this version of the term that has appeared in much subsequent writing, where it is used to suggest an omnipotent determination in the construction of subjectivity. Foucault himself has sought to redress this emphasis ever since the publication of *The Archaeology of Knowledge*. Again, in *The History of Sexuality*, he speaks of subjectivity as transacted within "a multiple and mobile field of force relations" that are never "completely stable" and thus do not produce static or completely preconstructed human subjects. Discourses, here, are always polyvalent, always subject to specific distributions. There is no monolithically imposed power structure but a "complex and unsta-

4. For a pertinent account of the "individual in history" problem, see Alex Callinicos, *Making History: Agency, Structure, and Change in Social Theory* (Ithaca: Cornell University Press, 1988), especially pp. 76–91. Callinicos poses as the major problem of his book "how to think of the relations between structures and agents" without massive reduction of the one to the other (p. 128).

5. Michel Foucault, *The Order of Things: An Archaeology of the Human Sciences* (1970; rpt. New York: Random House, 1973), pp. 307–18.

ble process whereby discourse can be both an instrument and an effect of power, but also a hindrance, a stumbling block, a point of resistance and a starting point for an opposing strategy."[6]

It is the model of the diversity of discourses that John Barrell's essay in this volume deploys so clearly. Although Barrell himself does not suggest the theoretical or empirical description of empowerment which Foucault hints at in *The History of Sexuality*, we can see that *this* Foucauldian formulation does come very close to a traditional Marxist explanation of positive class struggle, that is, struggle undertaken with the possibility of success. The "pop" Foucault so commonly encountered in literary criticism and quite familiar in much of the so-called new historicism is based on the earlier model of discourse as implied (though only implied) disempowerment. This tendency should probably be understood within the famously besetting preoccupation of Western Marxism and its related explanatory models with the experience of perceived failure—the failure of revolution, of democratic socialism, and hence of "praxis" in general—and the reciprocal political "success" of capitalism. Forms of expression have thus tended to be explained as forms of repression. This is of course a much simplified view of the history of the last hundred years, but it carries a certain generalizing conviction for intellectuals working within the academies of the "developed" world, not least because of their own (our own) professional interest in analyzing history through the mechanisms of culture and ideology.

These essays have another subject: materialism. Like Shakespeare as imaged by the Romantics, materialism is at once everywhere and nowhere in this volume. Its very openness to ongoing rather than achieved definition would seem to make it a promising term for describing the cultural criticism of the 1990s. And this kind of criticism—a materialist criticism—would seem to be the ambition of many among the theoretical and descriptive avant-garde in today's humanities departments. The more extreme adherents of deconstruction, with their attempt to pass off a reasonable attack on the weaker forms of historicism as a repudiation of historical criticism as a whole, no longer predetermine the conclusions of debates within the literary-critical

6. Michel Foucault, *The History of Sexuality*, vol. 1: *An Introduction*, trans. Robert Hurley (London: Allen Lane, 1979), p. 101. For a recent discussion of Foucault in relation to a strong-determination theory of power, see Frank Lentricchia, *Ariel and the Police: Michel Foucault, William James, Wallace Stevens* (Madison: University of Wisconsin Press, 1988), pp. 29–102; and Peter Dews, "Power and Subjectivity in Foucault," *New Left Review* 144 (1984), 72–95.

sphere, even though they must be acknowledged as providing a necessary vigilance over the "return to history." Feminist criticism, which has surely replaced deconstruction as the major unignorable term of inquiry (I do not say *essentially* replaced), has proved more and more (if never univocally) friendly to historical-materialist methods, whether they develop from the sexed body (a classical kind of materialism) or from the social-historical body/mind. But the very popularization of materialist methods, with their accumulating adjectival qualifiers—cultural materialism, historical materialism, and (let us not forget) dialectical materialism—brings with it another anxiety of definition. We may indeed be approaching the situation that Engels observed as characterizing German intellectuals in 1890: "In general, the word 'materialist' serves many of the younger writers in Germany as a mere phrase with which anything and everything is labelled without further study, that is, they stick on this label and then consider the question disposed of. But our conception of history is above all a guide to study, not a lever for construction after the Hegelian manner. All history must be studied afresh."[7] That is, the more familiar the words *materialism* and *materialist* become the less they will be thought upon or constructed specifically. As Engels observed, "*everything* can be turned into a phrase," upon which the critic's "relatively scanty historical knowledge" can seem to transform itself into "a neat system as quickly as possible" (pp. 61–62).

Against this perhaps inevitable domestication of terminologies, we might seek to uphold one of the most valuable principles of the poststructuralist initiative, that which requires all definitions to be understood as specific gestures *of* defining, without which they remain unacknowledged self-projections. In this context, we must inquire into every use of "materialist" for evidence of what is assumed to be *not* materialist, in exactly the spirit of inductive skepticism recommended by Engels. Otherwise—as with those other terms, ideology, class, and gender—our use of the critical vocabulary will remain precisely precritical, embedded within the very cultural matrices it is intended to call up for analysis. The maintenance of a more or less constant state of alertness is hard to achieve, whether in a single or a collective consciousness, but it should surely be projected as the ideal function of debate. One way of encouraging that it is (it can of course never be ensured) might be to develop the traditional eclecticism of

7. Friedrich Engels to Conrad Schmidt, Aug. 5, 1890, in *Marx, Engels: On Literature* (Moscow: Progress, 1976), p. 61.

literary criticism in the direction of a less opportunistic and more methodologically serious attention to the practices of other disciplines and subcultures. When we cease to raid anthropology, sociology, history, and other such inquiries for contingent illustrations and analogies and begin to engage seriously and in depth with the genesis of these disciplines *as* disciplines, then we will be well on the way to an understanding of our own. Reciprocally, we would then be in a more informed position to take seriously the divisions within literary criticism, which are currently often agreed to be subject only to political-consensual rather than analytic resolutions.

Those of us engaged in something that aspires to be a materialist criticism are certainly threatened as well as enabled by the tendency of the literary-critical subculture to label us an avant-garde, thereby proposing that in ten years or so the wave will have beached and the job will have been "done." (By the same logic, we should be wary—as I have tried to be—of passing "beyond" deconstruction, or anything else.) For those of us, meanwhile, still on the inside, the major problems arise from the increasingly evident false coherence of the term itself, *materialism*, the very term that would, if anything could, allow for the constitution of a movement or common cause vividly singular enough to command, say, a few photo opportunities for the *New York Times Magazine*. Partly this situation is the result of taking seriously the poststructuralist legacy that has made us suspicious of all definitions that go beyond the moment of defining itself and seek to roster themselves in the realm of the universal. Thus we are now more comfortable, and less socially out of line, when we employ the rhetoric of representations than when we speak of reality. In its classic forms, however, which will continue to inflect our usage even as we try to update them, materialism has privileged the language of reality, a reality that is either indifferent to the projections or modifications of human consciousness (as it is in the pre-Socratics, among whom subjectivity is simply not a concept for discussion) or is described in such a way as to contain and determine consciousness (as it is by most of the Enlightenment materialists) and to render irrelevant, except in exclusively sensational-physiological terms, all differences between one consciousness and another. Only Marxist or dialectical materialism (leaving aside those occasional deviations into naïve realism which are constantly emphasized by those hostile to the entire project of Marxist analysis) consistently offers examples of ways to explain how both representations and reality are necessary to an account of the produc-

tion and reproduction of cultural life, without either flattening out the
analytical model into a tautological indifference (representation is all
there is) or simplifying the relation between cause and effect to the
point that it is easily ridiculed by anyone armed with a few apt de-
constructive nostrums.

The Marxist tradition is, however, not only critically underrepre-
sented in most departments of English (as in the academy at large); it is
also, and reasonably, seen as radically deficient in its attention to the
major politicizing movement within the academy in recent years—
feminism. It is hard to justify the apparent underacknowledgment
of feminism by Marxist or proto-Marxist critics, whether one thinks
of the passionate defenders of a solidarity based principally upon
class consciousness (Raymond Williams, E. P. Thompson, Christopher Hill, for instance) or of the "high" theorists who have worked at
the construction of complex models of ideology and totality (Theodor
Adorno, Lucien Goldmann, Louis Althusser, Georg Lukács, among
others). This "sexist" legacy is hardly unique to Marxist theory. Feminism is a relatively recent element in the mass consciousness, and one
would not find it adequately represented in any critical movement
much before the 1970s. But Marxist theory takes the punch especially
painfully, because it has above all proclaimed itself in alliance with the
exploited and dispossessed, the vanguard of a better future. As such,
it might have been expected to have been more responsive to the
feminist avant-garde that was in place before the 1970s—in place
enough for even John Stuart Mill to take notice. Excuses may be found,
involving, for instance, the largely middle-class focus of most traditional (and indeed much contemporary) feminism. But the excuses are
not powerful enough to let a long series of male Marxist critics off the
hook, least of all for a generation whose own experience recognizes
the feminist moment as an unignorable fact of life.

The preceding remarks may serve as a brief and schematic rehearsal
of some of the questions pertaining to the specification of a "materialist" criticism. Conceived simply as definition, that specification is, I
suggest, impossible. And I do not mean to invoke the sort of glorifica-
tion of diversity that has proved to so many editors the most comfortable strategy for introducing other people's essays, least of all when
the very virtue of the present collection is its remarkable degree of
coherence in what it performs and in the problems it raises. The
implausibility of definition has in this instance much more to do with a

priority that Marxism and poststructuralism happen to share in their deliberate deviations from their inheritances: a commitment to breaking down the language of propositional logic and abstract theory. Poststructuralism is now quite well known for its efforts in this direction, mostly enacted within a linguistic frame of reference (it is "language," and/or its constitutive role within "metaphysics," which precedes us, makes us, and articulates us against or in spite of our conscious intentions). But Marxism also (and previously) gave us, albeit in vocabularies (those of historical and dialectical materialism) that have always been highly contested and often deemed anachronistic, a mode of thinking whose undermining of the language of universals remains the more powerful because of its capacity for constant updating and reinterpretation. This undermining is not limited to the reconceptualization of universal truth as historical truth, contingent on the rise and fall of the social-economic formations that give credibility to all such images of truth; it also includes (as poststructuralism seldom does) an inevitably (for us) uncomfortable confrontation with the complicity of *practice* in the very gesture of definition or interpretation itself.[8] Marxism is thus doubly historical, in both object and subject, and as such commits us to an engagement with the sorts of instabilities commonly known in the form of the hermeneutic circle, whose implications I will discuss in a moment. For now, let me just say that a Marxist-materialist method cannot function without reopening to critique those elements in the Marxist tradition itself which have seemed to rely upon what Althusser specified as a bourgeois ideology; that is, "the attempt to rediscover the world of history on the basis of *principles*."[9] This imperative, which is coincident with one of the major poststructuralist initiatives, is the more urgent to the degree that a Marxist literary criticism is already within an academic subculture that recognizes and rewards principally those intellectual achievements that are describable simply as such, as intellectual *achievements*. In this context, the easiest and most acceptable forms of "Marxist" criticism will be those (and this includes much of my own work up to now) that set out to objectify the social-historical dimensions of writings of the

8. I will surely be thought reductive here, since many critics insist that the recognition of the dimension of practice is the very essence of their poststructuralism. I would reply that recognition is not enough; the exact and particular implications have to be addressed in any analysis that purports to take this category seriously. Otherwise, we remain within the protective and self-confirming posture of irony and skepticism.

9. Louis Althusser, *For Marx*, trans. Ben Brewster (1969; rpt. London: Verso, 1979), p. 126.

past and in the past. Even these readings will surely prove threatening enough to those who propose the exceptionality of literature precisely by way of attributions of ahistoricality. But they are, fundamentally, within the fold, a fold that regards the past as another country, which may be accurately mapped without undue concern for the effects of the mapmakers and their tools.

The kinds of skepticism which inevitably follow upon a recognition of the roles of the mapmakers will, just as inevitably, sit very uncomfortably with that aspiration within the Marxist tradition which seeks to describe things as they are, or were, or will be. Against this aspiration, it has been the debate about the postmodern which has thrown up the most urgent ethical as well as epistemological objections. It is less helpful to speak of what the postmodern "is" than of what is being argued out around the term. Nor do the terms of the argument itself have an intrinsic and predetermined political valence. The case against rationality and totality has both a revolutionary and a conservative potential; it cannot be understood as a discourse with its own ineluctable laws, one way or the other, but can be evaluated only (if at all) within specific scenes and practices. As one commentator has observed, postmodernism "addresses a whole range of material conditions that are no longer consonant with the dominant rationality of modernism and its technological commitment to finding *solutions* in every sphere of social and cultural life."[10] If by "solutions" we understand proposed or experienced alternatives to the negative aspects of First World late capitalist cultures, then this prescription becomes quite conservative and could be taken to permit enjoying oneself as much as possible while the ship goes down, or onward. If, on the other hand, we take the negative attitude to "solutions" as stemming from a justified suspicion of the technologism and rationalism that have seemed to promise the experience of total control and total intelligibility while achieving, among other (and even some positive) things, the rape of the environment and the further subjugation of women, minority subcultures, and non-Caucasian cultures, then the political charge of this diagnosis becomes positively revolutionary. In the hands of those who are, like the critic just quoted, Andrew Ross, most astutely curious about the postmodern, this choice of ways is maintained as within the analysis, rather than as productive of simple

10. Andrew Ross, Introduction to *Universal Abandon? The Politics of Postmodernism*, ed. Andrew Ross for the *Social Text* collective (Minneapolis: University of Minnesota Press, 1988), p. x.

solution. The postmodern remains the site of a debate to which Marxist materialism must relate at all points. It cannot, however, simply acquiesce in the denigration of rationalism and totality as intrinsically repressive concepts.[11]

Totality, indeed, is another of those terms requiring more careful definition than it currently receives, not least because we tend to think less critically about what something "is" when we are in the habit of denying it.[12] There seem to be two models of totality now commonly argued against, the one diachronic and generally Marxist, the other synchronic and not at all Marxist. The second, non-Marxist understanding of the term employs it to describe the wholeness of a past moment, known as it was in itself, objectively. Much modern criticism contends that such knowledge is impossible, because we cannot remove ourselves out of our own present and cannot, indeed, know even that present except through the perspective provided by personal or subcultural interests. Being within history involves being subject to particular discursive or ideological constructions; there is no available position of disinterest and hence no possibility of claiming objectivity. The other model of totality, which is more properly Marxist, seeks precisely to involve the present (subject) in the construction of a whole that includes both past and present. This model too has raised some notorious problems, which I will describe in some detail later in this Introduction; its intentions, however, are clear and I think positive, both ethically and epistemologically. It seeks at once to describe the past and to recognize the principle of continuity which makes the past relevant to and constitutive of the present. Its goal is nothing less than an account of world history, and put in this way, it cannot but seem an implausibly grandiose aspiration. Indeed, its grandiloquence has been widely used to discredit the whole enterprise of Marxist theory. Nonetheless, the inevitable reductiveness of the grand vision should not be invoked to avoid what it does propose as a positive local imperative. For the failure to pursue the "global" connection has vitiated almost all literary-critical and historical work done within, and within the ideology of, the nation-state. To give but the most immediate example, all British literature, at least since the eigh-

11. On this subject see Fredric Jameson's exemplary recent statement: "Marxism and Postmodernism," *New Left Review* 176 (1989), 31–45.

12. For an attempt to expound part of the history of this concept, see Martin Jay, *Marxism and Totality: The Adventures of a Concept from Lukács to Habermas* (Berkeley: University of California Press, 1984).

teenth century and arguably well before that, has been inevitably situated within a national context itself implicated in the experiences of empire and colonization. But until quite recently the criticism of the national literature has been perfectly capable of devising accounts of its production and reception which are completely silent about this unseen dimension, the details of which have been eloquently available in the histories of Eric Williams and C. L. R. James, among others, but somehow passed over even by critics writing from the left. Recent literary criticism, most notably that written by Edward Said and Gayatri Spivak, has begun to redress this omission, so that it now seems almost as obvious to discuss the sources of Sir Thomas Bertram's income (in Jane Austen's *Mansfield Park*) as it had previously been to ignore them. And this curiosity about the "global" sphere only seems the more urgent in the light of the present crescendo of popular opinion identifying the breakup of the Eastern Bloc one-party states with "the end of Marxism." The recent efflorescence of work on the theory of race and its historical deployments adds yet another important dimension to this effort at transnational analysis.[13]

Marxism, then, seems to require a totalizing ambition for both its analysis and its praxis, as indeed for the articulation of any relation between the one and the other. Even if one holds to no grander claim than a continuing relation between surplus value and various forms of exploitation and domination, then one has the beginnings of a totalizing analysis. At the same time, the poststructuralist and postmodern suspicion and even negation of totality exercise a positive critical influence on this ambition, which should not allow itself to develop without the inspection of that influence.

I return to my earlier remark, that the 1990s would appear to be good times for materialist criticism. After all that has been said, perhaps I should be emphasizing the element of anxiety latent in the words "appear to be." Historical criticism, for example, is not necessarily materialist criticism, least of all when it forswears the experience of theory. What has emerged as the most fashionable literary-critical initiative since feminism (which is of course ongoing, and in many different ways) is the so-called new historicism. After a long period

---

13. For a powerful account of the consequences of an overrestrictive model, which we might call "pseudototal," in the work of Clifford Geertz, see Vincent P. Pecora, "The Limits of Local Knowledge," in *The New Historicism*, ed. H. Aram Veeser (London: Routledge, 1989), pp. 243–76.

through which one scarcely heard of any historicism except as a term of abuse, as the signifier of a naïve positivist practice, such a tendency to a *new* historicism might be expected to be good news for materialist analysis. But the exponents of new historical criticism have not escaped the accusation that their popularity may be based precisely on their inclination to avoid or deny theoretical self-consciousness (the anecdote replaces the proposition), either by pleading the innocence of the single occasion or contingent conjunction (a form of empiricism) or by affiliating with one or other of the aggressively simple theories derived from Clifford Geertz or from a particular reading of some arguments in Foucault. At these extremes, the new historicism would remain negatively as well as positively eclectic, never putting itself to any test other than that of self-evidence. H. Aram Veeser, editor of the recent collection *The New Historicism*, has found in the movement a seriously subversive threat to the "quasi-monastic" order of things in the academy but concedes that its exponents "eschew overarching hypothetical constructs in favor of surprising coincidences."[14] This celebration of contingency can, I think, be thought of as "subversive" only as long as it is nested within the postmodernist ethic of occasionality as in some sense libidinally liberating. Indeed, it seems more a symptom than a critique of what Stephen Greenblatt calls the "restless oscillation" and resistance to "fixed position" of a generally "capitalist" culture that for him comfortably includes both the past of the Renaissance and the present of critical attention.[15] This is an overhasty solution to the problem of writing about a past from a self-consciously present present: as long as we have this (distinctly overarching) "capitalism," no distortions or mediations need be considered. Frank Lentricchia, as so often, goes to the heart of such claims to self-reflexivity in finding them little more than a "badge of hermeneutical sophistication."[16] The gesture is made, but it is only a gesture, enacted to remove any distractions from the (illusory) immersion in the detailed richness of a historical past. It is this, indeed, that Marjorie

14. Veeser, Introduction to *The New Historicism*, pp. ix, xii.
15. Stephen Greenblatt, "Towards a Poetics of Culture," in *The New Historicism*, p. 8.
16. Frank Lentricchia, "Foucault's Legacy: A New Historicism?" in *The New Historicism*, p. 232. See also Walter Cohen, "Political Criticism of Shakespeare," in *Shakespeare Reproduced: The Text in History and Ideology,* ed. Jean E. Howard and Marion F. O'Connor (London: Methuen, 1987), pp. 18–46. Cohen argues that the new historicists' general denial of the effectivity of subversive energies signifies a "form of leftist disillusionment" masquerading as a "vaguely leftist sensibility" (pp. 33, 35).

                                                             David Simpson

Levinson has called *old* historicism, a practice whose fundamental project was "to restore to the dead their own living language, that they might bespeak themselves."[17]

Where the new historicism does propose a general model of determination for the events of the past, it has tended to embrace, as I have said, the "pop" Foucault of total domination or the Geertzian paradigm of semiotic saturation, wherein all facets of a culture are imbued with functional-expressive meaning, so that any interaction of text and context (or other text) is by definition charged with exemplary significance, representative meaning. Perhaps it is new historicism, then, rather than Walter Benjamin's "Arcades" project, that is most vulnerable to Adorno's criticism of that project. For Adorno accused Benjamin of, exactly, the worship of particularity, wherein details were "assembled but not elaborated," and the "conclusive theoretical answers to questions" were always held back in favor of the "wide-eyed presentation of mere facts." These facts could only arrest the critic and reader in a state of thrall, at "the crossroads of magic and positivism."[18] Adorno could see in Benjamin's work no "theory" to break the "spell" of this bewitchingly quotidian materiality and no explanation of the "mediation" that alone could position it within the structures of the *"total social process"* (p. 129). Terry Eagleton has warned us, in a similar spirit, of a certain aspect of the appeal of Benjamin to the liberal imagination in words that might, again, apply also to the appeal of extreme versions of the new historicism: "In the doomed, poignant figure of a Benjamin we find reflected back to us something of our own contradictory desire for some undreamt-of emancipation and persistent delight in the contingent."[19]

Benjamin's project is, however, mush more sympathetically and differently described by Colin MacCabe in this volume. Although it is possible to see more ambiguity and uncertainty in Benjamin's response to Adorno than MacCabe does in offering it as a paradigm of dialectical self-consciousness explained by analogy to an interpretation of cinematic montage, there is definite evidence for MacCabe's

17. Marjorie Levinson, "The New Historicism: Back to the Future," in Marjorie Levinson, Marilyn Butler, Jerome McGann, Paul Hamilton, *Rethinking Historicism: Critical Readings in Romantic History* (Oxford: Basil Blackwell, 1989), p. 52.

18. Adorno to Benjamin, in Ernst Bloch, Georg Lukács, Bertolt Brecht, Walter Benjamin, Theodor Adorno, *Aesthetics and Politics*, trans. Ronald Taylor (1977; rpt. London: Verso, 1980), p. 127.

19. Terry Eagleton, *Walter Benjamin, or Towards a Revolutionary Criticism* (London: Verso, 1981), p. 3.

major point, which emerges from within the (definitely poignant) articulation of the personal-historical despair afflicting Benjamin in 1938, a despair so powerful as to make Adorno's reactions positively cruel. MacCabe picks up and develops Benjamin's claim that the "base lines" of the "philological" construction must be seen to "converge in our own historical experience."[20] He suggests that it is this recognition of the biographical-historical present that breaks the spell of positivism, not the relocation of detail within a theorized social totality by way of an "objective" mediation, as Adorno had called for. We do not and can never have analytical access to a frozen structure whose details and interrelations map out an exact pattern of causes and effects in the historical past, for we must recognize at all times the constitutive energies of a historical present that is never static but always in process and always recombining models of cause and effect in whatever ways it requires to support its own foundational narratives.

This brings us back to a problem I have already raised, with the promise of a return: the problem of a Marxist-materialist response to the dilemmas generated by a recognition of hermeneutic circularity. MacCabe's interpretation of the exchange between Benjamin and Adorno might seem to have reduced the alternatives to the point of a near-Manichean schism: if one is right, the other must be wrong. If we are committed to a model of the past as available for analysis in scientific-objective terms, as Adorno seems to be, then we cannot factor in the present of the critic-analyst without wrecking forever the prospect of defining an autonomously coherent historical moment. Conversely, when we do factor in that present, and along with it the paradoxes of presence itself, we are committed to an always incomplete knowledge of our own moment of writing. Between the *an sich* and the *für uns*, there seems to be no place to stand: each becomes unknowable in the light of the other.

This is exactly the point, I suggest, at which a materialist criticism might begin its work, not by deciding for either Benjamin or Adorno (as here construed) against the other but by looking at possible ways of reconstructing the problem itself. Past and present need not be imagined as exclusive entities such that the integrity of the one demands ignoring the other. These are the fallacies of, respectively, the scientific-objective and the liberal reader-response traditions. We might instead

20. Benjamin to Adorno, in Benjamin, *Aesthetics and Politics*, p. 137.

think of the past-present interaction as producing determinate (because overdetermined) moments of intense interpretation, intense
because (like Wordsworth's spots of time) they somehow dramatize
those personal-historical conjunctions that motivate or provide an
interest to inquiry itself. Benjamin's "philological" method might then
require the moment of fixation upon detail precisely in order to move
us beyond it, into the theoretical-inductive procedure that Benjamin
calls "construction," which is itself what keeps us from "putting on the
waxen wings of the esoteric."[21] It is thus the puzzle of momentary
fixation (why this, why me, why now?) that moves us into a critical
reflection upon the variety of possible connections between our present and the past by which we are arrested. In this way, we may begin
to engage with the major questions of dialectical materialism as they
pertain to the interpretation of writing: what structures, what (possibly) objective continuities, if any, govern our (my) selection of some
details as more important than others in our construction of the past?
These questions are especially appropriate when large sequences of
historical time are under inspection (though they apply, of course, to
all writing, even that of the present), because it is in those large
sequences that the teleological aspiration of Marxist theory (the very
element that Althusser famously sought to decenter from *Capital* itself)
has depended on in order to describe the dynamic effects of class
struggle and modes of production. Lukács faced the problem boldly
enough, but only by resorting to explanations even less available to us
now than they were to many in the 1920s. He argued that the partial
perspective on history which the proletariat can adopt as the result of
its particular place in its present world (of the 1920s) must also come to
be seen by others as the objective truth of the whole of history. In other
words, the classless society that will result from the dictatorship of the
proletariat will produce a shared view of history which is also the truth
of history, the *end* of its evolution through time. The ideological will
disappear into the scientific because there will no longer be any division of interest to support different interpretations of the past. For
Lukács, this will not be simply a contingent development, happening,
as it were, through a series of unpredictable accidents: it is the fulfillment of the logic of history itself.[22]

   This is no place to take up the familiar problems of Lukács's He-

21. Ibid., p. 136.
22. See Georg Lukács, *History and Class Consciousness: Studies in Marxist Dialectics,*
trans. Rodney Livingstone (Cambridge: MIT Press, 1971).

gelian optimism. But his arguments remain important as a clear articulation of the problem we still face, with a much diminished political
idealism and a much more confused and complex intellectual apparatus—that complexity itself arguably the result of the disappointments
of the political sphere and the consequent need, so characteristic of
Western Marxism, to pay agonized attention to questions of ideology.
Let me give an (overbrief) autobiographical example. When I was
writing *Wordsworth's Historical Imagination: The Poetry of Displacement*
(1987), I was between jobs and between places, hoping to conclude, at
least for a while, a long series of displacements by "settling down." I
was, at that time, particularly exercised by the personal, historical,
economic, and emotional implications of work and property and their
implications for both public and private life. And I found these same
concerns all over Wordsworth's poetry (at least, up to 1807 or so). One
might conclude that because these things were on my mind they could
not be in any objective sense true to Wordsworth's writings, that I was
engaged in simple self-projection, reading myself through the com-
fortingly mediated forms of an invented past. But there is another
possibility, one that appeals to the density of what Benjamin called the
philological, to explain a conjunction between my own experiences
and the preoccupations of Wordsworth's writings. *My* finding these
things—anxiety about property and poetry, labor and leisure, class
and consensus, solitude and society—seemingly for the first time, was
neither a coincidence nor the result of any transcendent inspiration.
Quite the opposite: my own personal and social conditions (of which I
need not of course be completely, if at all, conscious) motivated a
preoccupation with the clues that led to a construction of an analogous
syndrome in Wordsworth. My professional (de)formation led me to
literature, a whole series of determinations led me to Wordsworth,
and so on into specific problems in/for Wordsworth. Once these determinations are brought to consciousness, then the inquiry must include
or even depend on an examination of the possible continuities between our two conditions, mine and Wordsworth's. This involves
no celebrative empathy of the traditional sort. In fact, it is an anti-
individualist method, which would look, for example (and I need only
be schematic here), at instances of complementary experiences of class
consciousness, professional insecurity, doubts about the usefulness of
one's "work" (is it even that?), and so on. From these moments of
philological fixation, one moves out into an attempt to construe the
continuities and discontinuities in class consciousness itself, and in

the energies that play on and within it. And at this point, we are on the way to a materialist history, and a dialectically materialist history at that. The question of how these analytical paradigms will be constructed and of what else there may be to say must remain an open one.

Such an analysis as the preceding paragraph sketches out would be one example of the gesture Marjorie Levinson has recently called for: to "articulate the past in such a way as to accommodate the contingency of the present," so that the present is read dialectically as the "delayed effect" of the structures of that past. In this way "our totalizing act thus becomes part of the movement by which history continually reorganizes itself."[23] This must always begin as a subjective criticism, which cannot assume, even as it hopes for, an intersubjective understanding of the paradigms it produces. For what is open to investigation is precisely the degree of general class or subcultural experience which determines such criticism in the first place. We do not yet live in the world that Lukács imagined, the classless society in which the experience of one is the experience of all, the desires of one the desires of all. The nonexistence of such a world has become almost an ethical first principle (diversity is all), as well as a perceived fact of life in both cultural and biological terms. And in the present political climate, it would be hard to argue that the effects of this understanding are anything other than positive. But literary criticism has not thoroughly accepted its implications insofar as it continues to write as if it were speaking to a professional subculture somehow unaffected by any determinations other than those derivable from an autonomous series of "literary" stimuli. Alternatively, where it has reached this understanding, its rhetoric is all too often uninformed by any aspiration toward a language that is not *just* (though it will always be) that of a special group interest. Whereas the achievement of total knowledge, knowledge of a totality, may well remain a utopian prospect, to deny it as an aspiration could well be to deprive our academic subculture, at least, of its one potentially effective motivation for reshaping the social world, for massive pressures are operating to dissuade us from combining diversities into any wholes more complex than that of "the people" or "our nation." As long as our aspiration for collective identity remains focused on the most implausibly totalized figments, those

23. Levinson, "The New Historicism: Back to the Future," in *Rethinking Historicism*, pp. 22–23.

most incapable of realization in social life (the people, the nation), then there can be no apparently attainable goals for social change.

It is Althusser, I think, whose writings still provide a provocative model for understanding these questions, both in general and as they pertain to the interpretation of writing. Interest in Althusser has been considerably deadened by the bitter polemics that arose around the discussion of his work in leftist circles in the 1970s.[24] But literary critics at least still have a lot to learn from them (I mean, of course, materialist literary critics). Arguing against attributing explanatory primacy to "His Majesty the Economy,"[25] Althusser made claims for a highly complex relation of cause and effect within social life, wherein a revolution in modes of production need not automatically and reflectively revolutionize those other elements we have tended to call (in what is itself a troublingly metaphorical word) the "superstructure." Whatever its immediate motivation as an attempt to explain (certainly not to justify) the coexistence of an apparently socialist economy with a Stalinist state and culture in the Soviet Union, Althusser's work still provides a useful prototype for formulating a materialist analysis in the wake of the poststructuralist project. His analysis of the social whole as marked by "uneven development" within the "structured unity of a complex whole" argues against both the Hegelian totality, with its single metaphysical energy, and that kind of economism whose "simple unity" Althusser forcefully demonstrated as untrue to the core of Marx's own writings (p. 202). Althusser was writing at a time when he could describe the vocabulary of totality as "very popular" (p. 203), and consequently all the more in need of definition. As I have said, the opposite conditions make the same demand, that of careful definition. Althusser argued that Marx's idea of history depended upon the principle of the *variation* of the forms of contradiction through time. This means, first, that they can be described only in terms specific to time and place and, second, that there is no possibility of an "essential section" (*coupe d'essence*)—a complete and objective representation of the historical past in any of its moments—without a lapse into empiricist history.[26] To believe in this possibility would be to deny the variations accruing since that time and modify-

24. For a fine account of the debate, see Perry Anderson, *Arguments within English Marxism* (London: Verso, 1980).

25. Althusser, *For Marx*, p. 113.

26. Louis Althusser, Etienne Balibar, *Reading Capital*, trans. Ben Brewster (1970; rpt. London: Verso, 1979), pp. 119–44, 177–81, 318.

ing the perspective of the present subject in its own history. But this effect does not cause Althusser to give up on the attempt to articulate "the structured unity of a complex whole." Instead, it makes different and difficult demands on that articulation, including, exactly, the diachronic component of the totality.

A reinspection of Althusser's habit of incremental totalization, cautiously but seriously pursued, seems especially important to a contemporary materialist criticism (and here I am again echoing Fredric Jameson). It is the postmodern ethic of incompletion—a validation of incompletion—that poses the most important challenge to any gestures toward totalization and constitutes the "grain" against which a renewed materialism must go, testing itself in the process of a creative antagonism. In its most familiar and practical implementations, the postmodernist privileging of disconnection and fragmentation takes on a spirited moral rectitude: let us not seek totality lest we turn into totalitarians. Seeking a way beyond what she perceives as the deadening dialectic of critique and ideology, Donna Haraway has argued for the libidinally liberating potential of the postmodern incoherence as leading to and stemming from a "subtle understanding of emerging pleasures, experiences and powers with serious potential for changing the rules of the game."[27] But totality as the goal of analysis and totalitarianism in political practice have not yet been proved identical, even if they are held to be so by some exponents of the strong argument for the synonymy of language and power or the unitary presence of power in language. It is certainly true that countercultural criticism has a tendency to collectivize and perhaps disempower the claims of all sorts of minorities preemptively, by the use of the language of "us" and "ours." But this is less a necessary condition of language per se than an unchallenged use of language in time and place. In fact, it is exactly because the identity of the marginal is *not* singular that the analytical aspiration toward totality remains important—important to an understanding of how the parts of the social formation are falsely collectivized into a whole, of how their various interests and opportunities are determined, of the exact forms of subordination they (variously) experience.

Althusser's emphasis on the "relative autonomy"[28] of those ele-

27. Donna Haraway, "A Manifesto for Cyborgs: Science, Technology, and Socialist Feminism in the 1980s," in *Coming to Terms: Feminism, Theory, Politics,* ed. Elizabeth Weed (London: Routledge, 1989), p. 196.
28. Althusser, *For Marx,* p. 111.

ments of social-cultural life that had all too often been located within a merely reflective superstructure—law, literature, and other parts of the "ideological state apparatus"—can still serve to direct fresh attention to the separateness of those elements, and to encourage the search for others like them at the subcultural level. Moreover, the explicitly Freudian language in which Althusser explained the operations of mediation—contradiction and displacement (p. 216)—makes his work especially fertile for an enterprise such as literary criticism, wherein the Freudian vocabulary is already well established thanks to its suitability for dealing with our commitment to the interpretation of linguistic and stylistic detail.

The potential complexity of Althusser's paradigm as applied to the encounter of a single human subject with a series of unevenly developed ideological state apparatuses also renders it particularly useful for an investigation of that element in the philosophical-sociological inquiry which has naturally proven most beguiling for literary critics: the category of subjectivity. That there has been little interest in this aspect of his project may be attributed largely to Althusser's own polemical commitment to a high theoretical mode in which theory (the *practice* of theory, no less) set itself deliberately against any dealings with the rhetoric of the various inherited humanisms, whether socialist, existentialist, or commonsense. Given this emphasis, any inquiry into the ideological behavior of single subjects (for example, writers or readers) must have looked to him like an acquiescence in the language of the opposition. Althusser's collaborator, Pierre Macherey, provided the most exhaustive application of the model to literary criticism, but his book (still in my view underappreciated) ran very much against the grain of the American avant-garde in the 1970s in its aspiration to nothing less than a "science of literary production" and to "criticism as knowledge"[29]—exactly the aspiration that deconstruction was most thoroughly calling into question. Macherey recognized this knowledge as a highly mediated identity, such that only critical rationality could expose the operations of contradiction, condensation, and displacement through which the literary artifact is produced. This artifact must, then, be "construed into a cognitive object" (p. 77) by the practice of criticism. But Macherey paid no attention to the moment of construal, to the position of the critic within his or her own historical

29. Pierre Macherey, *A Theory of Literary Production*, trans. Geoffrey Wall (London: Routledge and Kegan Paul, 1978), pp. 3–4. See also Terry Eagleton, *Criticism and Ideology: A Study in Marxist Literary Theory* (London: New Left Books, 1976).

moment. In other words, he paid no attention to the problem with which Lukács and Benjamin (variously) engaged, the problem that cannot be ignored by a Marxist-materialist project just because it is also the besetting platitude of a liberal-individualist culture, the problem that Althusser himself had at least recognized in his attempts to explain the absence, in Marx's own historical materialism, of a self-reflective theory.[30]

For these reasons, among others, that aspect of the assault on humanism represented by Althusser and Macherey has not yet sufficiently engaged literary critics in their inquiries into models of subjectivity, ideology, and history. Within literary criticism, indeed, the emphasis has been rather different. There were really two exemplary moments in the nineteenth-century departure from the philosophy of "man," and they were quite at odds with each other. They may be imaged in the names of Marx and Nietzsche, the first stressing the determining force of external or "macrocosmic" energies (class, economy, state, ideology), the second privileging the powers of the idiosyncratic and the perverse in mind and body. The first was used to justify an ideal of species solidarity and hope; the second proposed a posture of libertine resignation in the face of the likely disappointments of social and political life. It might be said that the bringing together of these two alternatives to the humanist legacy is the unfinished work of materialist criticism. This is of course no simple task, but it might, for example, expect to concern itself once again and in unprecedented detail with the activity and concept of *labor,* that intersection of the minuscule with the macrocosmic and the place where the grand impersonal forces of history register as the signatures of specialization and affliction, mental and physical. Althusser and Macherey remain, in terms of this schema, within the Marxist tradition.

But it has been the Nietzschean tradition (however far it may have diverged from the intentions of a philosopher who himself denied the authority of any such origins) which has tended to dominate (at least American) literary criticism in its curiosity about the relations of subjectivity to writing and history. The Nietzschean "genealogy," as recreated by Foucault, with its "relentless erudition" and its commitment to the preempting of any inquiry that assumes "the existence of immobile forms that precede the external world of accident and succession," has most effectively possessed the imaginations of literary critics, not least

30. Althusser, *For Marx*, p. 174.

because of its willingness to perform the "sacrifice of the subject of knowledge" and to renominate the "will to knowledge" as a malicious rather than a benevolent desire.[31] Where Macherey offers the apparently naïve ideal of criticism as a science, Foucault-Nietzsche insists on linking "historical sense to the historian's history" in a conjunction that is always "impure and confused" (p. 157). The "genealogy," in fact, readmits many of the classic categories of Enlightenment materialism: diet, climate, soil, physiology, and so forth (p. 148). But these are the categories that Fernand Braudel, for example, had used in the service of an anti-Marxist analysis. The interest of genealogy is not in the "dull constancy of instinctual life" (p. 153), however, but in the moments when that constancy is subverted and ceases to exist as such.

As an attack on the humanist notions of "truth and being" (p. 146), the genealogical is analogous to the Marxist project, but its emphasis on accidentality suggests a focus quite different from the Marxist. Just as Althusser's polemical situation led him away from any concern with a "subjective" level of detail, so Foucault's antithetical polemic leads him to underplay the definite potential in his own schema for a reconceived notion of totality (a tendency surely encouraged by the hostile criticisms of *The Order of Things* on precisely the grounds of apparent totalization, albeit on non-Marxist principles). But there may be nothing in the genealogical method that could not finally be worked into a Marxist-materialist paradigm, even if doing so involves some recognition of a larger measure of unpredictable and irrational accidentality than that paradigm has traditionally admitted.[32] And Foucault himself has elsewhere done much to encourage such a synthesis. Thus, in his famous essay of 1969 "What Is an Author?" Foucault made it very clear that the understanding of authorship as a historical construction requiring definition according to concepts of property and responsibility (capacity to be punished) did not involve abandoning questions of subjectivity but rather reconsidering them as discursive functions. We must then ask not how subjectivity gives meaning to writing but "under what conditions and through what forms can an entity like the subject appear in the order of discourse?"[33] This aspect of Foucault's

31. Michel Foucault, "Nietzsche, Genealogy, History," in *Language, Counter-Memory, Practice: Selected Essays and Interviews,* ed. Donald F. Bouchard, trans. Bouchard and Sherry Simon (Ithaca: Cornell University Press, 1977), pp. 140, 142, 162–63.

32. As a basis for such an attempt, see Frank Lentricchia, *After the New Criticism* (Chicago: University of Chicago Press, 1980), pp. 188–210.

33. Foucault, "Nietzsche, Genealogy, History," p. 137.

work seems to offer a fairly direct possibility of establishing relationships between the reproduction of discourses and the maintenance of the ideological state apparatuses.[34] But this relation remains, as yet, relatively unexplored, not least because Foucault's later work concerned itself more and more (despite the disclaimers I have discussed) with the analysis of punishment and repression as omnipotent forms of power, to the relative exclusion of models of complex mediation and of questions raised by the Marxist tradition at large.

A not dissimilar trajectory may be observed in the work of Roland Barthes, whose early critical writings were clearly responsive to the concerns of a broadly conceived Marxist tradition. Barthes was perhaps most of all responsible for directing us to imagine the writer as a textual rather than an ontological entity. But as his work developed, it gave less and less space to the historical-objective dimensions of textuality and more and more to the moment of reading itself as the function of a libidinal present. Even in *S/Z* (1970), arguably the most important piece of literary criticism of its generation and the book that performed its theoretical principles perhaps more exhaustively than any other of its time, we find that the motive for reading again (rereading) is explained not as the result of an intellectual aspiration toward knowledge—"to understand better, to analyze on good grounds"— but as the expression of a pleasure principle, as the desire for a "ludic advantage: to multiply the signifiers, not to reach some ultimate signified."[35] Barthes suggests that it is this pleasure in rereading, rather than any understanding it brings, that is most truly subversive of the rules of a commodity culture whose emphasis on suspense seeks to convince us that a book once read is finished, "deflowered" (p. 165), leaving its reader in a mood of longing, to be satisfied only by the searching out of something else to read. In this formulation, exemplary, I think, for postmodernism, understanding (the residual goal of a Marxist analysis, in its relation to practice) becomes a consolatory, second-order language. There can, it seems, be no pleasure in understanding itself which is not subject to the skepticisms called forth by the libertine philosophy in its negative attitude to postures of comprehension and incipient control. Barthes's Marxist peers, one sus-

34. I have discussed the explicitly non-Marxist and nondialectical implications of Foucault's work in "Literary Criticism and the Return to History," *Critical Inquiry* 14 (1987–88), 721–47.

35. Roland Barthes, *S/Z*, trans. Richard Miller (New York: Farrar, Straus, Giroux, 1974), p. 165.

pects, would have seemed to him not a little "uptight." And his emphasis on a disruptive present that was not itself situated in relation to any complex analysis of that present served finally to displace his efforts from a historical-materialist project. (A similar erasure of the historical may be attributed to the effect of Derrida's writings in their reluctance to distinguish the determinations of the specifically temporal-institutional elements of language from those argued to be general and atemporal, at least until the moment of breakdown of that Western metaphysics whose transitions Derrida never explained in terms other than those of language itself).

I suggest, then, that materialist criticism is still very much within and between Marx(ism) and Nietzsche, unsure of exactly how much of each can be worked into the other. Professional pressure is a hindrance rather than a help in this inquiry, insofar as it encourages affiliation to one or another special methodology within the field, maintaining a highly divided system of intellectual and pedagogical labor. Thus, quite unselfconsciously, many students move from one to another "approach" to see which suits them best. To the degree that we have any operative consensus at all, it tends to take the form of a general approval of the notion that all our theories should finally tell us something about that much-quoted creature, "the text." This is no bad thing, for if we cannot agree about much else, we may as well hold on to the faith that we are engaged in teaching reading and that reading is a complex activity. A materialist literary criticism will then tend to recognize the demands of this commitment to detail and will accord, at least in appearance, a good deal of respect to the language of induction. Feminism and gender studies, surely the most exciting of those methods that are familiar enough to be thought of as fashions, have raised so many so-far insoluble questions about "history" that the prospect of a newly defined totality seems farther off than ever. It is not, then, surprising to see that without prearranged coherence three of the following essays concentrate on the *career*. It is career that combines many of the elements of the materialist problematic—sex, gender, ideology, class, subjectivity—into an inquiry that has at least some (pseudo) empirical limits, a series of writings related by biographical or historical contiguity. In the explanation of the career, one finds variously weighted elements of the classic macrocosmic determinations (class, economy) woven into careful expositions of the details of particular writings and lives, the whole continually (and inevitably now) informed by an awareness of gender as functioning somewhere between the general and the particular. It is the career that evidences particular instances of the balance between action and reaction, initiation and reproduction, and shows us how structures can, in Alex Callinicos's words (following Erik Olin Wright), both "enable and constrain," both create and inhibit the powers that an agent has "in virtue of his or her position within the relations of production."[36] One should not be too confident that this site of mediations, the career, is not popular precisely as the projection of a generation of critics acutely conscious of the need to define for themselves a viable "window of opportunity," but as I have implied, this need not be a *reductive* connection: it may indeed be the very articulation that connects us with the exemplary bourgeois writers here discussed in these very terms. It may be, in other words, exactly that moment of "construction" which for Benjamin made possible a serious historical insight about both past and present.[37]

At the very least Levinson's Keats, Wilson's Emerson, and Lentricchia's Pound and Frost are textual-biographical vehicles for a whole range of determinations, not passive receivers of some inert totality but, to use Althusser's terms again, volatile participants in the "structured unity of a complex whole," wherein the complexity renders the structure itself unstable. Lentricchia thus finds in Pound and Frost not just authors but "signs of cultural forces in struggle." Against the grain of a critical convention that Marjorie Levinson aptly describes as committed to justifying (in Keats, but elsewhere too) "a march from alienation to identity," the critics in this volume collectively set forth and explore a plurality of determinations that redefine writing not just (and in the now familiar way) as the product of alienating energies but as expressive of the inwardness, idiosyncratic variability, and even integrity that those alienations assume. And it is the achievement of Levinson's reading of Keats's sonnet, of Lentricchia's reading of Frost's most famous poem, of Wilson's account of Emerson's *Nature*, and I hope of my own reading of Wordsworth, that these writings become more literary, more aesthetically complex, than they were before. The shrine of poetic complexity has been made what must surely seem a

36. Callinicos, *Making History*, p. 235.
37. Benjamin to Adorno, in *Aesthetics and Politics*, p. 136. That this conjunction is not just theoretically motivated but responsive to a long-abiding determination of capitalism in Protestant culture, might be inferred from John Guillory's important elucidation of *vocation* in Milton. See "The Father's House: *Samson Agonistes* in Its Historical Moment," in *Re-Membering Milton: Essays in the Texts and Traditions*, ed. Mary Nyquist and Margaret W. Ferguson (London: Methuen, 1988), pp. 148–76.

rich offering. But what does distinguish these readings from many others is the nonobservance of conventional assumptions about the differences between public and private, between the individual and the culture. (It is only one of the oddities of individualist criticism that it is generally so incurious about the cultural conditions that might be thought necessary to any account of individual distinction). These barriers have in the past tended to consign sexuality, for example, to the sphere of the private, but Keats, Wordsworth, Emerson, and Frost, as here read, are released from that privacy into a detailed historical-aesthetic typicality, yet a typicality that gives up nothing of its particularities (to a specific subgroup or class) and nothing of what we may recognize as individual genius. In demonstrating the synthesis of the personal with other determinations often consigned to the level of the alien or impersonal (class, work, the making of money) this criticism is attempting a comprehensive materialist analysis. There are now so many terms bidding for inclusion in such an analysis—race, class, gender, ideology, agency, and so on—that it has almost by definition to cast itself as an open and integrative account. If there is available no *assumed* master narrative that holds all these terms, and others, together, this materialist analysis would still be best served by addressing the question of which narratives *can* be proposed as connecting all these unignorable determinations. Without this attempt, our method will be indistinguishable from all those others which show themselves unconcerned with problems of totality and mediation and which are content to splice together luminous circumstances into exemplary images of history.

Much of the criticism in this volume remains recognizably literary and even canonical as it addresses the writings of Keats, Emerson, Frost, Pound, Dickens, and Wordsworth. That it does may be partly attributed to the requirements of the materialist method, which sets itself problems whose elucidations require detailed biographical as well as general historical information. This kind of information tends to be more available for the "major" writers, or at least more readily usable. The canonical turn, moreover, is a point of beginning rather than a significant conclusion, since the "literary" is always read back through its traditionally fetishized separateness and repositioned in relation to the vectors of more general social-historical energies. Thus, for Catherine Gallagher, *Our Mutual Friend* is to be seen within a tradition of critique of political economy based on an ideal of biological regeneration which is in fact shared with some of the political economists themselves but which turns out to be expressible only as premised on an antithetical condition of deanimation and reification. Dickens's novel is read against a general historical discourse that identifies the articulation of value with the extinction or suspension of life. Quite coincidentally, Mary Poovey's account of Edwin Chadwick's *Sanitary Report* shows how the image of housing functions as another form of deanimation, at once a response to the perceived threat of putrefaction, which was thought to follow from the urbanization of human bodies, and a prominent ingredient in the ideology of nationhood. Here, the boundaries between the literary and the nonliterary are completely erased as the rhetoric of public health is shown to mediate the languages of gender, class, career, and nationality. Again, John Barrell shows complementary syndromes at work in a little-known text as he describes William Pyne's negotiation of the demands of two antithetical discourses, both apparently necessary to the successful marketing (and even conceptualization) of his book and both responsive to the (various) positions of oil paint and watercolor along the spectrum between liberal profession and manual trade.

One could, of course, ask for more. None of us really manages to achieve a fully dialectical criticism of the sort Colin MacCabe sketches out as the legacy of a reinterpreted Walter Benjamin. But no one has yet produced that criticism, and if this volume signals its possibility and above all its desirability, then it will have done much. To have brought us to the point of understanding the need for such criticism may, indeed, be thought of as something of a breakthrough, in the propaedeutic sense. These essays, more than most, expose the inadequacy of the usual responses to the problem now widely associated with "reader response" criticism: the problem of specifying our own investments in and motivations for pursuing certain arguments and reading certain texts rather than others. After this volume, it should be much harder to make do with mere embarrassment, inarticulacy, jest, false modesty, or—an increasingly common tactic—a melodramatic, individualist, autobiographical pathos, as if we sense the need to admit the element of self but can find no critically historicized language for its presentation.

A materialist criticism, it seems to me, must now, and in the light of all the qualifications and self-disciplinary gestures I have described, call for exactly such a dialectical criticism, one that refuses both the liberal-individualist celebration of the present, with its pseudoepistemological confirmation of the ubiquity of "me," and the more widely discredited and equally implausible fantasy of a past history that is describable with complete disinterest. Since this criticism cannot (as Colin MacCabe makes clear) be arrested into fixed conceptual categories (in the sense of immanence) without bringing to an end the ongoing life of culture itself, materialist criticism will then be the Oliver Twist among methods: it will always find itself asking for more. It will ask for more both of its "objectivist" aspiration, that which at least *seeks* to understand the past as far as possible in its own terms, and of its subjectivist moment, that which seeks to understand the present as a function of both past and present. These poles are of course dialectically interdependent: neither can be specified without understanding the other. In response to the humanist tradition's privileging of the conscious subject and the special case, materialist criticism will beat the drum for all that is intersubjective in the formation of subjectivity and the definition of the exemplary. Reciprocally, in response to those who see only the crystalline structures of predetermination, it must search out a place for idiosyncratic deviation, the Nietzschean imperative—itself, after all, a variously materialist phenomenon as positioned along the spectrum between nature and culture. It cannot in principle choose *between* an empiricist and a dialectical history but must admit the evidence of both, using them against each other in the formulation of both connections and constraints. We need to know what can be said about how things, and texts, "happened," as well as about how they have come down to us and how they are currently expressed.[38] To those who recognize only one or two among class, gender, race, economics, and so forth, materialist criticism will set out to assess the operations of the others. It must even try to outdo the "classic" dialectical materialism in raising questions about the possible operations of an unworked nature, not assuming a determination already and always made over by culture, labor, or thought. Of course, no version of mere "Enlightenment" materialism will suffice as a complete description of the forms of interpretation, such as those principally addressed by literary criticism. As we have seen, such an account must reckon in the contemporary subject posi-

---

38. For important examples of each approach, see N. N. Feltes, *Modes of Production in Victorian Fiction* (Chicago: University of Chicago Press, 1986); and Peter Widdowson, *Hardy in History: A Study in Literary Sociology* (London: Routledge, 1989). Feltes details the variety of ways in which texts came before the Victorian and Edwardian publics and the effects of these means on composition and revision. Widdowson studies the afterlife of Hardy's texts in history—and not just literary history but also the history of the cultural and educational media.

tion in relation to any past that is being described, and it is therefore inescapably dialectical. At the same time, we would be ill-advised to lapse into the assurance that all questions about the past are to be mediated through the present subject position *in the same way* and with the same results. A predialectical materialism need not then be dismissed as simply the ideology of those professionally engaged in normal science. We can afford to ask, indeed, whether the model of a nonunitary nature—including, that is, an unworked or differently resisting nature—might not contain a more liberating and positive ethical moment than the kind of dialectical materialism (in science and philosophy) that has sponsored or accepted affiliations with technologism, Eurocentrism, and species imperialism.

Let me say once again that the kind of acquisitiveness I see as incumbent upon materialist criticism is not to be confused with mere pluralism, which admires the accumulation of diversity only insofar as it moves us away from any curiosity about totalities. And it is hard, given current institutional contexts and pressures—the demands, indeed, of our own *careers*—to imagine a community where the criticism here envisioned might be pursued to its most positive potential. In its utopian mode, nonetheless, materialist criticism can seek to present examples in which the consistent request for more is heard not as the one-upmanship of warring critics but as the articulation of a common concern. Some critics of course will have nothing to contribute to this effort; others actively try to discredit it or suppress it. Materialist criticism's common cause is not to be thought of as everybody's cause. Mental and verbal strife are not to be avoided. We do not live in a world in which we can expect to *prove* that a materialist criticism is the best or the only criticism. One can only ask for more in the hope that some relation emerges between what is asked for and the way the world goes. In turn, the way the world goes is not propositionally independent of what we ask of it, though it is tempting to deny as much in the face of academic megalomania of the sort that presumes an uncomplex effectivity for its pronouncements. To think upon these matters is already to do more than read and interpret "texts." At the same time, as professional literary critics operating within a recognized subculture, it is to texts that we must return and by which we will mostly be judged.

I cannot say whether I have efficiently answered a question raised at every point in the project that results in this volume: what *is* materialist criticism? At first, university administrators who were being asked to support a conference not unreasonably wanted to know what it was that they were funding. At the last, editors and readers have queried what can be said about this "materialism" in the light of a tradition of schools and movements—deconstructionism, new historicism, neo-pragmatism, and so forth—whose members have at least allowed themselves to be described as a collective, even though no oaths of membership have been sworn. If this "materialism" is not to be expressed in a series of memorable definitions, it may thereby at least hope to escape participation in the cycle of deification and demonization that so often constitutes academic notoriety. The compulsive openness to self-supplementation and self-correction for which I have called is going to seem to some readers a lack of commitment, to others a merely self-protective evasiveness. For similar reasons, presumably, Edward Said's model of "critical consciousness" has failed to catch on as a commonplace, definitive method.[39] That which sets out to respond to an ongoing history can never be reduced to a series of immanent propositions without betraying itself. There cannot be a finite theoretical paradigm for the prediction of situations within an evolutionary history (one that is yet, of course, composed of various kinds of temporary stabilities and relatively static structures): this, again, is the point of MacCabe's rereading of the Benjamin-Adorno exchange. But here is the all-important caveat (for today's market): to say this much is emphatically *not* to be against theory but to demand the fullest and most demanding engagement *with* theory, in every way and at every level. Totality and incipient generalization thus become methodological ideals: one looks for them, expecting that they may be there while refusing to settle for false promises. Perhaps "ideals," with its inevitable metaphysical connotations, is the wrong word, but perhaps, also, there is something at least a priori (and some would say metaphysical) about the terms with which one opens any analysis, until that analysis has gone through the process of exposition and set itself out in terms of a present consensus and a complex array of information from the past and, further, attempted some presentation of the possible relations between the two. Any place to start is just that, a place to start, and the kind of methodological purity invoked by those who regret the unavailability of absolute innocence can

39. Edward W. Said, "Traveling Theory," in *The World, the Text, and the Critic* (Cambridge: Harvard University Press, 1983), pp. 242, 247.

only serve to arrest *any* beginning and, ultimately, any actual self-consciousness, for once the transcendental is disavowed, then self-consciousness can never be without content.

In this way, materialist analysis is not to be identified with the inherited literary-critical worship of diversity and detail for their own sakes or, indeed, as polemical sticks with which to beat the explanatory ambitions of historians, social scientists, and others. The materialist commitment to incompletion must be accompanied by another commitment: always theorize, even when what is to be imagined is never a single theory or even a finished set of theories. This is a commitment to a constant exploration of possible relations between parts and wholes, pasts and presents, and of the various ways in which particularities compose themselves or are composed into aggregations by action and reaction. For reasons deriving from all these conditions, I have not sought, in this essay, to produce any absolute differentiation between Marxism and materialism, even though I have touched on some points where the traditional renderings of the terms have disagreed (for example, in the case of Enlightenment or pre-dialectical materialism). The academy has spent and is spending a good deal of time deciding what is and is not Marxism. But the afterlife of Marx's and Marxism's texts is so diverse and so central to *any* materialist project that it cannot be reduced to some prefigurative prototype or antitype. Instead, its flexibility and present potential are such as to exemplify the very point I have been making about the continuous articulation of presents, pasts and futures. Marxism, indeed, is so far from being out of date that it has hardly begun to be reckoned with by its disclaimers in any but the most vulgar and antagonistic terms.

So: much information is textualized; there are many kinds of texts; all texts are not the same. So: reading is continuously changing as the conditions that create it change, though in ways that are unpredictably (but eventually describably) mediated and not immediately reflective. So: subjects may be sometimes passive, sometimes active, and sometimes both at once in relation to different subcultural positions held simultaneously. These sets of qualifications may seem like wasted words to those of us with ambitions for immediate and enduring historical transformations, traditionally described as revolutions. But we do not know in advance the relation between any *work*, however apparently removed from the sphere of the practical, and the larger course of things. Thus we should beware, in the profound words of Raymond Williams, of "seeming to know in advance, and as a test of our political fidelity, the changing materialist content of materialism."[40] These essays stand, I suggest, as both exemplary summaries of recent changes and creative opportunities for a time yet to come.

40. Raymond Williams, *Problems in Materialism and Culture: Selected Essays* (London: Verso, 1980), p. 122.

1

The Revenge of the Author

Colin MacCabe

This essay is an attempt to bring into alignment two major and contradictory areas of my own experience. I have had few intellectual experiences that so deeply marked me as the introduction to the work of Roland Barthes in the late 1960s. Barthes's emphasis on the sociality of writing and the transindividuality of its codes has been a major and continuing gain in our understanding of literature and its functioning. At the same time, I have always been uneasy about the attempt to abolish notions of authorship entirely, and this uneasiness grew when, in the mid-eighties, I became actively involved in the making of films. The most general concern of the cast and crew of a film, not to mention the producer, is that the director know what film he is making, that there be an author on the set.

There is no more elegant statement of Barthes's opposition to the concept of the author than the extraordinarily influential essay titled "The Death of the Author," which summarized many of the most powerful theses of *S/Z*. Barthes's concern, in both the brief essay and the major study, was to stress the reality of the textual: the contradictory series of relations that a text enters into with the writings that precede it. The project may seem to have something in common with the New Critical attack on the author, but its aims are very different. New Criticism sought to liberate the text's meaning from the unfortu-

nate contingencies of an author's time and place. Barthes's attempt is
to liberate the text from meaning altogether. The author becomes for
Barthes the privileged social instance of this meaning. The massive
investment in the author which we witness in contemporary culture is
for Barthes an investment in meaning, an attempt to stabilize the
fragmentation of identity. Without the author as the crucial function
that grounds and identifies the text, we could begin to emphasize how
the text obliterates all grounds, all identities: "Writing is that neutral
composite oblique space where our subject slips away, the negative
where all identity is lost, starting with the very identity of the body
writing."[1]

Barthes emphasizes the priority of language in writing and derides
any aesthetic based on expression. All one is able to analyze in a text is
a mixture, more accurately a montage, of writings, and the writer's
only activity thus becomes that of editor—regulating the mix of the
writings. It is at the moment we grasp the nature of the textual that we
can also understand that the determination of the multiple writings
making up the text are to be focused on the reader and not the writer:
"The reader is the space on which all the quotations that make up a
writing are inscribed without any of them being lost; a text's unity lies
not in its origin but in its destination." But Barthes goes farther than
any orthodox kind of reception theory: "This destination cannot any
longer be personal: the reader is without history, biography, psychology; he is simply that someone who holds together in a single field all
the traces by which the written text is constituted."[2]

Where are we to locate this etiolated ghost of a reader liberated from
identity? How, historically, are we to place a reader without history,
biography, psychology, and how can we socially situate his, her, or (as
the lack of determination obviously includes gender) its emergence?
The answer is to be found in considering modernism as a response to
educational and social developments that posed readership as a major
problem. It is Derrida who has stressed a constant fear of writing in
terms of the inability of an author to control the reader's construction
of reading. Derrida's concern has been to indicate how this lack of
control is general to all situations of language use. What Derrida does
not stress, however, is the historicity of this problem, the particular
ways in which technological advances pose this problem in specific

1. Roland Barthes, "The Death of the Author," in *Image-Music-Text: Essays,* selected
and translated by Stephen Heath (New York: Hill and Wang, 1977), p. 142.
2. Ibid., p. 148.

forms to which there are specific responses. The advent of printing radically altered the relations of writer and reader, and our familiar category of author can be read in relation to that new technology. Whereas before printing all reading involved the prior transmission of an individual text, printing suddenly produced an audience with which the author is not, even in the attenuated relation of individual copying, directly related.

If we look back to the Renaissance, we find that the etymologically prior meanings of the word *author* stress the notion of both cause and authority without any special reference to written texts, but it is in relation to the new technology of printing and the associated new legal relations that our own concept of author is elaborated.[3] Once tied to the printed text, the national author of the vernacular languages re- placed the classical authorities—and replaced them by virtue of his or her individual power. There are few clearer examples of this process than Milton. It is rarely stressed that in beginning his famous attack on Parliament's attempt to regulate printing Milton explicitly excludes "that part which preserves justly every man's copy to himselfe,"[4] for its ordinance of June 14, 1643, was the first properly to recognize copyright. But Milton's interest in copyright and his minute concern with the exact details of his printed text[5] make clear how the new category of author relates to legal and technological changes.

Most important, however, is the new relation to the audience which is thus figured. The dialogue implied in both the popular dramatic forms and the circulated manuscripts is replaced by a literal petrify- ing of meanings. Milton's first published poem, one of the prefatory poems to Shakespeare's Second Folio, uses the metaphor of readers turned into marble monuments to Shakespeare's "unvalu'd book." The audience may not be universal, may be fit though few, but it is certainly not an audience actively engaged in dialogue with the text. The act of composition is the poet's alone. Milton's blindness and the image of his solitary composition is almost an essential part of his literary definition. But the solitary author gains, in complementary definition, the possibility of a national audience.

3. See Raymond Williams, *Marxism and Literature* (Oxford: Oxford University Press, 1977), p. 192.

4. *Complete Prose Works of John Milton*, ed. Don Wolfe, 8 vols. (New Haven: Yale University Press, 1953–82), 2:491.

5. See, for example, Mindele Treip, *Milton's Punctuation and Changing English Usage, 1582–1676* (London: Methuen, 1970).

When this conception is given a Romantic turn, the author ceases to authorize a national vernacular, but the new definition in terms of the solitary imagination and a local speech continues to presuppose, in its very definition, a potential national audience, although an audience now seen as at odds with the dominant social definitions. What brings the categories of both author and national audience under attack is the universal literacy of the nineteenth century, the production for the first time of a literate population. As the capitalist economy responded to this new market with the production of those mass-circulation newspapers that herald the beginning of our recognizably modern culture, we entered a new historical epoch of communication in which any author's claim to address his or her national audience became hopelessly problematic. Mass literacy spelled an end to any such possibility. There is now no conception of the national audience not threatened by a vaster audience that will not listen; the traditional elite strategies that defined the audience by those who were excluded are irredeemably ruined by those who will simply not pay attention. This historical situation is one of the crucial determinations of modernism, when all universal claims for art seem fatally compromised. Barthes's fundamental aesthetic is borrowed from the modernist reaction to this problem—a writing for an ideal and unspecified reader, for that reader who, in Nietzsche's memorable phrase is "far off," that ideal Joycean reader who devotes an entire life to the perusal of a single text.

There seems to me to be a historical explanation of why we get such a powerful resurgence of the modernist aesthetic in France, and it is to be found in the delayed but very powerful impact of the consumer society there in the decade from the midfifties to the midsixties. The fascination with, and distaste for, mass culture which runs through work as diverse as that of Barthes, the Situationists, and Godard indicates the extent to which the dissolution of the relations that supported traditional culture were widely felt and perceived. The paradox of modernism is that it fully lives the crisis of the audience while postulating an ideal audience in the future, it fully explores the slippage of significations which becomes so pressing as a securely imagined audience disappears while holding out the promise of a future in which this signification will be held together. The form of this future ideal audience has been conceived across a range of possibilities throughout the twentieth century. After 1968 in France, however, the favored solution was the alliance of avant-garde art and revolutionary politics which had marked postrevolutionary Russia and pre-Nazi

Germany and which theorized the audience in terms of a political
mandate authorized by a future revolutionary society.

Barthes's classless, genderless, completely indeterminate reader is
yet another version of the solution to the modernist dilemma, but it
preserves the crucial relation of author and reader bequeathed by the
national literary tradition. Indeed, that preservation can be seen in the
way that Derrida's project (closely related to Barthes's) was so eagerly
seized in the United States as a way of preserving the traditional
literary canon against radical curricular reform. Foucault in a famous
and almost contemporary article signals this danger. Speaking of the
concept of *écriture* and its emphasis on the codes of writing, he warns
that the concept "has merely transposed the empirical characteristics
of an author to a transcendental anonymity" and that it thus "sustains
the privileges of the author."[6]

It is the case, however, that Foucault shares Barthes's commitment
to those aspects of literary modernism which concentrate on the difficulty of the author's position. Beckett's "What matter who's speaking,
someone said, what matter who's speaking" acts as a kind of epigraph
for the essay.[7] Despite Foucault's emphasis on the need to look beyond
literature if we are to understand the functioning of the author and
despite his concern to trace the history of authorship, the entire article
is still written with an emphasis on the untenability of the traditional
Romantic valuation of the author as the originator of discourse. In
Foucault there is no consideration of the new forms of education and
entertainment which have rendered that position untenable but, in
the same moment, have opened up new possibilities.

It is significant that when Foucault does mention that he has limited
his discussion to the author of the written word, he catalogs his
omission in terms of painting and music: arts whose development is
contemporary with, and indeed dependent on, the evolution I have
sketched within national cultures. Foucault offers no discussion at all
of the cinema, which not only displaces the dominance of the written
word but also introduces radical new relations between texts and
audiences. This omission is in some way all the more surprising since a
mere decade earlier *Cahiers du cinéma* had half elaborated a new concept of the author in relation to cinema. I say half elaborated because

6. Michel Foucault, "What is an Author?," in *Language, Counter-Memory, Practice:
Selected Essays and Interviews,* ed. Donald F. Bouchard, trans. Bouchard and Sherry
Simon (Oxford: Basil Blackwell, 1978), p. 120.

7. Ibid., p. 93.

the *Cahiers* critics, François Truffaut, Eric Rohmer, Jean-Luc Godard, and Jacques Rivette, never saw their task in theoretical terms. Their concerns were polemical and specific. Above all they were concerned to accomplish two logically unrelated tasks. The first was to dispute the importance of the script for the construction of a film. They saw the weakness of French cinema in terms of its overvaluation of the written element in film, which failed to take account of the mise-en-scène, the whole composition of film, in which design, lighting, shot sequences, acting were articulated together to provide the very specific reality and pleasure of the cinema. The foregrounding of the mise-en-scène was accomplished by emphasizing the role of the *metteur-en-scène*, the director. This emphasis went hand in hand with the second task: the redescription of the huge archive of Hollywood cinema by selecting from its thousands of films a series of corpuses that could be identified through the consistent use of mise-en-scène, the consistency being provided by those directors (John Ford, Raoul Walsh, Howard Hawks—the names are now familiar) who could be called "authors."

The project is thus curiously at variance with the literary use of the term *author*. For Barthes the author is the figure used to obscure the specificity of the textual. For *Cahiers* the author, while sharing the Romantic features of creativity, interiority, etc., was the figure used to emphasize the specificity of the codes that went to make up the cinema. It is exactly that mix which makes for the interest and pleasure of those articles and no one was more elegant than Truffaut in his juxtapositions: "You can refute Hawks in the name of Ray (or vice versa) or admit them both, but to anyone who would reject them both I make so bold as to say this: *Stop going to the cinema, don't watch any more films, you will never know the meaning of inspiration, of a view-finder, of poetic intuition, a frame, a shot, an idea, a good film, the cinema.*"[8] The emphasis of this sentence, which I reemphasize, is the necessity of understanding film in terms of the relation between the fundamental articulations of the cinema (viewfinder, frame, shot) and the fundamental themes of great art (inspiration, poetic intuition, idea). The scandal of *Cahiers*, however, is that it insisted on the relevance of themes of great art to a form whose address to the audience neglected all the qualifications of education, class, and nationality which the various national cultures of Europe had been so concerned to stress.

8. François Truffant, "A Wonderful Certainty," in *Cahiers du Cinéma, the 1950s: Neo-Realism, Hollywood, New Wave*, ed. Jim Hillier (Cambridge: Harvard University Press, 1985), p. 108.

This position is interesting because it is a theory of the author produced both in relation to the materiality of the form and also, and this
is crucial, from the point of view of the audience.

The attempts, in the late sixties and seventies, to develop this concern with the materiality of the form and to analyze further the cinematic codes that *Cahiers* had been the first to bring into discursive focus
ran into inevitable epistemological and political impasses because they
attempted to undertake this development without any recourse to the
category of the author. The difficulties are clear in the pages of *Screen*,
which most consistently attempted to carry out this theoretical project.
The logic of the codes revealed in analysis was not located in any
originating consciousness but was immanent to the text itself. The
emphasis on the textuality of meaning, independent of the conditions of either production or reception, brought great gains, but like
Barthes's project of the late sixties (to which it was very closely allied),
it rested on very precarious epistemological ground, constantly veer-
ing between freezing the text outside any but the most general prag-
matic constraints (provided by psychoanalysis) and collapsing it into a
total relativism and subjectivism where the reading inhered in the
reader.

Parenthetically one might remark that it is not clear even from close
reading of the *Screen* of this period that the category of author was ever
abandoned according to the theoretical program. Perhaps the most
powerful single piece from that period, Stephen Heath's exemplary
analysis of Orson Welles's *Touch of Evil*, unites formal and narrative
determination in the attempt by the detective Quinlan (Welles) to keep
control of his cane.[9] When we consider the significance of the signifier
cane in Welles's own biography, then it is obvious that Heath's text as
we have it is radically incomplete, needing elaboration in terms of
Welles's own life and his relation to the institutions of cinema.

Screen's aim of producing readings independent of their grounding
within specific determinates of meaning was always suspect. If there
was great importance in emphasizing the potential polysemy of any
text, its potential for infinitization, and if there was fundamental significance in analyzing the transindividual codes from which any text
was composed, it is still the case that texts are continuously determined in their meanings. The question is how we are to understand

9. Stephen Heath, "Film and System: Terms of Analysis," *Screen* 16 (1975), 1:7–77,
2:91–113.

those determinations without producing, on the one hand, an author autonomously producing meanings in a sphere anterior to their specific articulation and, on the other, an audience imposing whatever meaning it chooses on a text.

It may be helpful in answering this problem to consider from a theoretical perspective the process of film making. However one is to understand the collectivities at work in the production of a written text, it is obvious at a very simple level in the production of films that it is directly counterintuitive to talk of one responsible author. Even a very cheap feature film involves thirty to forty people working together over a period of some six months, and the mass of copyright law and trade union practice which has grown up around film has largely as its goal the ever more precise specification of "creativity," the delineation of areas (design, lighting, makeup, costume) where an individual or individuals can be named in relation to a particular element of the final artifact. The experience of production relations within a film makes clear how one can award an authorial primacy to the director without adopting any of the idealist presuppositions about origin or homogeneity which seem to arise unbidden in one's path. If we are to talk of an audience for a film, then, at least in the first instance, that audience cannot be theorized in relation to the empirical audience or to the readings that audience produces. So varied are the possibilities of such readings and so infinite the determinations that enter into such a calculation that it is an impossible task. Indeed, were it possible to calculate the readings produced by any specific film, then the Department of Reader Response would be the most important section of any film studio, and Hollywood would be a less anxious place with much greater security of tenure.

Any future audience can be approached only through the first audience for the film—the cast and crew who produced it. It is the director's skill in making others work together to produce a film, which is of necessity invisible at the outset, which determines the extent to which the film will be successfully realized. It is the collective determination to make visible something that has not been seen before which marks the successful production of a film, and it is insofar as the producers of the film are also its first audience that we can indicate the dialectic that places the author not outside the text but within the process of its production. It might be said further that such an analysis provides an ethic that is certainly important and may be crucial in differentiating among the numerous productions of the new popular forms of capitalist culture. I venture to suggest that those elements in popular culture which genuinely mark important areas of desire and reflection are those where the producers have been concerned in the first place to make something for themselves. Where the determination is simply to produce a work for a predefined audience from which the producers exclude themselves, one will be dealing with that meretricious and toxic repetition that is the downside of the new forms of mechanical and electronic production. A further generalization would be that genuine creativity in popular culture is constantly to be located in relation to emergent and not yet fully defined audiences.

The process of film making indicates not only how the moment of creation integrally entails the figuring of the audience but also how that audience is figured in relation to a reality that thus achieves social effectivity. This is a solution to the problem of realism which avoids both the trap of representation (which elides the effectivity of the textual) and the snare of endless textuality (which endlessly defers the text's relation to the real). The repositioning of the reader or viewer by the work of art in relation to a social reality is thereby altered by the repositioning that allows the traditional heuristic and oppositional claims of realism without its traditional epistemology.[10]

Considerations of this order enable us to conceptualize the author as a contradictory movement within a collectivity rather than as a homogeneous, autonomous, and totalizing subject. If the process of film making allows us an obvious way of seeing the author in a plurality of positions, it should not be taken as an empirical formula for the studying of authors. If one were to take a specific film and attempt to constitute the author in relation to this first audience, one would be faced by a multiplication of the determinations on that audience to a level that makes any exhaustive analysis not simply technically but theoretically impossible. The usefulness of the film analogy, and the usefulness of the *Cahiers* critics who deliberately adopted a position similar to that of experienced technicians, is that it indicates the multiplicity of positions in which we must locate the author. It should not be thought, however, that the theoretical task is to specify a typology of positions which would then allow us to specify the determinations that would limit the possible meanings of the texts in relation to possible positions in which it could be produced and received. Such a

10. For details of this argument, see my "Realism: Balzac and Barthes," in Colin MacCabe, *Theoretical Essays: Film, Linguistics, Literature* (Manchester: Manchester University Press, 1985), pp. 130–50.

dream of scientific rigor discounts that our own position as reader is always present in any such calculation and that the very fact of a future allows for positions as yet unaccounted for. It should be stressed at this point that infinity once again becomes a real term in the analysis.

The difference between this conception of infinity, however, and Barthes's, is that whereas Barthes's is located in some atemporal and idealist account of meaning, this infinity is rooted in a historical and materialist account of significations. Marx so dominates our thinking about materialism that it may seem at first that any conception of infinite determinations is hostile to materialism. For over two millennia, however, it was the commitment to an infinity of worlds that distinguished materialist thought from the variety of religious views to which it was opposed. Indeed, it may well be that Marx's own unwillingness to produce the philosophy of dialectical materialism derived from his understanding of the centrality of infinity to any materialist philosophy.

If we are to understand the implications of these considerations for any practice of criticism, there is no doubt that the only place to start is with the most important example we have of materialist criticism: Walter Benjamin's fragments, *Charles Baudelaire: A Lyric Poet in the Era of High Capitalism.*[11] In a stunning tour de force Benjamin commences with an analysis of Baudelaire's physiognomy and its resemblance to that of a professional conspirator and then weaves in and out of the social and literary text as he moves from the taverns where the political conspirators gather to the question of the wine tax and how the tax relates to the poem on the ragpicker. He reintegrates the question of wine into the social spectacle of Paris—as the drunk family weaves its way home—and into its political economy: the *vin de la barrière* produced by the wine tax absorbs several social pressures that might otherwise threaten the government. Benjamin's method is to start with the *doxa* of nineteenth century life and to work through until connections begin to reveal themselves. Eschewing any theory of mediations, he uses montage to imbricate the literary and social text. There is no question of judging this method in terms of cause and effect within a social totality (all of which categories in this context become idealist): the crucial causal relation is between the analyst and the past and is a truly dialectical one in which the proofs of a reading

11. Walter Benjamin, *Charles Baudelaire: A Lyric Poet in the Era of High Capitalism*, trans. Harry Zohn (London: New Left Books, 1973).

develop in the analysis. Such methods are extremely alien to academic thought, and it is not surprising that the academic Theodor Adorno was so repelled by this text. In that most discouraging of letters which he sends to Benjamin in November 1938 he takes almost personal exception to "that particular type of concreteness and its behavioristic overtones" and warns Benjamin that "materialist determination of cultural traits is only possible if it is mediated through the *total social process.*"[12] But to imagine that the social process can be totalized is to misunderstand the living relation of the present, which determines that the past can be totalized only for now. It has no totality in itself but rather an infinite number of possibilities vis-à-vis a future it cannot know but which will bring it to life.

Benjamin saw quite clearly that the notion of "totality" and its associated concept of mediation were attractive because they were an attempt to fetishize the past into a controllable finitude and to avoid the risks of scholarly engagement in the present. His reply to Adorno stresses the personal basis of his own study and his need to keep the contradictions of his personal concerns in tension with "the experiences which all of us have shared in the past 15 years." He distinguishes sharply between this productive contradiction and a "mere loyalty to dialectical materialism." Indeed, so deep and productive is the opposition between the personal and the social that Benjamin refers to it as "an antagonism of which I would not even in my dreams wish to be relieved." And he goes on to state that "the overcoming of this antagonism constitutes the problem of my study."[13] It seems to me that his disagreement with Adorno was to dominate his thoughts for the short period of life that remained. The major text of that period is the fulgurant and elliptical paragraphs which compose the theses on the philosophy of history. I now find it impossible to read those paragraphs except as a prolonged and meditated reply to the *bêtise* of Adorno's letter. The constant opposition between the historicist and the historical materialist is fully comprehensible only if we read the text, in large measure, as an expression of the opposition between Adorno and himself. Every line of that remarkable text repays study, but for current purposes I want merely to quote the first half of the sixteenth thesis: "An historical materialist cannot do without the notion of a present which is not a transition, but in which time stands still

12. Adorno to Benjamin in Ernst Bloch, Georg Lukács, Bertolt Brecht, Walter Benjamin, Theodor Adorno, *Aesthetics and Politics* (London: New Left Books, 1976), p. 129.
13. Benjamin to Adorno, in *Aesthetics and Politics*, p. 136.

and has come to a stop. For this notion defines the present in which he himself is writing history. Historicism gives the 'eternal' image of the past; historical materialism supplies a unique experience with the past."[14]

Benjamin here makes clear the extent to which the critic enters into a full relation with the past in which his or her present reveals the past as it is for us. The crucial problem here is how we are to understand that "us." How does the critic's (and notice that the term must here be considered interchangeable with historian) personal constitution relate to any wider social collectivity? Where Adorno relies on concepts of totality and mediation to constitute a fixed social past, Benjamin in the theses relentlessly uses the concept of "class struggle" to locate us in a mobile social present. The virtue of the concept is that it emphasizes contradiction and division; its weakness is that it is very doubtful that any current definition of class, either Marxist or sociological, will not limit its contents to a reductive notion of the economic. The rhetorical function this concept plays in the theses cannot be sustained when it is given any substantial investigation. Benjamin would find himself limited to another form of the Adorno criticism from those who would demand "political correctness" in the present rather than "the total social process" in the past.

To elaborate Benjamin it would be necessary to build some notion of a social unconscious into the notion of class struggle. It is interesting that in early drafts of the "Arcades" project Benjamin had relied on Jung, for it is Jung, of course, who does propose a transindividual unconscious. Unfortunately Jung's concept of the collective unconscious is so historically unspecific that it is completely unequal to the task proposed. But the references to both Jung and Georg Simmel are not to be condemned from the pious position of the orthodox Adorno. They indicate a dimension that must be added to notions of class struggle which would radically transform that notion.

Without presuming on the content of such a transformation, one can indicate some of the effects of introducing the unconscious into the investigation of the past. The historical critic, the critical historian, brings to the past the currency of his or her own epoch; the effort to make the past speak must inevitably draw on resources of which the critic is unaware and which appear only in the construction of the past.

14. Walter Benjamin, *Illuminations: Essays and Reflections*, trans. Harry Zohn (London: New Left Books, 1973), p. 264.

The risks are considerable and there can be no question of guarantees. Adorno recalled Benjamin's remarking that each idea of the "Arcades" project had to be wrested away from a realm in which madness reigns, a realm in which the distinction between the nonsensically individual and the significantly collective disappears.[15] In this respect a critical work shares significant similarities with the creative work it analyzes. The author finds him- or herself in their audience.

15. Adorno to Benjamin, in *Aesthetics and Politics*, p. 127.

2

The Bioeconomics of
Our Mutual Friend

Catherine Gallagher

Our Mutual Friend draws on an antithesis that John Ruskin had named in *Unto This Last* (1862) a few years before the novel appeared: that of wealth and illth. In developing this antithesis, Ruskin began with a question that anticipated in striking detail the opening chapter of Dickens's novel: "If we may conclude generally that a dead body cannot possess property, what degree and period of animation in the body will render possession possible?"[1] In the first chapter of *Our Mutual Friend*, Gaffer Hexam also insists on the absurdity of the idea that a dead man can possess property. He raves: "Has a dead man any use for money? Is it possible for a dead man to have money? How can money be a corpse's? Can a corpse own it, want it, spend it, claim it, miss it?"[2] Gaffer seems to think that these questions automatically call for a negative reply: "No, a dead body cannot possess property." The novel, however, not only leaves this issue open but also goes on to ask Ruskin's more complicated question, the one that introduces the pos-

This essay first appeared in *Fragments for a History of the Human Body: Part 3*, ed. Michel Feher, Ramona Naddaff, Nadia Tazi (New York: Zone Publications, 1989), pp. 345–65. Thanks to Zone Publications for permission to reprint it here.

1. John Ruskin, *Unto This Last and Other Essays on Art and Political Economy*, ed. Ernest Rhys (New York: Dutton, 1932), p. 169, hereafter cited in the text.

2. Charles Dickens, *Our Mutual Friend* (London: Oxford University Press, 1974), p. 4, hereafter cited in the text.

sibility of "illth": what degree of health, of life, of animation, is necessary before the body can be properly said to possess something? Ruskin's question turns into an anecdote, like the one that opens *Our Mutual Friend*, of drowning and dredging up:

> Lately in a wreck of a California ship, one of the passengers fastened a belt about him with two hundred pounds of gold in it, with which he was found afterwards at the bottom. Now, as he was sinking—had he the gold? or had the gold him?
>
> And if, instead of sinking him in the sea by its weight, the gold had struck him on the forehead, and thereby caused incurable disease— suppose palsy or insanity,—would the gold in that case have been more a "possession" than in the first? Without pressing the inquiry up through instances of gradually increasingly vital power over the gold . . . , I presume that the reader will see that possession . . . is not an absolute, but a graduated power; and consists not only in the . . . thing possessed, but also . . . in the possessor's vital power to use it. (Pp. 169–170)

Ruskin, it seems, begins his investigation into the nature of economic value with death in order to root wealth in bodily well-being. Wealth, he concludes, is the possession of useful things by those who can use them. Useful things are those that nurture life, and those who can use them are those who are (at the very least) in a state of bodily animation. To the degree that possessions cause bodily harm, as in the story of the drowned man, to the degree that they incapacitate or make people ill, they are "illth."

The hero of *Our Mutual Friend*, John Harmon, is closely identified with, indeed, is identified as, the drowned body dredged up by Gaffer Hexam in chapter 1. As a possessor of gold, he has also suffered the action of illth, for he has been murdered for the sake of his money. We might say that this story is Ruskin's retold, although in Dickens's version both the man and the gold have surrogates. George Radfoot takes Harmon's place and, as Harmon later explains, is "murdered for the money" by "unknown hands," conceived merely as extensions of what Harmon calls "the fate that seemed to have fallen on my father's riches—the fate that they should lead to nothing but evil" (p. 370). Thus, John Harmon is officially drowned and dredged up at the novel's outset, a victim of illth. After being proclaimed dead, he staggers dazed through the novel's opening episodes, as if, following the stages of Ruskin's inquiry, he had reached the state of merely being wounded in the forehead by his would-be riches. The question that drives the plot is the same as that asked by Ruskin: what degree of animation in the formerly dead man would be necessary to render possible his possession of (instead of by) his money? "Should John Harmon come to life again?" the hero keeps asking. If he were to reanimate himself, gradually working his way from dead to ill to well, could he change illth to wealth?

The point of making these parallels between *Unto This Last* and *Our Mutual Friend* is not to argue that Dickens got the germ of the novel from Ruskin. It is rather to direct attention to a pervasive pattern of mid-Victorian thought, a widespread insistence that economic value can be determined only in close relation to bodily well-being. In several key texts on economics, sanitation, social theory, and aesthetics, this "new" way of restructuring economic investigations around the human body took the dead body as a starting place and tried to move toward reanimation. As I hope to show through an analysis of *Our Mutual Friend*, however, this operation often resulted in the reseparation of value (equated with life) from any of its particular instantiations (or bodies). That is, the attempt to resituate the human body at the center of economic concerns, to rewrite economic discourse so that it constantly referred back to the body's well-being, paradoxically itself tended to do what it accused unreconstructed political economists of doing: separating value from flesh and blood, conditioning value on a state of suspended animation or apparent death.

Ruskin and Dickens were by no means pioneers in the attempt to pose the question of value in terms of bodily well-being. Indeed, their effort has a history within political economy itself. We normally think of Ruskin and Dickens as part of a specifically literary moral reaction against the Victorian forces of commercialism and social alienation, and political economists are often singled out as the ideological vanguard of heartless laissez-faire capitalism. Certainly, this was often the self-understanding of Ruskin and Dickens. Ruskin quite explicitly wrote *Unto This Last* as a polemic against classical political economy, and Dickens, although far from systematic in confronting any system, nevertheless wrote of the "dismal science" as an enterprise devoted to the justification of particular human suffering. Ebenezer Scrooge epitomizes this bland insensitivity to individual pain when he suggests that the indigent ought to die and "reduce the surplus population."

As this quotation suggests, Thomas Malthus's epoch-making *Essay on Population* (1797) was often identified as the most outrageously hardhearted book in the whole hardhearted economic canon. Malthus was accused of setting population increase against economic well-being, of viewing a populous nation as one on the brink of disaster. Ignoring the complexities of Malthus's argument as well as its polemical situation within the debate over the perfectibility of man, his humane critics saw only a devaluation of human life in his essay and accused him of trying to found the wealth of nations on the death of babies. The zest with which he is alleged to have described the positive checks to population (death by starvation, infanticide) scandalized many reviewers, who characterized Malthus as a ghoul. He had built death, physical misery, and vice (the prevention of conception) into the base of the economic structure. He had inaugurated what was seen as a negative bioeconomics in which economic well-being (a balance of resources and consumption) could be achieved only through the devastation or prevention of life.

Like Dickens in his portrayal of Scrooge, Ruskin also implies that Malthusianism is the original sin of political economy, the most blatant division of economic value from embodied human life. He tries to reconnect economic and bodily health rhetorically, through etymology, deriving value from "*valor* from *valere*, to be well, or strong . . . ; strong *in* life (if a man), or valiant; strong, *for* life (if a thing), or valuable. To be 'valuable,' therefore, is to 'avail towards life'" (p. 168). Ruskin faults the political economists for calculating the values of commodities without regard either to their potential for sustaining and enhancing life or to the ability and willingness of their possessors to activate that potential. Ruskin's economic essays constantly return to this theme: the political economists have abstracted value, severed it from flesh and blood. "The true veins of wealth," he writes, "are purple—and not in Rock but in Flesh . . . ; the final outcome and consummation of all wealth is in the producing as many as possible full-breathed, bright-eyed, and happy-hearted human creatures" (p. 144). That contrast—blood veins in flesh versus metalic veins in rock—is at least as old as the Midas myth, but in the nineteenth-century it took on a new urgency and specificity. It was directed not simply against human greed or miserliness but against what many of Ruskin's contemporaries saw as a terribly destructive economic orthodoxy that was determining social reality.

Ruskin's statement about the purple veins of wealth, like Dickens's characterization of Scrooge, asserts the rights of human bodies against the doctrines of political economy generally and those of Thomas Malthus specifically. In fact, however, on this point Malthus himself fully anticipated these self-proclaimed anti-Malthusians. The relationship between bodily well-being and economic value was not, as Ruskin and Dickens seemed to think, a blind spot of political economy but, rather, one of that discipline's most problematic obsessions. And no one had treated the issue in terms closer to Ruskin's own than Malthus himself. I do not have space enough here to describe the paradoxical complexity of Malthus's *Essay on the Principle of Population*.[3] Suffice it to say that although Malthus undeniably made bodies socially and economically problematic, he did so, paradoxically, by ceding all value to them rather than removing value from them. Malthus, like Ruskin and Dickens, also polemicized against the abstracting tendencies of other political economists, and although he certainly feared overpopulation, he gave (at least in the first edition of the essay) no definition of value which can distinguish it from flesh. It was Malthus who first deplored Adam Smith's failure to distinguish among commodities on the basis of their *biological* usefulness; indeed, Malthus at times seems an even more fanatical proponent of the idea that value is embodied in flesh than Ruskin, for he goes so far as to suggest that the only productive labor is that which produces working-class food, that is, that the production of more laboring flesh is the sole proper outcome of labor. By this logic, purple veins would indeed be the only true source of the wealth of nations.

When writers such as Dickens and Ruskin insisted that health and illness be introduced into the calculation of economic value, they were not adding ideas drawn from some moral discourse distinct from political economy but unwittingly emphasizing one element of the logic of political economy itself. The biological aspect of political economy, the emphasis on value derived from flesh, follows from its central premise, the labor theory of value. But this very theory simultaneously dislodges considerations of physical well-being from calculations of value. The doubleness of Malthus's attitude toward living flesh, then, was just one instance of the following systematic ambivalence.

Political economists such as Adam Smith took labor to be the source or measure of all exchange value and often calculated the value of labor by the value of the commodities (primarily the food) necessary to replenish the body for the hours of labor expended on another com-

3. The following argument is developed in detail in my article "The Body Versus the Social Body in the Works of Thomas Malthus and Henry Mayhew," *Representations* 14 (Spring 1986), 83–106.

modity.[4] Thus the exchange value of any commodity was rooted in biological need; the worker's body was the primary nexus of exchange through which the value of those commodities that reproduce its labor largely determines the value of all other commodities. Adam Smith, for example, argues that all economic exchanges are ultimately rooted in the toiling body. The use of money merely covers over what political economists insisted on revealing: "What is bought with money or with goods is purchased by labour as much as what we acquire by the toil of our own body."[5] It is precisely because the "toil of the body" is a universal equivalent determining exchange value, however, that commodities can acquire abstract value independent of their biological usefulness. The very ability to calculate, through the common measure of labor, the relative values of commodities led away from a hierarchy of commodities based on ultimate biological usefulness. The labor theory of value could "equate" a bushel of corn, for example, with a bit of lace, even though, from a different physiological point of view, the corn would seem more intrinsically valuable. The humane critics of political economy resemble Malthus in accepting the premise of the labor theory of value while rejecting its implications. The value of a thing, they claim, is at least equivalent to the cost of keeping the artisan for the length of time it takes to make the article "in bread and water, fire and lodging," as Ruskin phrased it (p. 25). Biological regeneration is the foundation of all value for the critics as well as the proponents of political economy. But the critics, beginning with Malthus, claim that because the laboring body is the source of all value, commodities that immediately sustain more laboring bodies should be assessed as more valuable than those without direct physiological benefits. Thus the critics often accord a privileged position to the commodities that are most easily turned back into flesh. Malthus and Ruskin alike, then, wanted economic exchange to proceed from flesh back to flesh by the least circuitous route: life expended immediately converted into life replenished.

4. This discussion of the labor theory of value is admittedly extremely crude. It ignores the distinctions between Smith's and David Ricardo's theories, and between imagining labor to be a common measure of exchange value and imagining it to be the source of that value. It also fails to touch on the relationship between exchange value and other forms of value as well as the vexed question of how the value of labor itself as a commodity might be either determined or measured. It follows Malthus's analysis of the flaw in Adam Smith's thinking, but I believe it is nevertheless accurate in its description of the central role both given and denied to the laboring body in political economy.

5. Adam Smith, *The Wealth of Nations* (New York: Dutton, 1970), p. 26.

Viewed within this context, the emphasis on death in Ruskin and Dickens seems an extension of those very tendencies in political economy which claim to valorize life most fully. For these are the tendencies stressing the need for a life-giving potential in the commodity which makes up for its life-draining origins. In other words, the humane critics of political economy imagine the commodity, the bearer of value, as freighted with mortality, as a sign of spent vitality, in order to demand all the more strenuously that it have a vitality-replenishing potential.

This is the curiously death-centered bioeconomics that *Our Mutual Friend* draws out to its most paradoxical lengths. We have already seen that death from illth and the possibility of reanimation are at the core of the main plot, but the obsession with the place of human bodies within systems of economic accumulation and exchange goes far beyond John Harmon's story. The novel possesses an overall bioeconomics, which can serve to illuminate that story.

To begin once again at the beginning, the introduction to the theme shows us the dead body as a nexus of two kinds of economic exchange. John Harmon is not the only person interested in restoring "his" dead body to life. As one of the many kinds of garbage that Gaffer and Lizzie Hexam fish out of the river, the corpse forms a part of their livelihood. It is from this fact that Lizzie is trying to avert her own attention in the opening scene, as she and her father tow the putrefying corpse, which will later be identified as John Harmon's, to shore. In Lizzie's reluctant conversation with her father, the corpse and the river merge in the impersonal pronoun "it": "I—I do not like it, father." "As if it wasn't your living!" replies Hexam. "As if it wasn't meat and drink to you!" (p. 3) The shocking power of this metaphor, which immediately turns Lizzie "deadly faint," is its removal of all mediations between the girl's "living," her sustenance, and the corpse's moldering flesh, which becomes, in this oddly literalizing image, her food. Lizzie's physical reaction is another literalizing metaphor of denial: she would rather turn her own body into the dead white thing than keep it alive on such carrion. This first suggestion of how death might be exchanged for life is the most primitive and horrific of the biological economies presented in the novel.

Gratefully, we seem to move immediately on to another. We are relieved to learn as the passage continues that although the river has yielded many things that have directly nurtured Lizzie ("the fire that warmed you," "the basket you slept in," "the rockers I put upon it to make a cradle of it"), the dead bodies have been only *indirect* sources of life. They have brought money, the wherewithal to purchase food; they have not been food itself. Gaffer robs the bodies before turning them over to the police and also collects inquest money for having found them. Hence the bodies seem to be part of a thoroughly civilized network of economic circulation. Yet Lizzie is also disturbed by this exchange of the body for money; indeed, she claims that the sin of pilfering from the corpses is the root of her shame. Coming to us as it does in the context of the primitive alternative presented in Gaffer's metaphor, however, the intervention of money has a double moral impact. On the one hand, it brings the Hexams' living inside the pale of civilization, but on the other hand, the intervention of money seems just another metaphor, one that is intended to (but can't quite) cover over the reality of living from carrion, which is emphasized by Gaffer's and the narrator's insistent metaphorizing. The metaphors of the corpse as a living and Gaffer as a bird of prey give the trope of economics—the mediation of money—the air of a euphemism directing our attention from that which the explicit metaphors reveal: the real exchange *is* life for life.

We are, then, given two ways in which a corpse can be a "living" in this passage, but the distinction between them is collapsible. The more acceptable account (in which the human body is an item of exchange in a money network that fails to distinguish it from other items) is disturbing. But the source of the disturbance seems to be the deep secret that money is always ultimately taken out of flesh. That is, the horror is not that human flesh becomes money but that money is just a metaphor for human flesh. In this respect, the exchange made through the corpse is really not different from any other economic exchange, since all value is produced at the expense of life.

The opening of *Our Mutual Friend*, then, while echoing *Unto This Last*, also carries its logic to a nightmarish extreme: any commodity qua commodity is expended life. The commodity as dead body merely emphasizes this universal truth, and the further typical humanitarian suggestion that it should immediately become nutrition is then indistinguishable from Swift's modest proposal. The opening pages of the novel reveal that the humanitarian critique, wishing as it does for the shortest possible circuit between spent and augmented life, conjures up as a reductio ad absurdum of itself a fantastic, worse than cannibalistic bioeconomy.

As many critics have noticed, Gaffer and Lizzie Hexam are not the only scavengers in the book, the only people making a living out of the dead husks of life. Most of the economic enterprises amount to trading in human remains. The Boffin-Harmon dust mounds, the assembled debris of a vast number of lives, are only the most elaborate example. These become, through Mortimer Lightwood's metaphor, the spewed-forth life of old Harmon himself: "On his own small estate the growling old vagabond threw up his own mountain range, like an old volcano, and its geological formation was Dust. Coal-dust, vegetable dust, bone dust, crockery dust, rough dust and sifted dust,—all manner of Dust" (p. 56).

This is an image of peculiar fixity, seemingly ill assorted with the characterization of old Harmon as a "vagabond." It de-emphasizes the circulation of debris in the dust trade and transforms the enterprise into Harmon's simultaneous spending and hoarding of his own substance. The expense of his life is a self-burying; dust erupts from him and settles on him, so that accumulation and interment are the same thing. The last we hear of old John Harmon makes his death seem the merest extension of the activity of his life: "He directs himself to be buried with certain eccentric ceremonies and precautions against coming to life" (p. 15).

Old Harmon's whole existence seems to have consisted in "precautions against coming to life." He is the prototypically illthy individual, causing, in Ruskin's phrase, "various devastation and trouble around [him] in all directions" (p. 171). He oppresses and anathematizes his own living flesh and blood, his son and daughter, while he builds up his geological formations of dust, epitomizing the political economists, who, in Ruskin's analysis, devalue the true veins of wealth (purple and in flesh) in favor of the false veins (gold and in rock). The conflation of gold and rock in mountains of dust turns both to death, as Mortimer Lightwood, in telling old Harmon's story, makes explicit. But at the same time he calls attention to the clichéd nature of these associations: "[Harmon] chose a husband for [his daughter], entirely to his own satisfaction and not in the least to hers, and proceeded to settle upon her, as her marriage portion, I don't know how much Dust, but something immense. At this stage of the affair the poor girl respectfully intimated that she was secretly engaged to that popular character whom the novelists and versifiers call Another, and that such a marriage would make Dust of her heart and Dust of her life—in short, would set her up, on a very extensive scale, in her father's business" (p. 14).

One cannot simply dismiss the associations made here among dust, money, and death. Old Harmon is a death-dealer: he trades, like Gaffer Hexam, in the remains of life, and he converts life into those remains. But the presentation of these associations as sentimental commonplaces should make us take a closer look at them, a look that reveals how Harmon's business, like Gaffer's, emphasizes that value *as such* is always life spent and accumulated, stored up, in inorganic form. Old Harmon's conversion of life into death, his death dealing, is no different in principle from any other process of realizing value. Moreover, it is certainly preferable to the primitive directness of the carrion economy briefly figured in the opening chapter. Although the passing of life is legible in both Harmon's and Gaffer's commodities, the inorganic garbage already represents the achievement of several steps in the economic process of liberating value from the body.

Despite the dust-vs-flesh, death-vs-life dichotomies in the passages that introduce us to the dustmen, the transmission of life into inorganic matter and thence into gold is not truly presented as life destroying in the novel. On the contrary, it is portrayed as a sanitizing process in which a pure potential called life is released. This elongated circuit between life expended and life augmented becomes increasingly abstract as a life-transmitting potential, or power, finds itself outside of human bodies for a long time. And the liberation of such a vital power turns out to be the very means of making life seem valuable.

Little wonder, then, that the revaluation of old Harmon's legacy is accomplished not by its attachment to a worthy body (as Ruskin would have it) but by its sustained suspension through the apparent death of young John Harmon. Apparent death is the structural principle of the narrative. Young Harmon, as we've seen, describes himself as being dead but having the potential for reanimation. He is, like riches themselves, the possibility of embodied life in a state of suspended animation. And it is only in this state, when he has not claimed his money but has instead, by sloughing off his supposed body, achieved a kind of ontological oneness with the money as pure vital potential, that he can change illth into wealth. He is dead as its inheritor and yet he manages the fortune as Mr. Boffin's secretary. "The living-dead man," as the narrator calls him, resolves to remain in this state of suspended animation until he has effaced even his function as manager, until he is a mere "method" by which the money manages itself: "The method I am establishing through all the affairs . . . will be, I may hope, a machine in such working order as that [anyone] can keep it going" (p. 373).

Apparent death becomes the only direct access to the essence and value of life. Apparent death is the condition of storytelling and regenerative change. It reveals the value of his own story: "Dead, I have found the true friends of my lifetime still as true, as tender, and as faithful as when I was alive, and making my memory an incentive to good actions done in my name" (p. 372). As John Harmon becomes merely a name, a memory, and a fortune, the nugget of value that the story of his life contained is scattered and proliferates. From this vantage point, John Harmon, like an omniscient narrator, can see the complete pattern and know its worth. Even better, like an omnipotent narrator, he can change the story to create more value. This he does by remaining apparently dead as John Harmon to win (disguised as a poor man) the love of the mercenary girl who would otherwise have married him simply for his money. Hence, although the final aim of the dust plot is to prevent Bella's reduction of herself to a commodity, its machinations all depend on Harmon's merger with the fortune, his organic death into it.

John Harmon's plot, then, demonstrates that value, even the value of life itself, is only discoverable from some vantage point outside of the body. The novel repeatedly relocates value outside the body through processes that resemble the substitution of inorganic wealth for live bodies, even though the origin of wealth in bodies is never effaced. There is a fascination with macabre commodities. If the organic "death" of young John Harmon and his merger with his fortune is one example of the connection between money and the release of vital power, the commodities of Mr. Venus, a preserver of animals and birds and articulator of human skeletons, recapitulates the same point in a grotesquely comic form. While the consciousness of the living-dead John Harmon hovers around the Boffin residence as secretary, the mortal remains of the man whose death has enabled this suspended animation are themselves suspended, it would seem, in Venus's shop. "I took an interest in that discovery in the river," Venus tells Wegg. "I've got up there—never mind, though" (p. 84). Venus buys and sells body parts and also labors to make them dry, stable, and hence valuable. Of course, he also has a few fleshy organisms (various preserved babies), but most of his trade is in turning bodies into inorganic representations of themselves. It is this activity that releases value from the body and makes it a "living" for Venus but also bizarrely restores a kind of life to these bodies of representation themselves. As he hands a stuffed canary to a customer, Venus triumphantly remarks, "There's animation!" (p. 81).

The same drawing out of value from the organic body and storing it up, suspending it, in the inorganic characterizes Jenny Wren's doll-making trade. Jenny imagines that the great ladies whose clothes she copies to make her dolls' dresses are working for her as models. She imagines that her own effort of "scud[ding] about town at all hours" (p. 435) to see these fashionable clothes is matched by their owner's pains in trying on the dolls' dresses: "I am making a perfect slave of her" (p. 436), she says of one of her "models." And the result of all this sweat is the thing of value, as in Mr. Venus's shop, the inorganic body: "that's Lady Belinda hanging up by the waist, much too near the gaslight for a wax one, with her toes turned in" (p. 436).

All this metaphoric and imagistic insistence on the bodily origins of the commodity and on its disembodiment, on its transcendence of its organic origins and simultaneous conversion into vital potential, finds its culmination in the explicit vitalism of Rogue Riderhood's revivification. In this episode, life takes on its pure reality and absolute value only because it has been entirely disembodied. Rogue's body itself is merely a "dank carcase," and no one (besides Rogue's pathetic daughter) has any interest in the fate of the man himself. It is neither body nor spirit that is of concern in this scene, "but the spark of life within him is curiously separable from himself now, and they have a deep interest in it" (p. 443). For the sake of this abstracted entity, "all the best means are at once in action, and everybody present lends a hand, and a heart and soul." But when that potential and hence essential life begins to instantiate itself in the particular body of Rogue Riderhood, its value dissolves: "As he grows warm, the doctor and the four men cool. As his lineaments soften with life, their faces and their hearts harden to him" (p. 446). "The spark of life," the narrator comments, "was deeply interesting while it was in abeyance" (p. 447).

"Life in abeyance" characterizes the temporary condition of Rogue Riderhood and the longtime condition of John Harmon. Indeed, as we've seen, it is the condition underlying the narrative itself. Moreover, especially for those who insist most strenuously on the flesh-and-blood origins of economic value, "life in abeyance" is the definitive condition of commodities and their representation, money. As Rogue Riderhood's suspended animation shows clearly, the curious separation of life from the body is the refinement and purification of vitality itself. The humanitarian attempt to place and hold the human body at the center of inquiries into the nature of value thus has a paradoxical result; it leaves the body suspended, apparently dead,

while the newly valorized essence, vitality, achieves ever more inorganic and even immaterial representations.

This, then, is the destiny of the illth/wealth distinction and of the
bioeconomy on which it relies: those transfers of vitality at the heart of
a body-centered economic theory keep proving the dependence of
vitality on the suspension of animation in the body, on its apparent
death. In Dickens's novel, the illth/wealth duality cannot be said to
collapse, but the two terms enter into a dynamic fluctuation that
breaks their immediate one-to-one pairing with their supposed physiological reference points, illness and health. The storytelling, value-
creating consciousness, like the consciousness of love, like economic
value and the vital force itself, is released from bodies and exists in its
pure form only while it remains outside of bodies. In the name of life
itself, the humanitarian critics of political economy repeat the logical
trajectory of their antagonists and dislodge the body from the center of
their discourse.

Or perhaps it would be more accurate to say that the body remains
at the center but is deanimated, that what remain at the center are the
bodily remains. And these must be disposed of. *Our Mutual Friend* is
interested not only in getting a living from dead or apparently dead
bodies but also in getting a living from them as *garbage*, as waste that is
being at once disposed of and retrieved, salvaged. We have already
seen that in the novel corpse commodities remind us of the life-
draining nature of all commodities, contain in themselves the illth/
wealth duality. But in order to explain why the body should addi-
tionally be presented as potential waste and why the novel should be
divided between a watery world and a dry, dusty one, I would like to
turn briefly to a slightly different controversy, one that overlaps the
concerns of political economy but is not identical to them: the controversy over urban sanitation.

It is difficult for us to recapture the metaphysical weight that sanitary issues bore in mid-Victorian England.[6] The question of how to
dispose of decomposing matter was by no means merely technical. It
was intermeshed, perhaps even more than political economy, with
proofs of God's providence, of nature's beneficence, of human responsibility. Both sides in the heated debates over how to dispose of decomposing matter agreed that such matter had a deeply dual nature. It

6. This description of the sanitarian's debate is heavily indebted to Christopher
Hamlin's excellent "Providence and Putrefaction: Victorian Sanitarians and the Natural
Theology of Health and Disease," *Victorian Studies* 28 (Spring 1985), 381–412.

was both illth and wealth. One popular belief held that each nation had a God-given capital of fertilizing elements, including human waste and decomposing human bodies, which generated its food as interest. A way had to be found, sanitary reformers argued, to return this capital to the food-producing earth, for if it were not returned, it would, first, not bear sufficient interest as food to keep the population alive and, second, become itself the seed of death rather than life. For despite considerable disagreement over how large concentrations of decomposing matter caused disease, everyone agreed that they did. Hence dead and decomposing human matter was organized into the sanitarian's bioeconomy as both potential illth and wealth.

For many, the illth/wealth distinction was aligned with a distinction between wetness and dryness: decomposing matter allowed to rot in the river was illth; decomposing matter buried in the ground was wealth. The hero of Charles Kingsley's novel *Yeast* makes this distinction between the wet and the dry; he looks down at the Thames,

> at that huge, black-mouthed sewer, vomiting its pestilential riches across the mud. There it runs . . . hurrying to the sea vast stores of wealth, elaborated by Nature's chemistry into the ready materials of food; which proclaim, too, by their own foul smell, God's will that they should be buried out of sight in the fruitful, all-regenerating grave of earth; there it runs; turning them all into the seeds of pestilence, filth, and drunkenness.[7]

Dickens was a vocal supporter of sanitary reform, and he wrote *Our Mutual Friend* while London was undergoing one of its greatest sanitizing projects, the embankment of the Thames. It is not surprising, then, that the book draws on these organizing concepts, imagining the Thames to be a potentially pestilential open sewer full of human refuse. The narrator describes the very waterfront as a place "where the accumulated scum of humanity seemed to be washed from higher grounds, like so much moral sewage, and to be pausing until its own weight forced it over the bank and sunk it in the river" (p. 21). If political economy alone suggests the equation of commodity and life-drained body and suggests that the out-of-body state is the most valuable of all, the bioeconomics of the sanitarians lets us see why the novel arranges its inquiry into the nature of wealth around the disposal of human remains. It is within this discourse that the division of the world into wet and dry begins to make sense, that the heroism and

7. Charles Kingsley, *Yeast*, in *The Works of Charles Kingsley*, 7 vols. (Philadelphia: J. D. Morris, 1899), 4:280.

horror of dragging bodies out of the river come into sharper focus. This is the discourse that allows us to understand why Bradley Headstone's internal rot expresses its essential sterility in images of churning water, why the dust world is the place of transformations, why dry burial mounds would be the sites of regeneration. Further, it allows us to perceive the association between the river and the potential for tragedy. Characters in the river plot frequently undergo reductions; they have fewer and fewer options as the plot proceeds. On the other hand, the inhabitants of the dust world only apparently reduce themselves. As in the cases of John Harmon, Boffin, and Bella, deathliness, insensibility, are only stages in the process of preserving and releasing vital power. That suspended animation on which the release and transfer of vitality depend requires removing the body from the river and entombing it, as Eugene's body is entombed, in a dry place.

Hence, if political economy provides the metaphors that allow value to rest on suspended animation and even to require discardable bodies, the bioeconomics of the sanitarians gives us more insight into the novel's obsession with the disposal of the very bodies its own paradoxical logic keeps discarding. The recycling of such garbage-bodies, their conversion from illth to wealth, is the prototypical act of value creation in this novel. In it, once again, the deanimated body, vitality, and value become indistinguishable, depriving the terms *illth* and *wealth* of their physiological reference points.

The whole richly contradictory and fertile mixture is perhaps best summed up in the last conversation between Lizzie and Eugene, who, like John Harmon and Rogue Riderhood, must undergo a period of apparent death, of suspended animation. For Eugene this period follows Lizzie's retrieval of his garbage-body from the river, where it has been dumped, as John Harmon's was dumped, after a murder attempt. The two love plots work on a complicated series of parallels and inversions centering on images of suspended animation and discardable bodies, but it would take far too much space to trace those complexities here. The salient point for my purposes is that the period of suspended animation or apparent death is the moment when Eugene's life takes on value, and he is able, as John Harmon was able under similar circumstances, to give and receive love. Thus the familiar pattern is repeated: suspending the body's animation allows the liberation of value.

But furthermore, since Eugene's apparent death is not accomplished with a surrogate body, the equation of the hero's own body first with floating refuse and then with a broken "thing," that is, the emphasis on the body as garbage, is far more pronounced in Eugene's story than it was in John Harmon's. In his speech to Lizzie as his body returns to a state of animation, he stresses this equation of garbage and wealth by turning her into both: " 'You have thrown yourself away,' said Eugene, shaking his head. 'But you have followed the treasure of your heart. . . . you had thrown that away first, dear girl!' " (p. 753). Eugene and Lizzie are equally garbage and treasure to each other; indeed, they are treasure because they are garbage. And it is therefore perfectly rational for Eugene to fear the returning health of his body: "In this maimed and broken state, you make so much of me." Lizzie can make much of him, add value to him, only while his body is thus broken. Only while the vitality is somewhere outside his body can he possess this treasure, which is the squandering of Lizzie's life.

And so we seem to be witnessing the regenerative inversion of the horrific life transfer suggested in the opening scene, for now Lizzie's life becomes the wealth of the cadaver; instead of getting a living from the garbage-body, she spends her life on it. But in *Our Mutual Friend* reversals are never so neat. The expense of Lizzie's life is experienced by Eugene as a heavy debt: "It would require a life, Lizzie, to pay all; more than a life." Instead of inverting the novel's opening scene, Eugene's last words recapitulate it. There really is only one thing he can do to discharge his debt to Lizzie and keep himself in the condition of value he has achieved; we are right back where we started when Eugene concludes, "I ought to die, my dear."

Our Mutual Friend incessantly requires the body's suspension as a condition of the valuable life; illness unto death brings wealth. The location of both mortality and vitality, both fatality and regeneration, in decomposition makes us acutely aware that illth and wealth are alike abstractions from the body's particularity. They are alike poised on the vanishing point of those "full-breathed, bright-eyed, and happy-hearted human creatures" the literary humanitarians had set out to vindicate.

It is remarkable that, despite Eugene's reference to the squandering of Lizzie's life, all the commodity corpses, the discarded and suspended bodies in *Our Mutual Friend* are male. I would like very briefly to sketch how the apparent death of the male body is linked in this novel to the commodification of women and to the presentation of the author.

Both of the main plots, as well as several of the subplots, are driven by attempts to save women from becoming commodities. Bella, having escaped the fate of passively "being made the property of others," must then be saved from offering herself on the marriage market. Lizzie is also vehemently opposed to being a passive item of exchange between her brother and Bradley Headstone and must be rescued from the fate of becoming Eugene's mistress, his "doll," and then presumably passing into the world of the common prostitute. The novel reworks this material in tragic, comic, sentimental, satirical, and farcical modes in many of the minor plots as well. Even Pleasant Riderhood, who is engaged to Mr. Venus, expresses a fear of being confused with one of her fiancé's skeletal commodities. She breaks off the engagement because "she does not wish to regard herself, nor yet to be regarded, in that boney light" (p. 129).

Mr. Venus's solution to this problem, his plan for saving Pleasant from an identification with her body as commodity, is a humorous summary of the novel's operations: he promises to confine himself to the articulation of men. In this novel, then, women seem naturally prone to commodification, but commodification is also the fate from which they must be rescued by men who preemptively enact the condition of suspended animation, the condition, as we've seen, of the commodity itself. Men are knocked out, drowned, dried out, stored up, and finally reanimated ("There's animation!") so that women need not undergo any such self-alienation. The state of suspended animation is thus exclusively masculine in *Our Mutual Friend* because it is so naturally feminine.

This masculinity that is achieved through the incorporation of the feminine differs from femininity in its ability to survive apparent death. Only the men are capable of holding "life in abeyance"; only they have extra bodies at their disposal. Bella and Lizzie have no such out-of-body possibilities, and they are therefore debarred from the process of releasing value and being released as value, as pure vital potential, as *potency* itself.

Our Mutual Friend, then, provides an example of how apparent lapses in identity, breaks in the continuity of the self, and moments of self-alienation associated with the marketplace finally create the effect of an endlessly resilient and, in this case, emphatically male transcendent subject. Nowhere does this impression of broken, femininized, and hence enhanced male selfhood appear more overwhelmingly than in the postscript, where it applies to the author himself.

The postscript superimposes a series of authorial impressions, among which is the idea of Dickens as a principle of continuity suspended between the apparently discontinuous monthly parts of the novel. The final impression, though, is produced by an anecdote Dickens tells of a train accident that befell him as he was taking a monthly part of *Our Mutual Friend* to the printers. I'll close with this last final paragraph of the novels of Charles Dickens:

> On Friday the Ninth of June in the present year, Mr. and Mrs. Boffin (in their manuscript dress of receiving Mr. and Mrs. Lammle at breakfast) were on the South Eastern Railway with me, in a terribly destructive accident. When I had done what I could to help others, I climbed back into my carriage—nearly turned over a viaduct, and caught aslant upon the turn—to extricate the worthy couple. They were much soiled but otherwise unhurt. . . . I remember with devout thankfulness that I can never be much nearer parting company with my readers for ever, than I was then, until there shall be written against my life, the two words with which I have this day closed this book:—THE END

The author heroically risks his life to deliver his manuscript in this passage and then apparently dies into that commodity, where he remains immortally suspended.

3

Domesticity and Class Formation: Chadwick's 1842 *Sanitary Report*

Mary Poovey

This essay is about the "sanitary idea," which, along with the "statistical idea" and the "educational idea," has been credited with "energiz[ing] the system of national improvement that was state formation" in the early nineteenth century.[1] In the 1840s, in other words, the sanitary idea constituted one of the crucial links between the regulation of the individual body and the consolidation of those apparatuses we associate with the modern state. In order to grasp the implications of this argument, of course, we have to understand that the sanitary idea encompassed a number of related theories, technologies, and policies. Among the theories it implied, for example, was the medical thesis that disease was spread by miasma, the noxious fumes generated by decaying matter. Among the technologies associated with the sanitary idea were the house-by-house surveys of working-class neighborhoods, which were first conducted in the 1830s, and the compilation of data about these houses through statistics, that modern version of political arithmetic first institutionalized in 1833. The policies related to the sanitary idea, finally, constituted an arena of intense political debate in the 1840s. Such projects as laying sewers and ensur-

---

1. Philip Corrigan and Derek Sayer, *The Great Arch: English State Formation as Cultural Revolution* (Oxford: Basil Blackwell, 1985), p. 129.

ing continuous supplies of uncontaminated water sparked fierce bat-
tles between, in the first case, the newly consolidated central government and those local agencies that had traditionally governed England
and, in the second case, the private water companies, which sought to
keep prices high, and the urban public, who needed water but were at
the mercy of the companies that piped it in. My argument, then, is that
in the 1830s and 1840s, this dense network of interdependent theories,
technologies, and political disputes about policy simultaneously reor-
ganized individuals' relations to their own and their neighbors' bodies
and constituted the conditions of possibility for the formation of the
professionalized, bureaucratized apparatuses of inspection, regulation, and enforcement that we call the modern state.[2]

My breathless summary of the sanitary idea is not intended to put
you off or put you to sleep. My purpose in racing through some of its
components is to gesture toward the tentacular complexity of the
subject I'm about to address and to remind you what is at stake in such
an analysis. My specific subject in this essay is merely a modest part of
this larger network. In fact, by most historians' account, it is a pretty
modest subject altogether: I want to talk about domesticity and ideas
about the home. I will argue, however, that ideas about domesticity
played a crucial role in the sanitary idea and, through that, in the
process of state formation whose outlines I have sketched. My specific
argument is that Edwin Chadwick, author of what was probably the
most widely read government document of the Victorian period, deployed assumptions about domesticity that both brought the laboring
class into the newly forming social sphere and set limits to the role that
class could play in the government of "their" nation.

In 1839, at the time he began the *Report on the Sanitary Condition of the*

2. In addition to Corrigan and Sayer's *Great Arch,* readers interested in the relationship between the public health movement and the consolidation of English government
should consult the following: S. E. Finer, *The Life and Times of Sir Edwin Chadwick* (London: Methuen, 1953); R. A. Lewis, *Edwin Chadwick and the Public Health Movement* (London: Longmans, Green, 1952); M. W. Flinn, Introduction to Edwin Chadwick, *Report on
the Sanitary Condition of the Labouring Population of Great Britain* (Edinburgh: University of
Edinburgh Press, 1965); William C. Lubenow, *The Politics of Government Growth: Early
Victorian Attitudes toward State Intervention, 1833–1848* (Newton Abbot: David & Charles,
Archon Books, 1971), chap. 3; John M. Eyler, *Victorian Social Medicine: The Ideas and
Methods of William Farr* (Baltimore: Johns Hopkins University Press, 1979); F. B. Smith,
The People's Health, 1830–1910 (New York: Holmes & Meier, 1979); Anthony S. Wohl,
Endangered Lives: Public Health in Victorian Britain (Cambridge: Harvard University Press,
1983); and Frank Mort, *Dangerous Sexualities: Medico-Moral Politics in England Since 1830*
(London: Routledge and Kegan Paul, 1987).

Labouring Population of Great Britain, Edwin Chadwick occupied the
relatively subordinate position of secretary to the Poor Law Commission, which had been formed in 1834 as part of the New Poor Law
Amendment Act.[3] The three Poor Law commissioners, who disliked
Chadwick intensely, assigned him the sanitary inquiry partly in order
to ease him out of the office of secretary and partly to get rid of this
apparently trivial subject, which, on the face of things, had only a
tangential relation to the New Poor Law. In 1839, incidentally, Chadwick had no particular interest in or knowledge about public health or
sanitation. With characteristic determination, however, and with the
help of the fact-gathering apparatus of the New Poor Law, the bureaucrat par excellence transformed his ignorance into expertise and
his drudge work into professional gold. Despite the obstacles created
by his own unpopularity and the fall of the Whig government in 1841
(over public hatred of the New Poor Law), Chadwick pushed his
investigation to a conclusion, and in July 1842 the government published the *Sanitary Report.* Even though it was an official document, the
report was signed only by Chadwick, because the Poor Law commissioners were unwilling to take responsibility for it. Even though it was
originally a House of Lords paper (thus expensive, cumbersome, and
published in small numbers), the report obtained an enormous readership because Chadwick, ever the entrepreneur, arranged for a simultaneous printing in quarto size and large numbers at the same time that
he sent proof copies to luminaries such as Thomas Carlyle, John Stuart
Mill, and Charles Dickens, not to mention all the newspapers and
quarterlies likely to run a review.

The form of Chadwick's report, with its statistical tables, eyewitness
accounts, and summary of policy recommendations, has been naturalized by now as *the* conventional genre of government reports. But
the apparent inevitability of this kind of discourse should not blind us
to the constitutive role such early documents actually played in shaping what counted as authoritative and official. At the same time, of
course, such documents also helped constitute social norms, about,
for example, what counted as an "improved" population or an "overcrowded" apartment. As part of the establishment of social norms,
documents like Chadwick's *Sanitary Report* also contributed to the
consolidation of class identities during the period in which the eco-

3. Accounts of Chadwick's role in these enterprises can be found in Flinn, Introduction; and Finer, *The Life and Times.*

nomic basis of wealth (the definition of property) and the political basis of citizenship (the franchise) were both undergoing revision. In his depictions of the laboring population, Chadwick reveals one of the most important paradoxes of this process, for he simultaneously condemns members of the working class for failing to live up to middle-class standards (thereby implying that the classes could be alike) and suggests that the poor are—and will remain—fundamentally different from those who write about them. One effect of this paradoxical relation is to establish the "naturalness" of middle-class living habits by proclaiming their superiority in terms of health and longevity. Another is specifically to deny to members of the laboring population the opportunity for establishing the kind of relationships with each other that facilitated the consolidation of the middle class as a political entity. Central to both of these effects is Chadwick's representation of domesticity.

The importance Chadwick assigns to the domestic sphere is clear not only from the fact that Chadwick's sanitary reforms begin in the home and move outward,[4] but also from one of the biases evident in his use of statistics. The most prominent example of this bias occurs in chapter 4, which contains the widely cited discussion of "comparative chances of life in different classes of the community" (p. 219). In this section, Chadwick is intent on correlating life expectancy to the location in which one resides. His first task is to clear away material that might challenge his thesis. Thus, he must dismiss insurance tables that show the mean chances of life because they do not support the correlation he wants to prove and he must discount figures that indicate the prevalence of migrant labor because migrant labor complicates the idea of a fixed residence. Next, Chadwick breaks down his information by place and class. According to Chadwick's divisions, an individual's "class" is determined partly by the kind of work he does

4. Finer, *The Life and Times,* p. 222. Michael Cullen argues that between 1839 and 1841 Chadwick was converted to the belief that the solution to the sanitary problem lay in external drainage and sanitation rather than in the improvement of the actual houses themselves and that this conversion accounts for Chadwick's antipathy toward Robert A. Slaney, who advocated a general building act rather than Chadwick's "arterial system" (*The Statistical Movement in Early Victorian Britain: The Foundations of Empirical Social Research* [New York: Barnes & Noble, 1975], pp. 55–56). As I will argue, however, Chadwick's emphasis on the links between houses and sewers or water supplies places all these in one system, an urban or social body analogous to the individual body. In none of his projects does Chadwick fully turn away from his focus on the home. He never, for example, takes full account of the time individuals spent away from the home, especially in the streets, the workplace, and so on.

(that is, professional, trade, or labor) and partly by how and where he resides. (The conditions of one's birth or family do not figure here.) Even though Chadwick acknowledges occupation, however, he assumes that one's place of residence is more important than how (or even where) one works. Chadwick cites reporters from Aberdeen, for example, who were asked to mark maps first for the fever rates of various neighborhoods, then for the class affiliations of neighborhoods. "They returned a map so marked as to disease, but stated that it had been thought unnecessary to distinguish the streets inhabited by the different orders of society, as that was done with sufficient accuracy by the different tints representing the degrees of intensity of the prevalence of fever" (pp. 225–26). This statement assumes a strict correlation between place of residence, class, and susceptibility to disease. While class and neighborhood might well have been correlated, however, especially given the gradual subdivision of cities into suburbs and working-class areas, the transmission of disease could be tied to one's place of residence only if individuals spent all their time where they lived—or if the air where one worked could not carry miasmas.

Chadwick's elaborate tables, in other words, assume that "locality" means "place of residence," as becomes clear when he elects to divide his statistical findings according to gender. Acknowledging that a man "is subject to the influence of his place of occupation," Chadwick dismisses the death rates among men from his figures and asserts that women's mortality provides the most accurate index to general mortality because women spend most of their time in the home: "The mortality prevalent amongst the females is given separately, as probably indicating most correctly the operation of the noxious influences connected with the place of residence" (p. 231). In so organizing his data, Chadwick dismisses all occupational factors (such as hazards posed by machinery or toxic by-products); he takes all women out of the nondomestic workplace; and he effaces all the time a man or woman might spend outside the home as not contributing significantly to his or her health.

Several factors help account for Chadwick's focus on the homes of workers. In the first place, as Chadwick acknowledges early in the report, many of the earliest surveys of the poor, upon which the *Sanitary Report* is partially modeled, were based on house-by-house, neighborhood-by-neighborhood visitations by local medical men. This tendency to correlate neighborhood of residence with susceptibility to disease was reinforced by the cholera epidemic of 1831–1832, for the progress of the disease could be (and was) graphically charted by residential neighborhood. The fact that infant mortality accounted for such a large percentage of deaths also justified Chadwick's equation of "location" with "place of residence," as did the fact that, even in industrial cities like Manchester, so much work was still performed in homes, whether the work was "slop" (or piece) work or work requiring modest equipment, such as spinning or weaving.

When Chadwick instructed his informants to begin their surveys by going to schools and asking the sickliest children where they lived, then, he was simply responding to the fact that many members of the laboring population got sick and died where they slept.[5] But representing the working-class life as primarily domestic did not simply reflect the realities of Chadwick's contemporaries. It also produced ideological effects that had a strong moralizing—and, ideally, regulative—component. One example of the moralizing dimension of Chadwick's representation is the image implied by the recurrent word *overcrowding*, which conjures up its converse as well, a home that is *not* overcrowded but "normally" occupied—that is, occupied exclusively by members of the same family (and their servants), who are appropriately segregated within the home by age, sex, and class.[6] The moralizing assumptions that accompany the word *overcrowding* leap into relief in the section of the report that immediately follows Chadwick's decision to focus exclusively on women's mortality. Along with three and one-half pages of tables, this section includes some of the most explicitly moralizing passages in the report, which Chadwick characteristically presents through quotations from his informants. Here, for example, is the Reverend Whitwell Elwin, writing about Bath.

> Whatever influence occupation and other circumstances may have upon mortality, no one can inspect the registers without being struck by the deteriorated value of life in inferior localities. . . . The deaths from fevers and contagious diseases I found to be almost exclusively confined to the worst parts of the town. . . . Everything vile and offensive is congregated there [in Avon Street and its offsets]. All the scum of Bath—its low prostitutes, its thieves, its beggars—are piled up in the dens rather than houses of which the street consists. Its population is the most disproportioned to the accommodation of any I have ever heard;

5. See Flinn, Introduction, p. 48.

6. Alexander Welsh points out that the term *overcrowding* was new in the nineteenth century and that its use conveyed both a norm and the violation of that norm. See *The City of Dickens* (Oxford: Clarendon Press, 1971), p. 17.

and to aggravate the mischief, the refuse is commonly thrown under the staircase. . . . A prominent feature in the midst of this mass of physical and moral evils is the extraordinary number of illegitimate children; the off-spring of persons who in all respects live together as man and wife. Without the slightest objection to the legal obligation, the moral degradation is such that marriage is accounted a superfluous ceremony. . . . And thus it invariably happens in crowded haunts of sin and filth, where principle is obliterated, and where public opinion, which so often operates in the place of principle, is never heard; where, to say truth, virtue is treated with the scorn which in better society is accorded to vice. (Pp. 235–36)

The correlation that Elwin assumes between the filthy and overcrowded "dens" where the poor live and the "physical and moral evils" he associates with illegitimacy and extramarital cohabitation was made absolutely explicit by Chadwick's contemporary Horace Mann, who wanted the 1841 census to include information about religious affiliation. In trying to explain why the poor were alienated from organized religion, Mann pointed to the "vice and filth" of their "degraded homes." To these he contrasted the "religious character by which the English middle classes are distinguished [which] is the consequence of their peculiar isolation in distinct and separate homes."[7]

Chadwick's emphasis on the "overcrowded" working-class residence as the primary site of disease not only normalizes a "proper" form of domesticity, which is moral and sanitary (or moral *because* sanitary). It also produces the impression that working-class life not only ought to be but *is* centered in the home—however "degraded" these homes may be. At several points in his report, Chadwick contradicts this impression, as, for example, when he refers to the "migratory character of the population," which makes it impossible for him to construct tables accurate enough to prove his thesis (p. 243), or when he complains that the lack of domestic comforts in such homes drives working men into public houses for relief (p. 195). Such passing references to life outside the place of residence are echoed much more centrally in nearly all the "eyewitness" accounts of the 1840s and 1850s, which, by the same token, depict the insides of houses as almost completely devoid of human occupation. When Hector Gavin takes the reader into the homes of the poor in his *Sanitary Ramblings* (1848), for example, most of the houses are empty, depicted as places

7. Quoted in Cullen, *The Statistical Movement*, p. 72.

where people sleep, not live. Henry Mayhew's accounts of London in his *Morning Chronicle* reports, collected as *London Labour and the London Poor* (1849–1850), similarly show the streets teeming with people hawking their wares, while pubs and pantomimes fairly burst with the young and old. By contrast, the residences Mayhew visits are most often occupied only by his guide or the person he goes to see.[8]

Chadwick's 1842 *Sanitary Report* does contain a few extensive descriptions of working-class individuals who do not reside in anything remotely resembling a middle-class "home." Significantly, these passages constitute the most graphic and emotionally charged descriptions in the entire document. Their narrative vigor—especially in the light of other writers' reports that nondomestic activities prevail within the working population—suggests that Chadwick's emphasis on domesticity may actually perform a defensive and regulative purpose. We first glimpse the logic of Chadwick's emphasis in his depiction of French chiffonniers, men who earn their living by scavenging and selling bits of rubbish from city streets. Distinguished from other members of the laboring poor by their extremely "degraded and savage" living habits, the chiffonniers, according to Chadwick, are "outcasts from other classes of workmen; they sleep amidst their collections of refuse, and they are idle during the day; they are like all men who live under such circumstances, prone to indulgence in ardent spirits; being degraded and savage, they are ready to throw away their wretched lives on every occasion" (p. 163).

Perversions in every sense, these men not only hoard up refuse like treasure and squander their lives like garbage, but they also threaten both social stability and public health. As "conspicuous actors in the revolution of 1830," the chiffonniers are explicitly associated with political turmoil, and this revolutionary activity had recently been linked to the panic inspired by cholera. According to Chadwick's account of the relevant incident, the unsanitary accumulation of refuse that was exacerbating the epidemic prompted the French government to commission special garbage collectors to haul rubbish from Paris streets with their own carts. The chiffonniers, who opposed all sanitary improvements as threats to their livelihood, took this as a declaration of war. They

8. Hector Gavin, *Sanitary Ramblings, Being Sketches and Illustrations of Bethnal Green. A Type of the Condition of the Metropolis and Other Large Towns* (1848; facs. ed. London: Frank Cass, 1971); and Henry Mayhew, *The Unknown Mayhew: Selections from the "Morning Chronicle," 1849–50*, ed. Eileen Yeo and E. P. Thompson (Harmondsworth: Penguin, 1973).

rose in revolt, attacked and drove away the conductors, broke to pieces the new carts, threw the fragments into the river, or made bonfires with them. . . . The mobs of chiffonniers which collected on the following day were swollen by other crowds of ignorant, terrified, and savage people, who were persuaded that the deaths from the strange plague were occasioned by poison. "My agents," says the then prefet of police, in an account of this revolt, "could not be at all points at once, to oppose the fury of those crowds of men with naked arms and haggard figures, and sinister looks, who are never seen in ordinary times, and who seemed on this day to have arisen out of the earth. Wishing to judge myself of the foundation for the alarming reports that were brought to me, I went out alone and on foot. I had great difficulty in getting through these dense masses, scarcely covered with filthy rags; no description could convey their hideous aspect, or the sensation of terror which the hoarse and ferocious cries created. Although I am not easily moved, I at one time feared for the safety of Paris—of honest people and their property." (P. 163)

The contrasts in this passage between the mobs of savage, ignorant, and barely clothed rioters and the prefet of police, who is the vulnerable yet brave champion of the "honest people" and their property, refer English readers most explicitly to the contrast between France, where two violent revolutions had already occurred, and the more civilized Britain, where revolution continued (narrowly) to be averted. Chadwick does not underscore this nationalistic contrast, however. Instead, he insists that a subhuman population also inhabits Great Britain. Significantly, what distinguishes these people from the rest of the British population is that neither of the two groups that make up the subhuman population inhabits proper houses.

The first group, which Chadwick explicitly compares to the French chiffonniers, are the "bone-pickers," the lowliest occupants of the workhouse "bastilles" created by Chadwick's other major social "improvement," the New Poor Law. "The bone-pickers are the dirtiest of all the inmates of our workhouse," Chadwick quotes an eyewitness as reporting.

I have seen them take a bone from a dung-heap, and gnaw it while reeking hot with the fermentation of decay. Bones, from which the meat had been cut raw, and which had still thin strips of flesh adhering to them, they scraped carefully with their knives, and put the bits, no matter how befouled with dirt, into a wallet or pocket appropriated to the purpose. They have told me, that whether in broth or grilled, they were the most savoury dish that could be imagined. I have not observed that these creatures were savage, but they were thoroughly debased.

Often hardly human in appearance, they had neither human tastes nor sympathies, nor even human sensations, for they revelled in the filth which is grateful to dogs, and other lower animals, and which to our apprehension is redolent only of nausea and abomination. (Pp. 164–65)

The second group that arouses Chadwick's voyeuristic disgust had also been constituted, in part at least, by the New Poor Law. It includes members of the "vagrant population" who inhabit "common lodging-houses."[9] Chadwick devotes an entire chapter (chapter 8) and some of his most aggressive polemics to these itinerant poor. Here, for example, is Chadwick quoting Dr. Baron Howard on lodging houses in Manchester:

In some of these houses as many as six or eight beds are contained in a single room; in others, where the rooms are smaller, the number is necessarily less; but it seems to be the invariable practice in these "keepers of fever beds," as the proprietors were styled by Dr. Ferriar, to cram as many beds into each room as it can possibly be made to hold; and they are often placed so close to each other that there is scarcely room to pass between them. The scene which these places present at night is one of the most lamentable description; the crowded state of the beds, filled promiscuously with men, women, and children; the floor covered over with the filthy and ragged clothes they have just put off, and with their various bundles and packages, containing all the property they possess, mark the depraved and blunted state of their feelings, and the moral and social disorder which exists. (P. 413)

9. The New Poor Law encouraged migrant labor because it put an end to the assumption that one's parish would automatically provide relief. After 1834, manufacturers in northern industrial towns encouraged the Poor Law commissioners to help transfer redundant agricultural laborers to Lancastershire and Yorkshire. About four thousand laborers and their families were sent north under this scheme between 1835 and 1837. When industrial depression hit in 1837, however, many of the migrants found themselves out of work. See Michael Rose, ed., *The English Poor Law, 1780–1930* (Newton Abbot: David and Charles, 1971), pp. 102, 107–9.
    One could also argue that the number of itinerant workers was swelled by the unpopularity of Chadwick's New Poor Law. Many people would do anything—including tramp—rather than go to a workhouse. See Gavin, *Sanitary Ramblings*, p. 42. On the so-called wandering tribes, see Raphael Samuel, "Comers and Goers," in *The Victorian City: Images and Realities*, ed. H. J. Dyos and Michael Woolf (London: Routledge and Kegan Paul, 1973), 1:123–60. Samuel points out that "the distinction between the nomadic life and the settled one was by no means hard and fast. Tramping was not the prerogative of the social outcast . . . ; it was a normal phase in the life of entirely respectable classes of working men; it was a frequent resort of the out-of-works; and it was a very principle of existence for those who followed the itinerant callings and trades. Within the wandering tribes themselves the nomadic phase and the settled were often intertwined, with men and women exchanging a fixed occupation for a roving one whenever conditions were favourable" (pp. 152–53).

Chadwick devotes so much attention to lodging houses because he believes that they incarnate the "most serious and extensive" of all residential "evils." Like Dr. Howard, Chadwick maintains that the effluvia exhaled by "depraved" human beings is more poisonous than the miasma created by decomposing organic matter. Thus, having too many bodies in a small room is even more unhealthful than sleeping in rubbish. "It is my decided opinion," Chadwick quotes Howard as writing, "that the vitiation of the atmosphere by the living is much more injurious to the constitution than its impregnation with the effluvia from dead organic matter. . . . the 'human miasms' generated in over-crowded and ill-ventilated rooms [are] a far more frequent and efficient cause of fever than the malaria arising from collections of refuse and want of drainage" (pp. 413–14).

Whatever medical explanation underwrites his criticism of the irregular living habits of workhouse bone pickers and the itinerant poor, his singling them out for particular notice suggests that Chadwick's reforms are directed most pointedly toward exactly those all-male, nondomestic associations represented so horrifically by the French chiffonniers. Chadwick's tendency to associate such groups with "moral and social disorder" was also manifested in the temperance movement and in the chronic concern voiced by middle-class commentators about the working-class use of public space. Pubs, after all, were associated—in fact and in fantasy—not only with alcoholism and disorderly conduct but with radical working-class organizations and trade unionism in particular.[10] By the same token, the vibrant street life Mayhew describes in his series on the poor appeared as a kind of pandemonium where all kinds of boundaries and taboos were violated: children posed as adults, the poor mocked the rich, and boys lounged together on street corners or formed homosocial gangs led by a father-thief.[11] Such "irregular" associations—especially when they were exclusively male—smacked of those unspeakable parodies of the "regular" domestic relation, the homosexual "marriages" that were rumored to form in prisons, among sailors, or even in the boy gangs.

In specific contrast to these nondomestic males, Chadwick presents numerous portraits of "improved" members of the laboring population, whose improvement, not surprisingly, is figured in their domestic habits. Here is a description from Bedford, for example.

10. See Brian Harrison, "Pubs," in *The Victorian City* 1:175–81.
11. Mayhew's description of the pantomime displays many of these anxieties. See Henry Mayhew, *London Labour and the London Poor* (New York: Dover, 1969), 1:40–42.

I have much pleasure in saying that some cases of the kind have come under my own observation, and I consider that the improvement has arisen a good deal from the parties feeling that they are somewhat raised in the scale of society. The man sees his wife and family more comfortable than formerly; he has a better cottage and garden: he is stimulated to industry, and as he rises in respectability of station, he *becomes aware* that he has a character to lose. Thus an important point is gained. Having acquired certain advantages, he is anxious to retain and improve them; he strives more to preserve his independence, and becomes a member of benefit, medical, and clothing societies; and frequently, besides this, lays up a certain sum, quarterly or half-yearly, in the savings' bank. Almost always attendant upon these advantages, we find the man sending his children to be regularly instructed in a Sunday, and, where possible, in a day-school, and himself and his family more constant in their attendance at some place of worship on the Lord's-day. . . .

A man who comes home to a poor, comfortless hovel after his day's labour, and sees all miserable around him, has his spirits more often depressed than excited by it. He feels that, do his best, he shall be miserable still, and is too apt to fly for a temporary refuge to the alehouse or beer-shop. But give him the means of making himself comfortable by his own industry, and I am convinced by experience that, in many cases, he will avail himself of it. (Pp. 323–24)

The model of improvement contained in this description implicitly foregrounds gender as the bedrock of domesticity. Gender, moreover, is constructed as a strict binary opposition, which entails a complex set of assumptions about women, and female nature in particular. Among these are the assumptions that a woman's reproductive capacity is her most salient feature, that this biological capacity makes her naturally self-sacrificing and domestic, and that her more delicate nervous and physiological constitution makes her more susceptible both to her own emotions and to the influence of others. Because of this peculiar combination of self-denial and susceptibility, which women of all classes presumably shared, working-class women could be counted on to transport middle-class values into the working-class home. At the same time, because all women (ideally) reflected the labor of their husbands (instead of manifesting or profiting from their own wage work), working-class women could function as the sign of and incentive to the working-class man's successful performance as a disciplined, productive, "respectable" wage earner.[12]

12. See Mary Poovey, *Uneven Developments: The Ideological Work of Gender in Mid-Victorian England* (Chicago: University of Chicago Press, 1988), chap. 1.

At the same time that they depended on and reinforced this definition of women's nature, descriptions of improvement like the one I have quoted also represented the man's primary relation as his monogamous, legally sanctioned marriage to his wife. Beyond this, moreover, they also ensured that a man's most significant same-sex relationship would be formed *through* his wife to *himself*—to his "character." This relation, of course, was also the basis for a man's participation and investment in those institutions developed to promote the working man's "independence"—friendly societies, savings banks, religious organizations, and educational programs.

Despite the collective nature of such organizations, the form of "independence" they facilitated supported the model of domesticity I have just described. Both working-class societies and respectable domesticity, in other words, tended to link the individualized identity of the working man to his family *instead of* to any all-male association. The significance of this linkage becomes clear when we remember two things: the process by which men of the middle class consolidated and politicized *their* class identity and the forms of all-male association that were available to the working class in the 1830s.

During the eighteenth century, men of the middling ranks began to consolidate their identity as a class through a number of related activities, both economic and social.[13] Two of the most important of these were the constitution of social and economic alliances through networks of kin and the formation of same-sex relationships in such public meeting places as coffeehouses.[14] For the kin networks, the extension of a man's family through marriage was critical. As Leonore Davidoff and Catherine Hall have argued, the "hidden investment" a woman contributed to her marriage constituted a crucial addition to the family's worth both because her relations expanded the pool of potential economic resources and partners for her husband and because her judicious management of household resources could decrease unnecessary expenditures.[15] By contrast, the formation of nonfamilial alliances entailed the exclusion of women. In the public but informal meeting places provided by coffeehouses, men—but not

13. See Leonore Davidoff and Catherine Hall, *Family Fortunes: Men and Women of the English Middle Class, 1780–1850* (Chicago: University of Chicago Press, 1987), p. 199.

14. See Peter Stallybrass and Allon White, *The Politics and Poetics of Transgression* (Ithaca: Cornell University Press, 1986), pp. 89–90.

15. See Davidoff and Hall, *Family Fortunes*, pt. 2.

women—discussed ideas and news, founded the characteristic organizations of the middle class (including the stock exchange), and
developed shared standards for appropriate and effective behaviors.[16]

For both psychological and material reasons, then, men of the middle class tended to represent their social superiority partly in terms of
their domesticity. The middle-class man was recognizably different
from both the licentious, spendthrift aristocrat and the promiscuous
and improvident working man because he faithfully maintained an
orderly family. By the same token, however, the self-proclaimed domesticity of middle-class men was accompanied—especially after the
turn of the century—by an increasingly formalized segregation of the
sexes. Restrictions on property ownership, political representation,
and legal rights limited all (married) women's participation in social activities outside the home, just as increasingly rigid standards
of decorum and modesty limited the literal mobility of middle-class
women in particular. Thus, while the politicization of middle-class
men went hand in hand with the domestication of middle-class life,
this process had a dramatically asymmetrical effect on the historical
men and women who occupied the middle-class home.

When Chadwick generalizes the domestic values of the middle class
to society as a whole, he does so in such a way as specifically to deny to
working-class men the opportunity for those same-sex alliances that
constituted one critical component of the politicization of the middle
class. This denial, in fact, had a very specific historical referent, although it is mentioned nowhere in the *Sanitary Report*. Chadwick's
normalization of domesticity was composed during a period of intense
political activity on the part of the very group Chadwick sought to
individualize and domesticate. This activity was a response to a number of factors, from bitter disappointment at the inadequacies of the
1832 Parliamentary Reform to the anguish inflicted by the 1834 New
Poor Law to the hardships that accompanied the poor harvests of 1836
and 1837.[17] In 1836 a group of working men under the leadership of

16. Stallybrass and White, *Politics*, pp. 82–84, 94–100. See also Harold Perkin, *The
Origins of Modern English Society, 1780–1880* (London: Routledge and Kegan Paul, 1969),
chaps. 7, 8.

17. The literature on Chartism is vast. I found particularly useful Robert G. Gam-
mage, *The History of the Chartist Movement* (1854; rev. ed. Newcastle-on-Tyne: Browne
and Browne, 1894); Mark Hovell, *The Chartist Movement* (Manchester: Manchester University Press, 1918); Iorwerth Prothero, "Chartism in London," *Past and Present* 44 (1969),
76–105; W. H. Maehl, "Chartist Disturbances in Northeastern England, 1839," *International Review of Social History* 8 (1963), 389–414; Dorothy Thompson, *The Chartists: Popular*

William Lovett formed the London Working Men's Association. Two years later, Lovett and Francis Place published the People's Charter, demanding universal male suffrage among other things. The charter became a rallying point for the poor and wretched as well as the disenfranchised laboring population. By the end of 1838 Feargus O'Connor had founded the radical *Northern Star*, and torchlight meetings and marches were being held throughout England. In February 1839 the Convention of the Industrious Classes was held in London. On May 6, a petition bearing 1.2 million signatures supporting the charter was presented to Parliament and the leaders of the convention threatened a general strike. In July riots broke out, and they were repeated in November, when fourteen Chartists were killed. Thus, despite the dissolution of the convention, the arrests of Lovett and O'Connor, and the failure of the general strike, the Chartist movement had proved by 1842 that working men could and would organize in favor of political enfranchisement.

These politicized activities by working men constitute the implicit referent of the savagery of Chadwick's bone pickers and itinerant poor. But just as he used the French chiffonniers to incarnate (and displace) this barbarism, so Chadwick uses another nationalistic argument to further obliterate the class implications of his sanitary reforms. That is, just as Chadwick insists that the classes could (and should) be the same because women are the same, so he insists that England, Wales, Scotland, and Ireland could (and should) form one unified nation—a nation strong enough to resist the example and military force of the French. This rhetorical consolidation of "Great Britain," like the normalization of domesticity, serves to depoliticize difference and to authorize the precise form of "improvement" Chadwick wanted to substitute for political change.[18]

Chadwick's determination to consolidate "Great Britain" on the foundation of public health is clear from his initial response to the assignment he was given in 1839. Despite the fact that he was charged with surveying only England and Wales, one of Chadwick's first acts was to visit Edinburgh. There he urged sympathetic friends to petition

---

Politics in the Industrial Revolution (New York: Pantheon Books, 1984); and Gareth Stedman Jones, "Rethinking Chartism," in his *Languages of Class: Studies in English Working-Class History, 1832–1982* (Cambridge: Cambridge University Press, 1983), pp. 90–178.

18. For a discussion of nationalism as ideology, see Hugh Kearney, *The British Isles: A History of Four Nations* (Cambridge: Cambridge University Press, 1989), esp. chaps. 7 and 8.

that Scotland be included in the final report, and when this petition succeeded, Chadwick busied himself with obtaining the requisite information. In the *Sanitary Report* itself, Chadwick simply treats all of Britain as a single nation: he juxtaposes reports from Edinburgh to those from Manchester, and he draws figures about mortality from all parts of the United Kingdom. Only in the final paragraphs does Chadwick acknowledge arguments that have insisted on regional differences in the treatment of "British" health, and he specifically equates the nationalistic arguments of Scotland with the localist arguments of such towns as Carlisle. We see in this passage how Chadwick's claim that a "common interest" unites all British people is an argument for administrative "uniformity": as human beings, all Britons need the same protection; giving every individual the same protection will undermine the divisive "independence and separation" of discrete areas; making "Great Britain" one administrative unit will guarantee efficiency and economy of rule. Here is the final paragraph of the *Sanitary Report:*

> The advantages of uniformity in legislation and in the executive machinery, and of doing the same things in the same way (choosing the best), and calling the same officers, proceedings, and things by the same names, will only be appreciated by those who have observed the extensive public loss occasioned by the legislation for towns which makes them independent of beneficent, as of what perhaps might have been deemed formerly aggressive legislation. There are various sanitary regulations, and especially those for cleansing, directed to be observed in "every town except Berwick and Carlisle;" a course of legislation which, had it been efficient for England, would have left Berwick and Carlisle distinguished by the oppression of common evils intended to be remedied. It was the subject of public complaint, at Glasgow and in other parts of Scotland, that independence and separation in the form of general legislation separated the people from their share of the greatest amount of legislative attention, or excluded them from common interest and from the common advantages of protective measures. It was, for example, the subject of particular complaint, that whilst the labouring population of England and Ireland had received the advantages of public legislative provision for a general vaccination, the labouring classes in Scotland were still left exposed to the ravages of the small-pox. It was also complained by Dr. Cowan and other members of the medical profession, that Scotland had not been included in the provisions for the registration of the causes of death which they considered might, with improvements, be made highly conducive to the advancement of medical science and the means of protecting the public health. (P. 425)

Chadwick's concern with sameness shows its other face in his treatment of the Irish. On the one hand, Chadwick adamantly rejects the notion that the Irish are by nature different from the English or the Scots. On the other hand, however, Chadwick admits that in some instances at least, sanitary experiments implemented in Ireland have failed. Rather than present these failures as proof of Irish incompetence, however, Chadwick uses them to drive home one of his central principles: that administrative uniformity, fiscal responsibility, and executive efficiency can be guaranteed only by a system that combines administrative and technical expertise. What Chadwick has in mind is the consolidation of the areas to be governed and the centralization of the governing apparatus in a body of professional administrators whose technical knowledge ensures the efficiency and quality of their work. Chadwick's insistence on the national and class consolidation of Great Britain, in other words, is inextricably bound to the centralized government by experts which he imagines.

In order to appreciate the role played by a centralized, professionalized administrative unit in Chadwick's scheme, it is necessary to return once more to the other end of his plan—the individual working-class man. I have already argued that Chadwick's emphasis on the domesticity of the working class (ideally) works against those nondomestic, same-sex relationships working-class men had already begun to form and that the elevation of sexual difference underwrites this emphasis on domesticity. Even though Chadwick's focus on domesticity gives considerable power to women, however, it is important to recognize how limited this power really is. Specifically, women's power over men is limited to control over the domestic environment, which is limited by the enormity of the housekeeping task women face. Here is the example Chadwick offers to prove the limitations of women's power—or, as he phrases it, to show the "effect of the dwelling itself on the condition of a female servant." Before she married, Chadwick begins, this young woman "had been taught the habits of neatness, order, and cleanliness most thoroughly as regards household work." Such respectable domestic habits, not surprisingly, are also reflected in the woman's appearance, as Chadwick's lady informant reports:

> Her attention to personal neatness . . . was very great; her face seemed always as if it were just washed, and with her bright hair neatly combed underneath her snow-white cap, a smooth white apron, and her gown

and handkerchief carefully put on, she used to look very comely. After a
year or two, she married the serving man, who, as he was retained in his
situation, was obliged to take a house as near his place as possible. The
cottages in the neighbourhood were of the most wretched kind, mere
hovels built of rough stones and covered with ragged thatch. . . . After
they had been married about two years, I happened to be walking past
one of these miserable cottages, and as the door was open, I had the
curiosity to enter. I found it was the home of the servant I have been
describing. But what a change had come over her! Her face was dirty,
and her tangled hair hung over her eyes. Her cap, though of good
materials, was ill washed and slovenly put on. Her whole dress, though
apparently good and serviceable, was very untidy, and looked dirty
and slatternly; everything indeed about her seemed wretched and neglected, (except her little child,) and she appeared very discontented.
She seemed aware of the change there must be in her appearance since I
had last seen her, for she immediately began to complain of her house.
The wet came in at the door of the *only room,* and when it rained,
through every part of the roof also, except just over the hearth-stone;
large drops fell upon her as she lay in bed, or as she was working at the
window: in short, she had found it impossible to keep things in order, so
had gradually ceased to make any exertions. Her condition had been
borne down by the condition of the house. (P. 195)

This vignette sets out another of Chadwick's central tenets: that "circumstances that are governable govern the habits of the population,
and in some instances appear almost to breed the species of the
population." "Circumstances" therefore limit women's power to improve men (just as, in this description, circumstances displace women
as "breeders" of the human species). Significantly, of course, as Chadwick's formulations repeatedly emphasize, the circumstances that
govern women are themselves "governable"—not by political reform
but by the very army of bureaucratic experts who facilitated and were
required by a centralized government scheme such as Chadwick's
plan to improve public health.

The twin effects of every component of Chadwick's sanitary plan
were, on the one hand, to limit the ability of working-class men to
organize themselves into collective political or economic associations
and, on the other, to empower the kind of professionalized bureaucrat
that Chadwick himself represented. The role women are assigned in
this plan is strictly auxiliary, although it is crucial to the domestication,
individualization, and, by extension, depoliticization of working-class
men. Chadwick's plan therefore draws the working class into the
social but in a strictly limited way. Beyond the protective legislation of

the Poor Law lay the preventive legislation about public health—a scheme that figured the problem posed by the human body on such a gigantic scale that individual reform efforts, while necessary, could never be enough. Chadwick's tendency to translate the problem of the people into a condition of the environment therefore necessitated the very centralized preventive measures that also finally set limits to what the people could do for themselves.

Historians of this period have tended to divide on the issue of whether the demise of working-class political action after 1848 was a function of the kind of incorporation I've been describing here or a function of the development of indigenous working-class forms of collective organizations. This essay is intended to contribute to that debate by arguing that when historians of both sides have ignored the role played by ideas about domesticity in the making of the working class, they have overlooked one of the pivotal points of social organization and change. I am not going to take a position here on whether—and to what extent and in what locales—Chadwick's model of domesticity triumphed in the 1850s among members of the working class, for that would take me too far afield. I do want to pose the question, however, of what difference it would make if we revised our understanding of this period in terms of the bond forged among certain ideas about domesticity, the nation, and public health. By 1848, after all, even though Chadwick's beloved board had been dissolved and the regulation of public health had largely been returned to local government, the politicized working-class movement of Chartism was effectively dead, and working-class men had joined middle-class reformers in demanding the regulation of women's work for the sake of the "family wage." By 1848 political contests between the classes had been largely displaced by the struggles of men of all classes for the opportunity to achieve the domestic life normalized by Chadwick's report. The divisive issues of the 1850s were not about the right of the working class to vote but about women—their right to own property, to divorce, and to enter the wage-labor force—especially such professionalized occupations as Chadwick's own had become by midcentury.

4

Visualizing the Division of Labor: William Pyne's *Microcosm*

John Barrell

Since the late eighteenth century the idea of the division of labor has been a crucial tool in the attempt to isolate and define a notion of cultural modernity; but it has always been a double-edged tool. We are most familiar nowadays with the idea as it was used by Marx, and so with the notion that the narrative it recounts is a bad narrative, a story of alienation—from the unity of the productive process, from the social totality, from the self. But in the late eighteenth century, the idea of the division of labor functioned as a fully articulated discourse, offering a comprehensive account of human history which could be appealed to by aestheticians, linguists, literary critics, and speculative historians. It was predominantly associated, however, with the institution of political economy: with the celebration of economic expansion and industrial improvement and the attempt to vindicate the

Copyright © 1991 by John Barrell.
    The first version of this essay was written for the "Materialism and Criticism" conference (University of Colorado, Boulder, March–April 1988). A rather different version, delivered at the annual conference of the Social History Society (University of York, January 1988), appears in *The Arts, Literature, and Society,* ed. Arthur Marwick (London: Routledge, 1990). The present version will also appear in my book *The Birth of Pandora and Other Essays* (London: Macmillan, 1991). My thanks to Homi Bhabha, Tim Clark, Marcia Pointon, Jacqueline Rose, and David Simpson for help and advice with this essay, and to Routledge and Macmillan for permission to reprint and copublish.

structure of modern commercial societies as, precisely, a structure, as something that, despite its arguably chaotic appearance, was available to be known, to be comprehended. And for political economists, of course, it was a discourse that had, for the most part, a good story to tell. It posited a primal, presocial moment of undifferentiated occupational unity, when each person performed all the tasks necessary to his or her survival. The coming together of men and women in communities, however, enabled and produced a differentiation of occupations. As population increases and communities become larger, an ever-greater degree of occupational specialization is required and encouraged, and the products, whether of manual or of intellectual labor, become increasingly refined by being the products of progressively more specialized labor.[1]

As elaborated in writings on economics, the discourse of the division of labor acknowledges that specialization can be understood as a threat to social cohesion, for diverse occupations can also be seen as competing interests. To put it briefly, it is in the interests of each occupational group to sell its own product as dearly as possible and to acquire the products of other groups as cheaply as possible. The field of intellectual production is also acknowledged to be an arena of specialization and conflict, in which the various discourses of a culture can be understood as so many "faculty languages," or occupational idiolects, which severally attempt to interpret the world in terms of the different occupational interests they represent and articulate. But whereas in other fields of inquiry the discourse of the division of labor could be used to suggest that this atomization of occupations, interests, and discourses might lead in time to the corruption of the body politic, in political economy it enabled a new conception of social cohesion, as something that is itself predicated upon occupational division. When each of us produces only one thing or has only one service to offer, we are obliged to depend on each other for every other service and product that we need. Those apparently in competition are in fact dependent on each other; apparent economic conflict is the

1. What is, as far as we know, the first extended discussion of the division of labor occurs in book 2 of Plato's *Republic*. Plato's account was imitated in the eighteenth century by David Hume, *A Treatise of Human Nature* (1739–40), ed. L. A. Selby-Bigge and P. H. Nidditch (Oxford: Oxford University Press, 1978), pp. 485ff., and by James Harris, "Concerning Happiness: A Dialogue" (1744), in *The Works of James Harris* (London: Thomas Tegg, 1841), pp. 59–64. The fullest eighteenth-century elaboration of the discourse of the division of labor is Adam Ferguson, *An Essay on the History of Civil Society* (1767), ed. Duncan Forbes (Edinburgh: Edinburgh University Press, 1966).

basis of actual social coherence. This mutual interdependence, by which "the structure of the body politic," as the statistician Patrick Colquhoun described it, comes to be defined in economic terms, in terms of the structure of employment, and of the market, thus becomes a guarantee of the unity, and so of the health of society, and not a symptom of its corruption.[2]

The problem in this account, however, was that of defining the place from which that social coherence could be perceived, for the discourse of the division of labor seemed to deny the very possibility of the social knowledge it sought to invent. It represented every individual within a modern, commercial society as performing a specialized task, and so it represented every subject-position as partial, as defined and constrained by the specialization necessary to compete successfully in the market. What people could know was no more than a function of what they did: in Adam Smith's famous example, the philosopher and the street porter are both creatures defined by the propensity to truck and barter, and the relations between them are governed by an unspoken agreement: the porter would carry the philosopher's burdens on his back if the philosopher spared him the burden of philosophizing. The porter's knowledge of the world was no more than the knowledge of what was good for porters, and all the philosopher knew was what it was in the interests of philosophy to call knowledge. Everyone, therefore, has an occupational interest that must occlude the perception of occupational difference in the recuperated form of social coherence: that, after all, is why the mechanism that ensures that everyone, in acting for him- or herself, acts also for the common good was described by Smith as an "invisible hand."[3]

In short, the very invention of this account of social organization and social knowledge also required the invention of a knowing subject who, within the terms of the discourse, could not conceivably exist within any developed, commercial society. This problem is sometimes managed by delegating the task of comprehension to an abstract viewing position borrowed from the discourses of natural science, "the philosophic eye." It would probably take, we might reflect, such a

2. Patrick Colquhoun, *A Treatise on the Wealth, Power, and Resources of the British Empire, in Every Quarter of the World, Including the East Indies & c* (1815; facs. rpt. New York: Johnson Reprint, 1965), p. ix.

3. Adam Smith, *An Enquiry into the Nature and Causes of the Wealth of Nations* (1776), ed. R. H. Campbell, A. S. Skinner, and W. B. Todd, 2 vols. (Oxford: Clarendon Press, 1976), 1:28–29, 456, cited hereafter in the text.

disembodied observer to see an invisible hand at work; and the phrase has the additional advantage of maintaining the pretense that the discourse is articulated by no one in particular, that it represents no interest, that it is not, finally, a discourse at all.

But the problem is more usually managed by making a simple division, which is never clearly articulated, between manual labor and intellectual labor and thus between those whose labor is visible, who can be seen to do things, and those whose function Smith describes as "not to do any thing, but to observe every thing" (1:21). By this distinction, the diversity of manual labor is used as a synecdoche to represent all forms of doing, all occupational diversity. Society becomes divided between the observers and the observed, and the occupational identities of the observers are ignored. In his early draft of *The Wealth of Nations*, Smith had written that "philosophy or speculation . . . naturally becomes, like every other employment, the sole occupation of a particular class of citizens. Like every trade it is subdivided into many different branches, and we have mechanical, chymical, astronomical, physical, metaphysical, moral, political, commercial, and critical philosophers."[4] In the published version (1:21–22) this passage is considerably revised: the varieties of philosophy are no longer listed, and "trade" is replaced by "employment," with the effect that philosophy becomes less plural and less directly comparable with manual trades. More generally in the *Wealth of Nations*, though the philosopher is formally acknowledged in the opening chapters as a specialist participating in the market economy, he is quickly accredited with an impartiality, an integral subjectivity (manifested in the pronoun "we"), and a disinterestedness, which enable him to perceive the real history of society as the real and unchanging coherence of continuously subdivided activities and interests; and he is imagined as articulating that perception in terms that, because they cannot be identified as the terms of any specific occupation, elude the constraints of specific discourses as entirely as they elude determination by an economy of exchange. Knowledge becomes a disinterested knowledge of what the public is and of what is good for the public, and it becomes the property of a particular *social*, not simply a particular occupational, class. Ignorance too becomes the property of a particular

4. Adam Smith, *Lectures on Jurisprudence*, ed. R. L. Meek, D. D. Raphael, and P. G. Stein (Oxford: Clarendon Press, 1978), p. 570.

class, the class that is the object of knowledge, and so the object of the discourse.

I want to look further at the problem of authority in the discourse of the division of labor by offering a reading of an early nineteenth-century text, *Microcosm*, which consists mainly of hundreds of vignettes of figures engaged in agriculture, manufacturing, and the distributive trades. These vignettes were drawn and etched by the watercolorist W. H. Pyne and aquatinted by John Hill; an introduction, and what the title page calls "explanations of the plates," in the form of brief prose essays, were provided by someone called C. Gray. The first complete edition of the *Microcosm* was published in two volumes in 1806 and 1808; the plates had earlier begun to be issued in monthly parts in 1803.

The text has an alternative title that gives a fuller account of what its authors supposed to be their intentions: *A Picturesque Delineation of the Arts, Agriculture, Manufactures, &c. of Great Britain, in a Series of above a Thousand Groups of Small Figures for the Embellishment of Landscape*, and so on. These alternative titles disclose that the book has two separate objects, which the introduction to the first volume tries to represent as easily compatible. The *Microcosm*, it claims, "presents the student and the amateur with picturesque representations of the scenery of active life in Great Britain. And, by means of this, it, at the same time, places before them actual delineations of the various sorts of instruments and machines used by her in agriculture, in manufacture, trade, and amusement."[5] Now evidently what is imagined to be at stake in this "double object" is an opposition between "picturesque representations" and "actual delineations," where the actual is conceived of as extratextual, a real that can be directly reproduced by one kind of drawing but not by another. But as we shall see, the competition between the two is played out as a competition between discourses inside the text itself, discourses that must, I want to suggest, be incompatible.

One of these discourses is that of the division of labor itself; and its presence within the introduction is signaled by the claim that the *Microcosm* will represent the *variety* of occupations that together com-

5. Unless otherwise stated, all quotations from the *Microcosm* are from C. Gray's introduction to the first volume. For a brief bibliography of studies of Pyne's work (by A. E. Santaniello), see the facsimile reproduction of the 1845 edition of the *Microcosm* (New York: Benjamin Blom, 1971), p. 17.

pose the economic structure of Britain. Thus the *Microcosm*, the introduction argues,

> is devoted to the domestic, rural, and commercial scenery of Great
> Britain, and may be considered as a monument, in the rustic style, raised
> to her glory. While it assists the students of both sexes in drawing, and
> teaches them to look at nature with their own eyes, it sets before them,
> in pleasing points of view, the various modes in which her capital is
> invested, and by which her industry is employed: in short, the various
> ways by which she has risen to her present high situation, as one of the
> first among nations.

This acknowledgment of the variety of occupations, of labor, of employment in a modern commercial society, is a defining feature of the
discourse of the division of labor. But the acknowledgment is always
predicated on the ability of the discourse to produce some general
truth about that variety, such as will describe its *unity* when it is
examined by the eye of the economic philosopher. Thus Smith, for
example, after examining "all the variety of labour" that goes into the
production of a laborer's tools and woolen coat, continues:

> Were we to examine, in the same manner, all the different parts of his
> dress and household furniture, the coarse linen shirt which he wears
> next his skin, the shoes which cover his feet, the bed he lies on, and all
> the different parts which compose it, the kitchen-grate at which he
> prepares his victuals, the coals which he makes use of for that purpose,
> dug from the bowels of the earth, and brought to him perhaps by a long
> sea and a long land carriage, all the other utensils of his kitchen, all the
> furniture of his table, the knives and forks, the earthen or pewter plates
> upon which he serves up and divides his victuals, the different hands
> employed in preparing his bread and his beer, the glass window, which
> lets in the heat and the light and keeps out the wind and the rain, with
> all the knowledge and art requisite for preparing that beautiful and
> happy invention, without which these northern parts of the world
> would scarce have afforded a very comfortable habitation, together with
> the tools of all the different workmen employed in producing these
> different conveniences; if we examine, I say, all these things, and con-
> sider what a variety of labour is employed about each of them, we shall
> be sensible that without the assistance and co-operation of many thou-
> sands, the very meanest person in a civilized country could not be
> provided, even according to, what we very falsely imagine, the easy and
> simple manner in which he is commonly accommodated. (1:23)

The strategy and structure of this extraordinary sentence (which are
closely matched in some sentences by Mandeville on the same topic of

the "variety" of employment)[6] have the effect of instantiating precisely the transcendent form of knowledge which is taken to characterize the subject of the discourse of the division of labor. It begins with a proliferation of examples of the "variety of labour," and the sheer number of these examples, the random order in which they are mentioned, the listing of general categories and particular objects confusedly together ("the furniture of his table," the knives, forks, and plates), the multiplication of binary terms (sea and land, heat and light, and so on), and the tendency of some items to prompt reflections that delay the conclusion of the list (the glass windows, for example), have the effect of producing a consciousness that seems to be constituted by, and dispersed among, the numberless consumable articles that demand attention in a modern commercial society. The next sentence will contrast the vast number of such articles available to the European laborer with the frugal accommodation of "the African king."

But the conditional form of the sentence is available to rescue this dispersed consciousness and acts (so long as we do not lose sight of it) as a promise, whose fulfillment becomes the more urgent the more it is deferred, that order will finally emerge and that some general truth will be produced from all these confusing particulars. The conditional form is eventually reactivated, at "if we examine, I say," announcing the imminent fulfillment of the syntactical contract; more to the point, the parenthetic "I say" (Mandeville uses precisely the same expression, at precisely the same rhetorical moment in a similar sentence),[7] can be read as a guarantee—a claim at least—that one consciousness, the philosopher's, has never been bewildered: throughout this long recital, he has had his eye on the enunciation of a general truth, though the reader may have been blind to it, and a transcendent truth, because it will be produced by a transcendent subject.

6. Bernard Mandeville, *The Fable of the Bees* (1714–24), ed. Philip Harth (Harmondsworth: Penguin, 1970), pp. 359–60.
7. Compare Smith with this sentence from Mandeville (p. 360): "But if we turn the prospect, and look on all those Labours as so many voluntary Actions, belonging to different Callings and Occupations, that Men are brought up to for a Livelyhood, and in which every one Works for himself, how much soever he may seem to Labour for others: If we consider, that even the Saylors who undergo the greatest Hardships, as soon as one Voyage is ended, even after the Ship-wreck, are looking out and solliciting for employment in another: If we consider, I say, and look on these things in another View, we shall find that the Labour of the Poor, is so far from being a Burthen and an Imposition upon them; that to have Employment is a Blessing, which in their Addresses to Heaven they Pray for, and to procure it for the generality of them is the greatest Care of every Legislature."

The acknowledgment of *variety* in occupations and employments is therefore always predicated, in the optimistic version of the discourse of the division of labor, on the possession of a position of knowledge beyond discourse, beyond occupation and interest, and so on the possession of a knowledge of the effective *unity* of apparently divided labors (the "co-operation of many thousands"). It is this that enables the concern for variety in the first place, and it is this that accounts for and justifies the concern of the *Microcosm* to represent the various modes in which capital is invested and labor is employed and "the various sorts of instruments and machines" used in British agriculture, manufacture, and trade.

In offering to present an image of the unity of apparently divided labor, the *Microcosm* does not offer its reader an ascent to the elevated viewing position from which the knowledge of that unity originates. Its pedagogic address to "young people" offers that vision of unity in the more restricted, the more marketable, and the more easily consumable form of "useful knowledge"—as a "useful knowledge," for example, "of the practical part of various arts and manufactures." The educational movement of which this phrase was the watchword sought to represent as true knowledge only what it was "useful" to know, and its notion of usefulness was tailored to fit a subject more easily identifiable as an intelligent artisan or mechanic than as a member of the polite, more liberally educated classes.[8] This subject was imagined to be impatient with all knowledge not empirically derived and without practical application, and it is to young people destined to become just such subjects, to whom the useful and the practical were one and the same, that the introduction addresses itself.[9]

8. See Nicholas Hans, *New Trends in Education in the Eighteenth Century* (London: Routledge and Kegan Paul, 1951), pp. 152–60; J. W. Hudson, *The History of Adult Education* (1851; facs. rpt. London: Woburn Books, 1969), pp. 29–35; Thomas Kelly, *A History of Adult Education in Great Britain* (Liverpool: Liverpool University Press, 1970), pp. 78–79.

9. See, for example, the definition of *technology* in Jeremy Bentham, *Chrestomathia* (1817), ed. M. J. Smith and W. H. Burston (Oxford: Clarendon Press, 1983), p. 85: "From two Greek words: the first of which signifies an *art*. . . . a *connected* view is proposed to be given, of the *operations* by which *arts* and *manufactures* are carried on. . . . On this occasion will be to be shown and exemplified, the advantages, of which, in respect of *despatch* and *perfection*, the principles *of the division of labour* is productive. Here will be shown how, by the help of this most efficient principle, as *art* and *science* are continually making advances at the expense of *ordinary practice* and *ordinary knowledge*, so *manufacture* (if by this term be distinctively designed *art*, carried on with the help of *the division of labour*, and thence *upon a large scale*) is continually extending its conquests, in the field of *simple handicraft art*—art carried on *without* the benefit of that newly found assistance.

It was as a branch of "useful knowledge" that the teaching of political economy was legitimated in the early nineteenth century, for example, in Jeremy Bentham's plans for chrestomathic education and in the
Mechanics' Institutes;[10] and it was their occupational identity as mechanics, of course, which meant that those who attended such institutes could be thought of as acquiring only the conclusions at which
political economy arrived and not the principles by which those conclusions had been reached. I take it that the *Microcosm* is offering a
knowledge of the "variety of labour" on the same terms. It is predicated on the assumption that the knowledge necessary to produce the
book and the knowledge it seeks to impart are very different: the
authors are able to *initiate* a knowledge of how the body politic is organized; the young people who read it, will be able to do no more than
recognize that organization when it is presented to them and understand, perhaps, where they belong within it. Thus "useful knowledge," when it takes in political economy and the division of labor,
becomes a hybrid or transitional form of knowledge—neither one of
the variety of functions to be observed nor at the point where observation originates.

But the *Microcosm*, as we have seen, has a "double object": it seeks
also to offer "picturesque representations"; it wishes to please as well
as to instruct, and it is looking for a market among those whose
interest is in art as a polite accomplishment, as well as among those
concerned to acquire "useful knowledge," or concerned that their
children should acquire it. And in order to describe this second aim,
the introduction engages a discourse that, like that of the division of
labor, had come to be fully articulated only in the final decades of the
eighteenth century. This discourse of the picturesque, as originally
developed by William Gilpin, and subsequently by Richard Payne
Knight and Uvedale Price, can be understood as giving definition to
the aesthetic concerns of the connoisseur and the amateur gentleman
artist. In doing so, it represents itself as thoroughly hostile to the
values inscribed within political economy, but except in the later writings of Knight,[11] it seeks also to privilege the concerns of the gentle-

10. See J. F. C. Harrison, *Learning and Living, 1790–1960: A Study in the History of the English Adult Education Movement* (London: Routledge and Kegan Paul, 1961), pp. 79–84.
11. See Peter Funnell, "Visible Appearances," in *The Arrogant Connoisseur: Richard Payne Knight, 1751–1824*, ed. Michael Clarke and Nicholas Penny (Manchester: Manchester University Press, 1982), pp. 82–92.

man amateur over those of the professional artist, especially the professional artist in landscape and genre—and I use the word *professional* to mean simply the opposite of amateur, rather than to describe artists (we shall come to them presently) who thought of themselves as engaged in a profession, rather than a manual trade. For the discourse of the picturesque reinscribed the traditional distinction between the intellectual and the mechanical aspects of painting in terms that suggested that modern painters, if left to themselves and not guided by the gentleman connoisseur, would become preoccupied with matters of execution at the expense of a concern for correctness of taste.

A sign of these distinctions, between gentleman and economist and between amateur and professional, is the concern everywhere evinced within the discourse of the picturesque with the visible appearances of objects to the entire exclusion of a consideration of their use or function. This concern is often expressed in connection with a disdain for manual labor: the discourse represents itself as capable of being articulated only by a subject who is sufficiently remote from the need to regard the material base of economic life to be able still to consider an interest in the useful as a mean interest, an interest in the mechanic at the expense of the liberal arts. Here for example is Gilpin, on the objects worthy to be represented in a picturesque landscape: "We hardly admit the cottage, and as to the appendages of husbandry, and every idea of cultivation, we wish them totally to disappear."[12] Or here he is again, on the "vulgarity of . . . employment," which, he says, "the picturesque eye, in quest of scenes of grandeur, and beauty, looks at with disgust."[13] And here he announces a primitive version of the Group Areas Act: "In grand scenes, even the peasant cannot be admitted, if he be employed in the low occupations of his profession: the

12. Quoted in C. P. Barbier, *William Gilpin* (Oxford: Oxford University Press, 1963), p. 112. Barbier's book is the best account of Gilpin and an excellent guide to the early phases of picturesque theory.

13. William Gilpin, *Observations Relative Chiefly to Picturesque Beauty, Made in the Year 1772. On Several Parts of England, Particularly the Mountains and Lakes of Cumberland and Westmoreland* (1789), 3d ed. (London: for R. Blamire, 1792), 2:44–45. Compare Archibald Alison, *Essay on the Nature and Principles of Taste*, 3d ed. (Edinburgh: Constable et al., 1812), 1:121: "The sublimest situations are often disfigured, by objects we feel unworthy of them—by traces of cultivation, or attempts towards improvement. . . . The loveliest scenes, in the same manner, are frequently disturbed . . . by the signs of cultivation . . . [and] the traces of manufactures." Alison is not truly a theorist of the picturesque; he bases his aesthetic on the association of ideas. The point of this passage is to prohibit the intrusion into aesthetic experience of mean associations, rather than to invite us to consider "sublime situations" independently of the associations they may evoke.

spade, the scythe, and the rake are all excluded" (2:43–44). And here, finally, he is more generous, acknowledging what was implicit in the previous quotation and allowing the peasant entrance into picturesque scenery if he leaves his tools behind:

> In a moral view, the industrious mechanic is a more pleasing object, than the loitering peasant. But in a picturesque light, it is otherwise. The arts of industry are rejected; and even idleness, if I may so speak, adds dignity to a character. Thus the lazy cowherd resting on his pole; or the peasant lolling on a rock, may be allowed in the grandest scenes; while the laborious mechanic, with his implements of labour, would be repulsed. (2:44)

The object of the picturesque, in that last quotation, is represented as depiction "in a picturesque light," rather than a "moral" light; and in the same way the subject of the discourse is sometimes identified as the "eye of taste," or the "picturesque" eye. The phrase has the effect of acknowledging that this subject is a partial subject only, one among the various discursive identities available to the inhabitants of the polite world. It is an acknowledgment essential to the legitimation of the discourse precisely because, especially in its lofty disdain for manual labor, for industriousness, it defines itself in contradistinction to the moral as well as the economic.

That this disdain for labor can also be read as the gentlemanly disdain of the amateur, however, enables the picturesque to lay claim to that transcendent viewing position which had through the eighteenth century been regarded as the perquisite of the gentleman, a transcendence (as I have argued elsewhere)[14] similar to that claimed by the political economist, in that it represents itself as disinterested, but distinct from it also, in that it is characterized by a tendency to overlook, rather than to comprehend, the details of trades and occupational identities. In an essay on his own sketches, for example, Gilpin had described a picture of the Colosseum, "adorned with a woman hanging linen to dry under its walls. Contrasts of this kind," he commented, "may suit the moralist, the historian, or the poet, who may take occasion to descant on the instability of human affairs. But the *eye*, which has nothing to do with *moral sentiments,* and is conversant only with *picturesque forms,* is disgusted by such unnatural

---

14. John Barrell, Introduction to *English Literature in History, 1730–1780: An Equal, Wide Survey* (London: Hutchinson, 1983).

union."[15] Gilpin represents the picturesque here as if it were a *faculty* of pure unmediated vision: it is the "eye," unqualified by any adjective, disjoined from any specific occupational and discursive identity, entirely disinterested. He considers three occupational identities, moralist, historian, and poet, and the vision of each of them is shown to be mediated by their specific interests, with the result that each is imagined to approve of a picture that, for Gilpin, depicts an "unnatural" union of forms and sentiments. As opposed to these, the "eye"—now not even the "picturesque" eye or the "eye of taste"—is pleased only by what is *natural*. The natural is located in picturesque forms devoid of ethical, political, or sentimental meanings. If they are not devoid of such meanings, he argues, they are "disgusting"; they appeal only to a partial or a perverted taste.

That this claim to a transcendent vision could serve to distinguish the amateur student of picturesque forms from the professional artist in landscape and genre will be clear enough, if we consider the rural-subject pictures produced in the 1790s by such artists as George Morland, James Ward, and Francis Wheatley, which are everywhere concerned with just such meanings as Gilpin rejects. But if we consider the art of painting in terms of its institutional history in the late eighteenth and early nineteenth centuries, it will be apparent that artists who painted for a living found no great difficulty in accommodating within their own self-image the opinions of the gentleman connoisseur on matters of taste, however much they resented the claim of the connoisseurs to dictate to them on such matters.[16] For the master narrative of that institutional history is the continual concern to represent painting as, precisely, a profession, a liberal profession, and not a mechanical or a manual trade, and thus to claim for the painter at least as much gentlemanly status as the practitioners of other professions laid claim to. The disdain for mere execution, for the manual aspects of painting, expressed by the picturesque connoisseur, could certainly be understood as a negation of this claim; but it could also be used to validate it. For to establish painting as a liberal profession, it was not sufficient simply to establish visible institutions, such as the

15. William Gilpin, *Three Essays on Picturesque Beauty; on Picturesque Travel; and on Sketching Landscape; with a Poem on Landscape Painting. To these are now added Two Essays Giving an Account of the Principles and Mode in which the Author executed his own Drawings,* 3d ed. (London: for Cadell and Davies, 1808), p. 165.
16. See Felicity Owen and David Blayney Brown, *Collector of Genius: A Life of Sir George Beaumont* (New Haven: Yale University Press, 1988), chaps. 9 and 10.

Royal Academy, and to substitute professional training for apprentice-ship. It was also necessary to appropriate such discourses as presup-posed a liberal, a gentlemanly subject to articulate them.

Painters of history were justified by the long tradition of amateur criticism to mobilize a version of the discourse of civic humanism to represent their aims and status. There was also a tradition of heroic landscape painting in oils, continued in the nineteenth century espe-cially by Turner, which could arguably be defined and defended in civic terms. Essential to the civic theory of painting was the claim that the painter of heroic subjects, at least, was an inventor, not a mere maker of objects, and thus the practitioner of a liberal art. But this discourse was not easily available to those who painted landscape and genre, not heroic actions or the ideal forms of humanity; and it was especially unavailable to artists in watercolor (Pyne himself was pri-marily a watercolorist and was to become an active propagandist of the medium).[17] The restricted size of landscapes in watercolor and the traditional use of the medium to produce images for the purpose of conveying factual information rather than moral instruction required that the professional aspirations of landscape artists in watercolor should be defined in other terms. What was taken to characterize the art of watercolor, especially in the newly popular technique of painting in watercolor, as opposed to coloring in or washing over a previously drawn image, was the spontaneous facility necessary to a medium in which mistakes could not easily be corrected. For artists in watercolor in the early decades of the nineteenth century, therefore, the disdain for labor and the concern for pure aesthetic values of the picturesque were a valuable resource in the representation of their professional and gentlemanly aspirations.

It was doubly necessary to represent painting in watercolor as a liberal, a polite activity, for what was at stake was not simply the status of the artist as practitioner but the economic viability of watercolor painting as an occupation. Professional watercolorists made their liv-ings not simply by selling their works; equally, if not more, important to most of them were the fees they received for teaching their art. To find paying students it was necessary to represent their art as an accomplishment suitable to the sons and daughters of the politer part of the bourgeoisie or of those aspiring to politeness.[18] For this purpose

17. In particular Pyne edited, in 1823–24, *The Somerset House Gazette,* a periodical largely devoted to publicizing the technique of painting in watercolor.
18. See Michael Clarke, *The Tempting Prospect: A Social History of English Watercolours* (London: British Museum Publications, 1981), chap. 5.

too the discourse of the picturesque, with its connotations of amateur status and gentility, could be a valuable resource. It became, therefore, the primary discourse employed in the numerous instructional manuals produced by watercolor artists in the early decades of the nineteenth century, and the *Microcosm*, as its full title indicates, offers itself as just such a manual. The offer is repeated in the claim that the book "presents the student and the amateur with picturesque representations." The "amateur" is the polite connoisseur of the picturesque; and the "student," I take it, is not here conceived as one studying to enter the profession: the students of art referred to later in the introduction may be "of both sexes" (this at a time when women were excluded from an institutional education in the fine arts) and are apparently studying art as an accomplishment and a pastime.

This pedagogic concern announces that the discourse of the picturesque is articulated in the *Microcosm* not by an amateur such as Gilpin but by a polite professional such as Pyne wishes to be considered. And in the terms of the discourse of the division of labor, the appropriation of the picturesque by such men as Pyne must identify it as a discourse that has forfeited its claim to be a disinterested, transcendent form of knowledge. It has come to be used to market a specific service, to define a specific interest, and to claim a specific status for the practitioners of a particular occupation.

On the one hand, then, the *Microcosm* intends to represent the "variety of employment" packaged as useful knowledge, and this intention is announced within the terms of the discourse of the division of labor. On the other, the *Microcosm* offers the pleasures of the picturesque, and that intention is inscribed within the discourse of what, within a commercial publication such as this, must be understood as a specific occupational interest, a defining characteristic of which is a disdain for the "vulgarity of employment," the very occupations the book is committed to representing. Thus, at a time when the importance of drawing was being increasingly emphasized as a useful part of mechanical education, the *Microcosm* is anxious to stress the accuracy of its illustration; and at a time when drawing was also becoming preeminent among the polite accomplishments, it is equally concerned to stress how well it combines the "agreeable" with the "useful."

There is no necessary incompatibility between these two intentions and concerns at the level of social practice: we need not even think of the *Microcosm* as addressing itself to two different markets, for it is not hard to imagine the existence of large numbers of parents among the

upwardly mobile or upwardly aspiring middle classes who would
have been anxious to encourage their children in both practical and
liberal pursuits. Nor, in the first decade of the nineteenth century, was
the distinction between technical and what we may call "aesthetic"
drawing as rigid as it soon became. The problem faced by the introduction is a discursive problem: it is a problem of how to describe two
social practices, which may not have been experienced as incompatible, in the terms of two discourses that are quite evidently so. The
problem is to make these two discourses act in concert and not in
conflict and contradiction, and the introduction seeks to manage the
problem by treating this discursive opposition as if it were a matter of
due balance between equal concerns and as if the pleasure offered by
the picturesque could be additional to, a supplement to, an "actual"
account of the variety and coherence of economic activities.

It attempts at one point to describe this balance by conceiving of the
illustrations themselves as divided into two discursive units, whereby
the machines carry the responsibility for the usefulness of the book,
and the figures are left free to give pleasure—a resolution hardly
compatible with the unwillingness of the picturesque to represent
manual labor. This solution is probably borrowed from the convention
established in the late eighteenth century for the illustrative plates of
encyclopedias of arts and sciences, whereby one half of a plate would
be devoted to a bustling atelier scene in which a number of artisans
pursued their divided labors with the tools and machine parts deline-
ated in the other half. But the basic strategy of the introduction remains to announce, simply, that the book does *this* and that it does *this*
too; it does so much of the one and the same amount of the other. It is
as if each discourse has a similar kind of status and authority, when
what is at stake is precisely the negation, by the division of labor, of
any claim that a merely occupational discourse might have to articulate
an objective form of social knowledge, and when one defining characteristic of the picturesque is such as to throw into doubt the very
knowledge that it is the object of the division of labor to impart.

But if the introduction can handle this discursive opposition only by
offering to recast that opposition as balance, the book itself constructs
a set of relations between the discourses of the picturesque and of the
division of labor in which their opposition is apparent, if not acknowledged, and in which each can be read as attempting to appropriate the
other. In the next two sections of this essay, I want to examine how this
discursive conflict is played out in the *Microcosm*.

I want to begin by concentrating on half of the "double object" of the *Microcosm*, the attempt to represent the various divided labors of commercial Britain and to grasp that occupational variety in the form of economic and social unity. From the point of view of the discourse of the division of labor, the picturesque as it has so far been characterized seems to be entirely disabled from assisting in that attempt by virtue of its reluctance to represent manual labor and also by virtue of the fact that, in the view of the economic philosopher, it must be identified, by that very reluctance, as an occupational and so an interested discourse. The profession of the artist, or more specifically of the landscape and genre artist in watercolor, is evidently in these terms one of the divided labors that the philosophic eye must attempt to comprehend in its vision of the social totality, rather than a situation from which a view of that totality can be advanced.

But equally evidently, if the illustrations to the *Microcosm* instantiate a visual discourse of the picturesque, they must embody a version of that discourse very different from the picturesque of Gilpin or of the artist whose claim to be a member of a liberal profession depends upon his lofty disdain for the mechanical. To depict, as this book does, picturesque groups of workers, is one thing; but to depict picturesque groups of workers actually *working*, as well as sitting idly around (see figure 1), is immediately to compromise that gentlemanly disdain for manual labor and, to that degree, also to compromise the occupational specificity of the picturesque. To the philosophic eye, we could say, picturesque drawing, once it has overcome that disdain, ceases to instantiate a discourse at all, in that it no longer instantiates a claim to define its own proper objects of attention and its own hierarchy of values and to generate its own specific kind of social knowledge. In the *Microcosm*, we could say, picturesque drawing has become a victim of the process by which social knowledge was increasingly defined in the late eighteenth and early nineteenth centuries as economic knowledge and the arts were increasingly denied a cognitive function. And so it has become, rather, a rhetoric, a style, and one that, I suggest, can usefully be appropriated by the discourse of the division of labor to give a visible form to its account of social organization.

Considered as a style, rather than as the instantiation of a mode of knowledge, picturesque drawing possessed characteristics that made it particularly appropriate to the representation of the unity of commercial and manufacturing economy. The picturesque, as I argued earlier, is concerned only with visible appearances to the exclusion of

Figure 1. *MICROCOSM*, plate 98, *Woodmen*. Lopping branches off timber.

the moral and the sentimental. The picturesque eye is a Polaroid lens that eliminates all sentimental and moral reflection. It is thus also absolutely hostile to narrative; and when it depicts figures, it attempts to do so in such a way as to raise no question about their thoughts or feelings or their interactions with other figures. Picturesque drawing—figure 2 is an example by Gilpin himself—seeks to represent figures as, precisely, figures, no more than that. It employs, for example, none of the conventional signs, physiognomic or pathognomic, by which other contemporary visual discourses encode the stereotypes of individuality. Accordingly, the working figures in the *Microcosm*—figure 3 is a case in point—are distinguished by the attitudes they adopt and the movements they perform, by their physical relations to the various objects they work with and work on, by their occupations, rather than by their thoughts or feelings about those occupations. They are what they do: identity becomes largely a matter of what movements they make and which implements they apply to which raw materials.

The non-narrative neutrality that characterizes picturesque delineations of the human figure is reinforced by a characteristic method of drawing. The picturesque line is often hardly a *line* at all: it is discontinuous, spiky, concerned to represent texture at the expense of outline. Texture is communicated in the *Microcosm* both by Hill's aquatinting, and by Pyne's etched lines, which are broken as if to represent the building up of an image out of rapid, successive scratches of the pen as it stumbles over the textured surface of handmade paper. The line seems to call attention to its own discontinuity, and so to the spontaneous movement of the masterly hand that produced it; but the notion of the "natural" in this sketching from nature represents "mastery" in terms not of the individuality of the artist's manner but of the "accuracy" with which it registers the visual appearances of objects supposed to be humble and informal. It is expressive of a neutrality, not an idiosyncrasy of vision; it instantiates a conception of "accuracy" which governs indifferently the representation of both people and things, in such a way as assimilates each to the other by suggesting that both are capable of being observed with the same kind of neutral aesthetic attention. The neutrality of picturesque vision can thus be read as the sign of a disinterested, not a partial observation. In short, the picturesque as style, applied to the representation of manual labor, becomes an ideal visual vehicle for the representation of an account of the various occupations by which the British economy is constituted, one

Figure 2. William Gilpin, "A few landscape-groups," illustration to his "Essay on the Principles on Which the Author's Sketches are Composed," in Gilpin, *Three Essays on Picturesque Beauty.*

Figure 3. *MICROCOSM*, plate 14, *Grinders. Left, above and below:* grinding a scythe. *Right, above and below:* grinding the blade of a hatchet.

that can reinforce the claim that the knowledge and understanding of that variety proceeds from no occupational interest or identity at all.

Each plate in the *Microcosm* consists of two or three but usually four or more small vignettes of individual figures, groups of figures, or occasionally implements of trade. For the most part each plate is devoted to a particular mechanical trade or occupation. And in each plate, there is evidence of Pyne's concern to pattern the various individual vignettes into a well-designed page. When two groups are illustrated on the same horizontal axis, they are carefully balanced or contrasted, as in figures 4 and 5. Where the page is arranged vertically, as in figure 6, it is usually organized into three tiers, with the largest vignettes at the bottom and the smallest at the top; sometimes a vignette may artfully invade the space of the tier above it, as in the same plate of sheep shearing.

More or less the same principles of organization inform the plates that are arranged horizontally, except that a good number of these are divided into four vignettes of about equal size, the composition of one answering that of the other on the same tier, as in figures 7 and 3. This careful patterning of separate vignettes on the same page clearly announces the genre in which Pyne thought of himself as working. In the 1790s George Morland in particular, but other artists as well, had taken to publishing volumes of etchings which purported to be reproductions of their private notebooks or sketchbooks. These volumes sometimes devote a single sheet to the reproduction of a single finished drawing, but as often a number of separate studies are grouped together on the same plate, with a careful attention to the balance of each composite sheet—though never, so far as I have observed, with quite as meticulous an attention as Pyne's.[19] This style of presentation, which became very common in nineteenth-century drawing manuals,[20] seems to have been governed by a specific aesthetic. Ten of Morland's published sketchbooks have the title *Sketches from Nature*, just as Pyne's vignettes are said on his title page to be "accurately drawn from nature." The notion involved here is that sketches and drawings from nature are, precisely, accurate, because, unlike fin-

19. For a list and discussion of Morland's sketchbooks, see Francis Buckley, "George Morland's Sketch Books and Their Publishers," *Print Collector's Quarterly* 20.3 (1933), 211–20.

20. See Ken Spelman, *Catalogue Four. The Artist's Companion: Three Centuries of Drawing Books and Manuals of Instruction* (York: Ken Spelman, n.d.); and Peter Bicknell and Jane Munro, *Gilpin to Ruskin: Drawing Masters and Their Manuals, 1800–1860* (London: Christie's, 1987).

Figure 4. *MICROCOSM*, plate 71, *Market Groups. Left to right, top to bottom:* groups selling fruit, onions, poultry, fish (two drawings), earthenware (two drawings), and geese.

Figure 5. *MICROCOSM*, plate 51, *Dairy. Left to right, top to bottom:* milkman driving his cows; dairymaid; woman milking; milking, with cows underneath a shed.

Figure 6. *MICROCOSM*, plate 45, *Sheep-Shearing &c. Left to right, top to bottom:* washing the sheep preparatory to shearing; shepherds; shearing the sheep, rolling the fleece and so on.

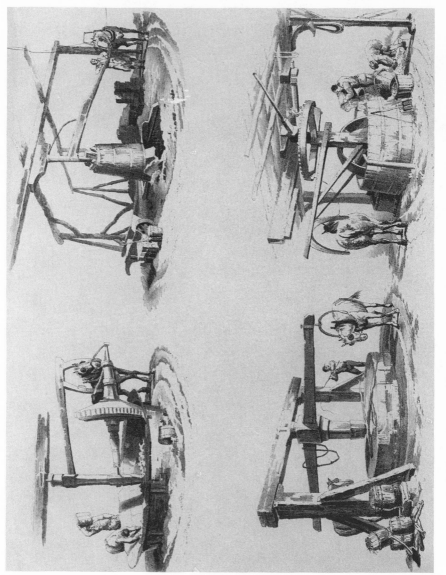

Figure 7. *MICROCOSM*, plate 65, *Mills. Left to right, top to bottom:* a bark mill used by the tanners, a potter's mill for grinding clay, machine for raising water, a mill for grinding chalk.

ished oil paintings, they instantiate, once again, a vision unmediated by fancy or sentiment.

But this specifically picturesque concern with the patterning of vignettes is useful to the aim of the *Microcosm* for more reasons than that the vignette-sketch can be taken to represent a vision of objects disjoined from narrative or from a concern with anything other than supposedly neutral visual appearances. For the patterned page, when it no longer depicts a random collocation of figures and objects, as in Morland's sketchbooks, but instead presents a deliberate sequence of actions, could of course also be used to propose a new form of narrative structure, different from the sentimental narratives that inform contemporary rustic genre painting and particularly useful to the representation of the *division* of labor, when the point is to make a claim for the *coherence* of divided labor or for the ability to understand it *as* coherent. Each vignette can be used to represent the various stages of a divided productive process. In the depiction of this process, the separate figures and groups may appear as preoccupied with their own particular tasks, and so as unaware of themselves as participating in this new form of narrative; and in this light, the *Microcosm* can be seen as depicting a fiction of alienated labor, labor in which the other various stages of production are conceived of as incomprehensible to those whose task is confined to just one of those stages.

The contrast with the bustling atelier scenes of collective work in the plates of late eighteenth-century encyclopedias could hardly be more marked. That contrast is to be understood in discursive rather than material terms. It is not that the work of artisans is being differently performed in 1800; it is being conceived differently, by those who do not perform it, as a collection of individual and separate operations.[21] By conceiving of manual and artisanal labor in this way, those who do not perform it—the readers of the *Microcosm*—can establish their superiority over and distance from those who do, by the claim that they (and only they—that is the fiction) can construct the narrative that links each operation to the others.

21. The history of encyclopedia illustration in eighteenth-century Britain is complicated by the fact that new encyclopedias might buy or copy the plates of their predecessors as well as those of the Diderot and D'Alembert *Encyclopédie*. By and large, however, it seems fair to generalize that the atelier scene more or less disappears around 1790. Such scenes appear, for example, in the first edition of *Encyclopaedia Britannica* (1771); in Hinde's *New Royal and Universal Dictionary of Arts and Sciences* (1771–72); and in Erasmus Middleton's *New Complete Dictionary of Arts and Sciences* (1778). There are none in George Selby Howard's *New Royal Cyclopaedia* (1788) or in Ephraim Chambers's *Cyclopaedia* (1791), and they are most uncommon thereafter.

That task is made easier in the *Microcosm* by the prose essays that accompany the plates (for the sequence of actions the plates illustrate cannot always be read from left to right and top to bottom—figure 8, of potters and leather dressers, is a case in point). The meticulous patterning of the plates positively invites us to understand these different stages of production as together composing not just a coherent story, with a beginning, a middle, and an end, but a unity. To understand *how* the different stages of a productive process cohere into unity, it seems, what is necessary is to take up a position outside that process. It is from there that its unity can be observed, from the place, so to speak, of the philosophic eye, and of the picturesque eye too, now that the picturesque has been reduced to a style and employed in the attempt to give a visible shape to the otherwise invisible structure of the division of labor.

So much, then, by way of justifying my contention that in the *Microcosm* the discursive conflict I identified results in an appropriation of the picturesque by the discourse of the division of labor: an appropriation, I have argued, which has the effect of divesting the picturesque of its character as an occupational idiolect, the discursive articulation of an occupational interest. I want now to represent another result of that conflict, in which the picturesque can instead be understood as resisting the totalizing and appropriating efforts of the discourse of the division of labor and as advancing its own competing version of social knowledge.

The point can be made by examining what occupations the *Microcosm* does and does not illustrate. In 1815 Patrick Colquhoun produced a table that attempted to "Estimate the New Property Arising Annually in Great Britain and Ireland, Arising from the Use of Capital combined with Human Labour and Machinery . . . as derived from *Agriculture, Mines and Minerals, Manufactures, Inland Trade, Foreign Commerce and Shipping, Coasting Trade, Fisheries, and Foreign Income: A Treatise on the Wealth, Power, and Resources of the British Empire*.[22] Colquhoun's estimates are for the year 1812, a few years after the publication of the collected edition of the *Microcosm*. His text is probably the most comprehensive contemporary attempt to understand the economic structure of Britain in terms of the discourse of the division of labor. When I tried to divide the occupations illustrated by Pyne into Colqu-

22. Colquhoun, *Treatise*, pp. 89–96.

Figure 8. *MICROCOSM*, plate 10, *Pottery* and *Leather-Dressing. Left to right, top to bottom:* removing the pots from the kiln (two drawings), packing the ware in crates, undescribed drawing, making heavy vessels in clay, staking the leather, two men withing leather (a process in the production of white leather), staking the leather, grounding the leather to soften it, soaking white leather to get rid of the salt.

houn's categories, I was struck by two things in particular. To begin with, I had somehow gained the impression that a far greater proportion of plates than was in fact the case were devoted to representations of agricultural employments. I had assumed, that is, and wrongly, that the claim made by the picturesque of a special privileged perception of "the natural" and the stated object on the title page to use the vignettes for the embellishment of landscape would have tended to privilege agricultural over manufacturing employments as suitable subjects for representation. The hostility of the picturesque to images of manufacturing industry is far greater than its hostility to images of industrious agricultural workers,[23] as Gilpin's distinction between the "laborious mechanic" and the "loitering peasant" has already suggested to us, for his implication is that we associate the mechanic with industry but that we can more easily associate the peasant with a sauntering disinclination to labor. But in fact, only about nineteen of Pyne's plates represent agricultural employments, while some twenty-nine depict what Colquhoun classified as manufactures, and some twenty-two depict subjects of inland distributive trades. Another three illustrate trades associated with mines and minerals, and about four each represent coastal trade and fisheries—the figures are approximate because not all the plates can be easily classified.

Second, however, I was struck by the fact that of what Colquhoun identifies as the four most productive manufacturing industries, Pyne chooses to illustrate only the leather industry, which appears in two plates. Thus, apart from one plate of sheep shearing, the *Microcosm* makes no acknowledgment at all of the textile trades in Britain and Ireland (cotton, woolen and linen manufactures), to the increasing mechanization of which Colquhoun, among others, attributed Britain's economic miracle. Of exportable manufactures, "by far the most extensive," according to Colquhoun, were *"cotton, woolen, leather, linen, fabricated metals, glass,* and *porcelain,"* in which he includes all ceramic manufactures (p. 68). Of these seven, Pyne illustrates only three, and of the sixteen most productive manufacturing industries, according to Colquhoun's estimates, only eight.

These two things are of course related. At the point at which woolen and linen production become manufacturing industries, they move,

23. See, for example, the reviewer in the *Somerset House Gazette,* June 5, 1824, presumably Pyne himself, of a watercolor by Joshua Cristall, whose "peasants, though truly English, are not the slouching boors and slatternly alehouse maids of George Morland. They are selected from the sequestered village, yet uncontaminated by the vicinity of manufactories," and they are "the healthy offspring of retirement and content."

for the most part, indoors and are lost to the landscape and the rustic genre artist. My impression of a bias toward images of agricultural employments resulted not only from the bias of my own interest in landscape but from the fact that, of Pyne's 121 plates, fewer than a dozen illustrate occupations that are carried on wholly or partly indoors.[24] Three of these are plates of cottage interiors and domestic work, a favorite theme of rural-subject painters, and in none of the others is the interior location suggested except by the absence of the usual landscape motifs. What purports, then, to be a "microcosm," a comprehensive and a disinterested delineation of the "various modes" in which Britain's "capital is invested" and "her industry is employed," turns out to be a thoroughly partial view from the vantage point of a particular occupation, that of the artist in landscape and genre.

Thus employments are divided and distinguished by Pyne according to the different possibilities they offer for the embellishment of landscape, and the potential of figures to embellish is so much more important a qualification for their inclusion in the *Microcosm* than their ability to contribute to Britain's wealth that in disregard of his own stated purposes and in deference to an imperative enunciated by Gilpin, Pyne devotes a number of plates to labor conceived of as so unproductive that it is not recognized as labor at all. In his poem "On Landscape Painting," Gilpin had advised the artist not only to exclude, as usual, the "low arts of husbandry" from "rocky," "wild," and "awful" scenes but to invite in their place "gypsey-tribes" and "banditti fierce," who would be as appropriately "wild as those scenes themselves."[25] Accordingly, Pyne devotes two plates to gypsies, who, for all their "sloth and idleness," as Gray describes it, "certainly afford us some very picturesque groups" (1:17).[26] There is a further plate devoted to smugglers, partly on the grounds that "the scenery . . . in which they are generally found, has much of the grand and the wild" and partly because they can stand as homegrown substitutes for the "banditti" who provide the conventional *staffage* of landscape painting in the style of Salvator Rosa (2:25).

24. These depict basket makers and coopers, brewing (half sheet), coppersmiths, cottage groups, cottagers, domestic employments, iron foundry, pottery and leather dressing, slaughterhouses, statuary, and wheelwrights.

25. Gilpin, *Three Essays*, p. 165.

26. For some useful remarks on attitudes to gypsies in the 1790s and early 1800s, see David Simpson, *Wordsworth's Historical Imagination: The Poetry of Displacement* (London: Methuen, 1987), pp. 43–44.

But in case there are some for whom only the real thing will do, Pyne also provides (figure 9) four vignettes of banditti in the genuine Calabrian style, wearing armor, lounging on rocks and under trees, and contributing only in the most unimaginably indirect way to the economic progress of Britain. By plates like these, but also by the nearly exclusive concentration on outdoor employments, social knowledge is defined as knowledge useful to the landscape artist. And in this connection, it is worth noticing that when the book was republished in 1845, by which time a clearer division had been produced between technical and decorative drawing, its title was changed. "Microcosm" was dropped, the main title became *Picturesque Groups for the Embellishment of Landscape*, and reference to whatever useful application the book still aspired to was relegated to the small print of the title page.

In this process of resistance to the totalizing aspirations of the discourse of the division of labor, that discourse is itself revealed as an occupational, an interested discourse, with its own specialized account of what knowledge is. For the whole point is that gypsies, smugglers, banditti (or armed robbers, for that is how they are treated in the accompanying prose essay) were indeed *participants* in the economic structure of early nineteenth-century Britain. They performed a variety of labor, which was, however, ignored in accounts of the division of labor, not because it was illegal but because it was invisible to the philosophic eye. And it was so because economic philosophy conceived of society as structured like a market in which people exchanged the goods and services they had to offer for the goods and services they needed or desired. Gypsies, who were almost universally regarded as thieves, robbers, and smugglers, were all excluded from the visible market; the goods they had to exchange had not been acquired by anything that a political economist could understand as labor or could recognize as an act of exchange.

The absence of such occupations from the economic and social totality envisaged by the discourse of the division of labor reveals, as I say, that this discourse offers a restricted and an interested account of what social knowledge is. It could be argued that the presence of such occupations in the *Microcosm* and the absence of images of large-scale manufacturing industry reveal the occupational bias of the picturesque. But it could equally be argued that the picturesque, by virtue of its ability to notice and to represent the activities of criminals and others who are invisible within the commercial market, and by virtue too of its ability to represent leisure as well as industry—the *Microcosm* includes plates of archery, cricket, hunting, skittles, and so on—pro-

Figure 9. *MICROCOSM*, plate 60, *Banditti*

duces an account of the variety of social activities no less expansive, though certainly less methodized, than that revealed to the economic philosopher.

I have not been able to compress my account of the plates sufficiently to allow me to discuss the accompanying essays at any length; so I can only give the most general idea of what interests me about them. It is that they seem unable to produce an account of the various occupations they describe which can represent them as other than divided, and as divided beyond the point of being comprehensible in terms of their participation in what might be, however invisibly, a coherent form of social organization.

We have seen how the possibility of envisaging a coherent society depended, for the discourse of the division of labor, upon the production of a unified and disinterested subject to articulate that discourse. The visual discourse of the picturesque, deployed through the plates, could produce the illusion of such a subject by bestowing the same kind of alienated attention on all the objects illustrated. There is no equivalent coherence in the essays, because there seems to be no similarly coherent discourse available to govern the representation of all the various occupations they describe. Their incoherence arises partly from the fact that many of those occupations present themselves to the writer as far more thoroughly inscribed within their own individual discursive histories: the shepherd within the pastoral, the plowman within the georgic, the haymaker within the comic, the soldier within a discourse of popular patriotism, and so on. It arises also from that hospitality to discursive variety which characterizes the essay genre in the eighteenth and early nineteenth centuries. Thus, some employments are discussed in terms of their history and some in terms of the supposed moral condition of their practitioners; of others, Gray simply observes that there is nothing much to say about them. Interwoven with all these discourses is the discourse of the division of labor, which attempts to establish a unified subject with a stable viewing position and a coherent grasp of each occupation in particular and the structure of the body politic in general. But it is unable ever to silence those other discourses for any length of time and so becomes just one of a hubbub of voices, which together produce the representation of a society irretrievably atomized and dispersed.

One of the major preoccupations of the conference for which this essay was originally prepared was the question of what "materialism" might mean for criticism in the humanities. David Simpson, in opening the proceedings, spoke of the disintegrated condition of materialist criticism, divided, as he put it, between the view that all efforts at integration (totality) are inevitably totalitarian and the view that the refusal of totality is itself nothing more than a reflection of the dominant ideology. As long as the division is construed in this way, my own essay would seem to subscribe to the first version of materialist criticism, whose direction Simpson specified as the patient and precise reconstruction of particular events and occasions in the past. I am happy enough with this account of what my essay has tried to do, but only if this notion of precise reconstruction is not predicated on the assumption that we can somehow reconstruct a real history from the traces of the past. The past is available to us only in the form of representations, and it was, equally to the point, available to the past only in the same form. To attempt to reconstruct the precise occasions of history is to attempt to reconstruct them in the only form in which they are or were available to be known, as representations articulated within the different discourses that combine and compete to represent the "real."

The problems of constructing a totalizing materialist account of the history or the culture of a society have been reiterated often enough to require no lengthy rehearsal here. Materialism announces that human subjects are not coherent and independent entities but the incoherent products of a history it defines as a material history. It conceives of subjects as constrained by the discourses they articulate and by the ideology inscribed within those discourses. A totalizing account, on the other hand, which makes a claim to be true, to be a quasi-scientific description of what is really the case, must presuppose an integral and a transcendent subject, undetermined by discourse and ideology. And yet if materialism does not attempt to produce such accounts, it deprives itself of the possibility of constructing the narratives of change and conflict which seem to constitute its raison d'être; it is reduced, at best, to the analysis of isolated and arbitrary moments, which can be connected within larger narratives only with an equal arbitrariness.

It is with this problem of authority, the problem involved in defining the place from which the real processes of history can be perceived, that my essay has been concerned, with whatever degree of indirection. What interests me about the *Microcosm* is the competition played out within it between the discourse of the division of labor and the discourse of the picturesque, a competition in which the first attempts to arrogate to itself the privilege of being the totalizing discourse that includes and can account for the other forms of discursive representation within the text, and in which the picturesque responds by elaborating a field of knowledge no less expansive, which in turn localizes and particularizes the claim to generality, to totality, of the discourse of the division of labor. The totalizing discourse is thus revealed as the discourse of a subject that defines its own partiality even as it denies it; it operates as a form of oppression in that it defines what knowledge is in accordance with its own exclusive interests; and in doing so, it calls up a resistance to itself in the form of a competing discourse, which can articulate the interests it excludes.

I am offering this conclusion not as a means of endorsing one side of the division in materialist criticism which Simpson has located but rather as a contribution to the archaeology of that division. In recent debates, the question of the loss of the possibility of totalization has been described in terms of the transition from the modern to the postmodern. What I have been trying to show is that that issue has always been present in the competition among the various discourses of capitalism to claim the totality for themselves.

5

Emerson's *Nature:*
A Materialist Reading

R. Jackson Wilson

Autobiographical accounts of mystical experiences, transports, or ecstasies have to confront, sooner or later, the tough problem of getting back to the ground, to the realm of ordinary experience. It is, after all, only the implicit notion of the normal that gives force to the idea that it can be transcended. And the assumption behind any verbal report of an ascent into the wondrous is that it has to be written "down," in ordinary language, time, and space. But perhaps no transcendental experience has ended so abruptly and mournfully as in Ralph Waldo Emerson's *Nature*. Emerson brought the figure he sometimes called "the poet," sometimes "a man," and sometimes "I" back from a mystical ecstasy by plunging him into mourning:

> Nature always wears the colors of the spirit. To a man laboring under calamity, the heat of his own fire hath sadness in it. Then, there is a kind of contempt of the landscape felt by him who has just lost by death a dear friend. The sky is less grand as it shuts down over less worth in the population.[1]

This dark passage is a curious ending for Emerson's first chapter, where he proposed a joyful solution to the problem he had set forth in

1. I have used *"Nature," with an Introduction, a Note on the Text, and a Bibliography Prepared by Warner Berthoff* (San Francisco: Chandler, 1968), p. 14, hereafter cited in the text.

a brief introduction: how can an alienated age, accustomed to taking experience at second hand, recover an "original relation" with Nature,[2] and find union between the self and "all that is not me"? The fulgent solution was laid out in a schematic narrative of several pages, climaxing in the poet's glad possession of Nature. In the narrative, Emerson leads his autobiographical figure out of society but also out of his own "chamber," first into the streets, then to charming landscapes, across bare commons, and finally into the woods. The narrative is one of progressive and increasingly solitary release from constraint, a heightening assurance that the protagonist truly possesses the "horizon."

The tone of the familiar passages is increasing exhilaration. Early in the narrative, Emerson talks of how his poet figure had felt exalted in Nature, even if Nature came in the shape of a muddy common under a lowering sky: "Crossing a bare common, in snow puddles, at twilight, under a clouded sky, without having in my thoughts any occurrence of special good fortune, I have enjoyed a perfect exhilaration. Almost I fear to think how glad I am" (p. 8).[3] A bit later, Emerson moves his figure farther away from society, into the woods, where he can reclaim the perpetual, the perennial, and the millennial:

> In the woods, too, a man casts off his years, as the snake his slough, and at what period soever of life, is always a child. In the woods, is perpetual youth. Within these plantations of God, a decorum and sanctity reign, a perennial festival is dressed, and the guest sees not how he should tire of them in a thousand years. In the woods, we return to reason and faith. There I feel that nothing can befal me in life,—no disgrace, no calamity, (leaving me my eyes,) which Nature cannot repair. (p. 10)

2. In this and in other similar instances in what follows, I observe Emerson's portentous capitalizations of key concepts, in order to preserve distinctions between his idiosyncratic meanings and the common meanings of such terms.

3. Emerson had developed this passage, like many others, through his journals. In 1834 he wrote, "I do not cross the common without a wild poetic delight notwithstanding the prose of my demeanor." But this must not be taken to mean that he actually *had* one or more such experiences of wild delight. His journals, like the essays and lectures he took from them, are more about experiences as they might come to some imagined person than they are about what actually happened to him. The journals are a writer's journals, and the few passages that record real experiences that probably went deepest—such as the one recording Ellen's death or the entry in which he reported that he had opened her coffin months after she was entombed—are usually quite brief and without flourish. William H. Gilman et al., eds., *The Journals and Miscellaneous Notebooks of Ralph Waldo Emerson*, 16 vols. (Cambridge: Belknap Press of Harvard University Press 1960–82), 4:355. I shall cite this invaluable collection by volume and page, giving dates for entries only if they are material to the point under discussion. The laconic entry about opening Ellen Tucker Emerson's coffin is at 4:7.

In these woods, Emerson's figure of the poet completes his bold project. He becomes as completely at one with Nature as Emerson's most careful use of the language could make him. He vanishes into the world but simultaneously takes the whole world into himself. There is a transaction in which he loses his private identity and becomes nothing in order to see all. But in the transaction, he gains spiritual liquidity: his head is "bathed," "currents" flow through him: "Standing on the bare ground,—my head bathed by the blithe air, and uplifted into infinite space,—all mean egotism vanishes. I become a transparent eyeball. I am nothing. I see all. The currents of Universal Being circulate through me; I am part and particle of God" (p. 13).[4] This moment of transcendence enables the poet to cut the last remaining ties that bind him to the world of ordinary men. He has already abandoned whatever learned profession kept him in his chamber, reading and writing. He has relinquished property, and even the idea of property. Now, in his climactic ecstasy, he surrenders what remains of his social identity. Family and friends, acquaintances and servants—all the relationships of town and village life—are quite lost to consciousness: "The name of the nearest friend sounds then foreign and accidental. To be brothers, to be acquaintances, master or servant, is then a trifle and a disturbance. I am the lover of uncontained and immortal beauty. In the wilderness, I find something more dear and connate than in streets or villages" (p. 13).

To this point, the tone has been one of mounting gladness. But then Emerson passed, without transition, to his mournful observation about Nature always wearing the color of the spirit. Without a hint of warning or preparation, he suddenly turned from ecstasy to mourning, and so ended his first chapter, seemingly undisturbed by the odd rhetorical blunder a quizzical reader might think he had committed. In his narrative—the most important chapter in Nature—Emerson had been insisting on a view of experience in which the sky confers worth on the solitary individual and makes him glad. Now, almost offhandedly, he reversed epistemological gears and admitted that the sky itself

4. Emerson had anticipated this in his journal for 1835: "Standing on the bare ground, with my head bathed by the blithe air, and uplifted into the infinite space, I become happy in my universal relations." But again, he was not necessarily reporting an actual experience. In fact, the way this entry runs out of rhetorical steam (with words like "bathed," "blithe," and "infinite" cooling into the meager phrase "happy in my universal relations") is very like the journal entry in which "wild poetic delight" decays into "notwithstanding the prose of my demeanor." It is fallacious to reason from the seeming urgency of prose to the urgency of any experience that might have prompted it. *Journals and Notebooks* 5:18.

is less grand as it shuts down on less worth in the population. At the climax of his venture into Nature, the poet finds in the wilderness something more "dear" than in streets and villages; but suddenly he drops into mourning a "dear friend" and fretting over the worth of the "population" that inhabits those same streets and villages. The social relations that had a moment before been "foreign and accidental" all at once become essential and determining. In his ecstasy, he had been a spiritual island, but Emerson suddenly has him remember his Donne and acknowledge that the social toll exacted by death makes grand poetic vision impossible. (How often in his years as a clergyman must Emerson have fussed with ministerial formulas for explaining to grief-stricken parishioners—and to himself—how a benign Unitarian God could send death even into the pews of his Second Church?)

Nor does the little paragraph seem to make any sense with respect to what is to come after. On the facing righthand page begins a new chapter with the cheering title "Commodity," only the first of several chapters in which Emerson methodically counts the ways Nature serves man. In these chapters nothing answers to the sudden invocation of loss and grief at the climactic point of chapter 1. Nature, he argues in the rest of the book, "serves" man incessantly and prodigally. He begins "Commodity" by talking about how even the "private poor man" lives in luxury, for he enjoys the fruits of social and economic development, which are all part of Nature. The poor man "hath cities, ships, canals, bridges, built for him. He goes to the post-office, and the human race run on his errands; to the book-shop, and the human race read and write of all that happens, for him; to the court-house, and nations repair his wrongs. He sets his house upon the road, and the human race go forth every morning, and shovel out the snow, and cut a path for him" (p. 17). This "poor man" seems to have money to buy stamps and books, and the leisure to read them. He can pay lawyers. He has a house and apparently pays the property taxes necessary to support snow removal. As a locus of value, he is at odds with the gloomy phrase that ends chapter 1: "less worth in the population."

So the little paragraph of mourning seems to be a textual anomaly, out of joint with what comes immediately before and after, and out of joint also with the cheering tone and character of the book as a whole. Some textual anomalies are no doubt lapses that ought to be ignored. One possible way of explaining, or explaining away, the mourning passage would be to attribute it to haste or carelessness. A quite widely held view of his practice takes Emerson to be a kind of quilter, piecing together oddly shaped and colored bits of fabric, mostly taken from his journals, into a patchwork held together only very loosely, as though any piece might be taken out or moved around with no damage to the whole. If this is so, there might not be anything at all interesting about the presence and placement of any one rhetorical patch. But whatever may be the character of many of Emerson's other essays, *Nature* is a very carefully designed piece of work. In particular, the introduction and the first chapter are extremely careful exercises in planning, with joinery work as intricate and careful as might be found in any piece of writing.[5] The mourning passage is given a highly privileged place at the end of a chapter. So it ought to be approached with care, and on the assumption that Emerson had some fairly definite ideas about its purposes. It is even possible that this apparent textual anomaly could turn out to have a decisive bearing on the general import of *Nature*.

Perhaps the most obvious—and certainly the most popular—explanation of the mourning passage is that it was a reflex of Emerson's own experience of loss and grief. One informal critical tradition holds that Emerson was quite deliberately reaching into his own life, remembering his own loss of "a dear friend"—his brother Charles, perhaps, but more probably his first wife, Ellen Tucker Emerson. Her death had grieved him profoundly and even driven him to thoughts of suicide, or at least to thoughts of poems about suicide:

> And o perhaps the welcome stroke
> That severs forever this fleshly yoke
> Shall restore the vision to the soul
> In the great Vision of the Whole.[6]

There is no useful reason to doubt the depth and sincerity of Emerson's grief for both Charles and Ellen. It might even be sensible to suppose that writing about the poet's great gladness in nature would surely remind him of those passed. After all, the poet has come to Nature like a bridgegroom. He has put off his faded wardrobe. He is

5. I have discussed *Nature*, and some of his other work, at much greater length in *Figures of Speech: American Writers and the Literary Marketplace, from Benjamin Franklin to Emily Dickinson* (New York: Alfred A. Knopf, 1989).

6. *Journals and Notebooks* 3:230–31. Something like this "welcome stroke" comes to *Nature*'s poet, making him dead to the world, in order to baptize him in universal being.

"bathed." He is the "lover of uncontained and immortal beauty." Surely such language could not have failed to evoke intense memories of the "unmeasured affection" Emerson said he had had for Ellen Tucker.

But treating Emerson's grief and its mnemonic residue as an item of experience which found voice in the mourning passage has unfortunate implications. It is the kind of interpretative maneuver that sometimes gets called "historicist." But in fact, like much of what passes for "historicism," it abstracts—and so *de*-historicizes—experience. Emerson mourned for Ellen in a historically definite way, a way that was shaped by the course of his experience at large. His grief was not grief as such. It had a particular import and mattered to him in particular ways. Specifically, it was directly linked to the urgent vocational choice he had made soon after Ellen died, to quit his ministry and to "write and be a fine thinker, all by himself."[7]

Career and marriage were closely linked in Emerson's mind. About the career there had at first been no doubt: He would go to Harvard, then on to the Divinity School, and when he was old enough he would follow generations of Emerson men into the pulpit, almost certainly in Boston or one of the nearby towns. In 1824, as he was about to turn twenty-one, he was conscious that he was about to become "*legally* a man," and he made his commitment explicit in his journal: "I deliberately dedicate my time, my talents, and my hopes to the Church."[8] Then in 1826 he was "approbated," licensed to give sermons occasionally but not yet to hold a pulpit in any Unitarian church. But all this— finishing college, dedicating himself at twenty-one to a ministerial career, studying in the Divinity School, and even being permitted to preside over church services from time to time—was only so much preparation. Until he had a congregation of his own and a wife to go with it, his manhood would be merely legal. And when these two things did come to pass in 1829, when he was about to become minis-

7. This was the language of Emerson's brother Charles. At least it was Charles who committed the language to paper. But it could well have been Emerson's own phrasing, since during the period after Ellen's death, Emerson's career had been a principal subject of conversations and letters among his mother and brothers. At the point of Emerson's resignation from his ministry, Charles wrote: "Now things seem to flying to pieces, and I don't know when they will again be put together and he [be] harnessed in . . . the labors of a daily calling. . . . I do not doubt he may write and be a fine thinker, all alone by himself; but I think he needs to be dragged closer to people by some practical vocation, however it may irk his tastes." Quoted in James Elliott Cabot, *A Memoir of Ralph Waldo Emerson*, 2 vols. (Boston: Houghton, Mifflin and Co., 1893), 1:174.

8. Entry for April 18, 1824, *Journals and Notebooks* 2:237.

ter of Boston's Second Unitarian Church and to marry the pretty
nineteen-year-old daughter of a wealthy merchant family, he understood the events as paired elements in an equation whose outcome
was "manhood." He dramatized the moment in his journal in a way
that linked his betrothal and his ordination, and prayerfully draped
over both a mantle of divine will: "My history has had its important
days within a brief period. I enjoy the luxury of an unmeasured
affection for an object so deserving of it all & who requites it all. I am
called by an ancient & respectable church to become its pastor. I
recognize in these events . . . the hand of my heavenly father. . . . I
feel my total dependance. O God direct and guard and bless me."[9]

Emerson was ready in principle to admit that his pulpit and his bride
were not rewards he had earned, although the "dependance" he chose
to acknowledge in his journal was only on his "heavenly father." In
truth, he was dependent in many other ways on less spiritual kinds of
guardings and blessings. He had always enjoyed important familial
and institutional advantages. He had been entitled to what he called
"great expectation," indeed, just about every expectation any young
man of his social class in New England could hope for.

R. Waldo Emerson (his own initial choice of a professional name)
was the son, grandson, and great-grandson of ministers. He was even
the stepgrandson of another, since the eminent Reverend Ezra Ripley
of Concord had married the widow of his predecessor, Emerson's
paternal grandmother. His grandfather Emerson had held the pulpit
of the church at Concord. Emerson's father was minister of Boston's
grandly prestigious First Church. Stepgrandfather Ripley still minis-
tered to the Concord church while Emerson was growing up. The first
sermon Emerson ever preached was given from his uncle Samuel
Ripley's pulpit in Waltham. He preached his second sermon in his
father's old church, the First. It was also in the First Church that he
gave his first sustained series of sermons during the years between his
approbation and his ordination. When he was ordained at the Second
Church in March of 1829, the ceremony was a tableau of ancestral and
institutional continuity. The first ritual step, the "charge" to the new
minister, was administered by Grandfather Ripley—who had also
charged Emerson's own father thirty-seven years before. The ordination sermon was delivered by Uncle Samuel Ripley. The "right hand of
fellowship" welcoming the new minister to his congregation was of-

9. Entry for Jan. 17, 1829, *Journals and Notebooks* 3:149–50.

fered by the man who had replaced Emerson's father at the First Church, Nathaniel Frothingham.[10]

This intricate and dense network of family and professional relationships was the defining context of Waldo Emerson's youth. It limited the choices he could consider, but it sanctioned the choices he made. It took him through Harvard College and the Divinity School. It made his selection of a bride plausible not only to him but also to Ellen Tucker and her family. It made his ordination much more than the symbolic ratification of a contract between him and the Second Church—made it into a public rite, a ceremonial declaration of the claims and privileges of family and history.

But one persistent problem, one gap in the "great expectation," had threatened to negate the entitlements that defined young Waldo Emerson: there was no money. His mother got very little of the merchant wealth that belonged to her side of the family, and when Emerson's father died in 1811, he left a forty-three-year-old widow with six children ranging in age from eleven to three. From that point on, Emerson's life had been shaped by charity. It had come in the form of patronage, channeled through the same familial and professional systems that eventually led Emerson to his marriage and his position at the Second Church. The First Church had provided the widow Emerson with a seven-year annuity of five hundred dollars a year. Waldo had been only eight when his father died, but the annuity lasted until he was ready to enter Harvard. Then the church voted money to help pay for his education. (It was the income on a bequest that had already been used to help Emerson's elder brother through college.) Emerson's headmaster at the Boston Public Latin School was able to get him an appointment as the "President's Freshman"—a sort of messenger and orderly—which paid his tuition and room for the first year, and his uncle Samuel Ripley, who was running a school, completed the arrangements. He gave Waldo a job teaching there during the winter vacations to augment his income.[11]

When he graduated from Harvard, Emerson tried to get a position teaching at the Latin School, but he was turned down because his

10. *Journals and Notebooks*, 2:98n; Ralph L. Rusk, *The Life of Ralph Waldo Emerson* (New York: C. Scribner's Sons, 1949), p. 119; Gay Wilson Allen, *Waldo Emerson, a Biography* (New York: Viking, 1981), pp. 93–94. Emerson's inaugural sermon at Second Church was "The Christian Ministry." *Young Emerson Speaks: Unpublished Discourses on Many Subjects* (Boston: Houghton Mifflin, 1938).

11. Cabot, *Memoir* 1:27; Allen, *Waldo Emerson*, p. 38; Rusk, *Life*, p. 62.

record at Harvard had been poor (he ranked below the middle of his class). Nevertheless, he was able to fall back again on family connections and teach for several years in a school for girls which his elder brother William had started in Boston. Even in matters of health and leisure he depended on patronage. When he became convinced that he had tuberculosis—though he could find no doctor willing to accept his self-diagnosis—he resorted once more to family. In 1826, during the winter after his approbation, he traveled to South Carolina and Florida with the financial help of his uncle Samuel.[12]

The obvious contrast between inherited "expectation" and practical "dependance" occasionally chafed. In student days, Emerson grumbled from time to time over his family's preoccupation with "pedigree." He could even declare that ancestry was irrelevant and that "my business is with the living." But such moments of brave impatience were exceptional and probably kept quietly confined to his journals. (In any case, two years later, he labeled the front cover of a notebook "Genealogy" and set down about fifteen pages of notes on his ancestry.) When he was ready for what he thought of as manhood—career and marriage—his deepest sense of himself was as a man who would finally be able to earn a good living and gain a degree of celebrity doing what generations of Emersons had done. On this point, as in the matter of pedigree, he had occasional moments of quiet unease. Once or twice, during his apprenticeship as a minister, he joked that he might leave the profession and "commence author" if only the "muse" were not "unwilling." But such speculations were few and not at all serious. From the time he was an undergraduate, he dreamed of "fame," but for his ambitions, the Unitarian establishment seemed an ample and safe stage. Indeed, it seemed to him the only plausible institutional setting for a career. And this same career was what made it possible for him to have the "luxury" of fastening his unmeasured affection on a girl like Ellen Tucker.[13]

And so, as he set out on his marriage and career, Emerson thought of his life as defined by continuities of time and place. "History," he

---

12. Allen, *Waldo Emerson*, pp. 60–80; *The Letters of Ralph Waldo Emerson*, ed. Ralph L. Rusk, 6 vols. (New York: Columbia University Press, 1939), 1:80.

13. Emerson's most famous complaint against the idea of "pedigree" was in a journal entry of Jan. 1825 which ended: "But the dead sleep in their moonless night; my business is with the living." *Journals and Notebooks* 2:316. The notes on his ancestry are at 3:349–53. The notion that he might "commence author" was put in a very lighthearted letter to his brother William in 1827, *Letters* 1:201.

stuffily said, "is premiere in the cabinet." And he could write to a friend, before he had even met his future wife: "I am in the pleasant land of my fathers, and of my sons and sons' sons peradventure." He could travel to Charleston and St. Augustine, but the idea of a life any distance from the land of his fathers was unthinkable. A year after he was licensed to preach, the possibility developed of a call to a congregation in New York. He recoiled, saying that he would rather "be a doorkeeper at home than bishop to aliens."[14]

To be a minister was to take up what he called a "priestly" vocation, to become the moral voice of a congregation, "a hundred other hearts to which God has united us."[15] It was a career that led emphatically away from nature toward institutions, away from solitude toward community. The congregation was not an audience but a constituency. The "priest" spoke not to strangers but to families he knew intimately. And this relationship was manifested concretely in the legal contract that bound the minister to his congregation, with a definite income, in principle for life. The duties were clear and fixed by powerful traditions. He could count his visits to the sick and the grieving; he could keep track of the numbers of people he married or baptized. There were sermons to prepare, and he could carefully number these, too. There might be times when the prospect of having to write one every week seemed "terrifick." But ministering to the Second Church meant having definite, limited tasks, performed for an almost changeless constituency, at close range, and for measured rewards.[16]

Emerson's understanding of his profession was almost perfectly opposed to any possibility that he might "commence author." In the career of a writer, both the tasks and the rewards were undefined. The work of an "author" was produced not for a familiar constituency but for a marketplace full of strangers, and it carried no certainty whatever of profit. Little wonder that the idea of becoming a professional writer surfaced in his mind only from time to time and was usually written into his journal as a slightly sheepish joke. Little wonder either that whenever his elder brother hinted that he might abandon his own career as a lawyer in New York to take up lecturing or newspaper

14. Emerson to John Boynton Hill, June 19, 1823, to William Emerson, Jan. 6 and Oct. 31, 1827, *Letters* 1:132, 185, 218.

15. This notion of the congregation was put in a sermon written in June 1827, during the first year of his approbation. It is in *Journals and Notebooks* 3:90–91.

16. The remark about the "terrifick" obligation to write four sermons a month was in a a letter to his stepgrandfather, March 22, 1829, *Letters* 1:26.

editing, Emerson was alarmed. He urged William to stick to the "comfort and respectability" of his learned profession.[17]

In less than three years after Emerson attained his "manhood," his own neat world of comfort and respectability unraveled. Ellen Tucker Emerson died early in 1831. A year and a half later, in September 1832, he went into the pulpit of Second Church to resign.

The ostensible reason for his resignation was a disagreement with the proprietors of the Second Church, but Emerson himself provoked the quarrel. He abruptly refused to continue to administer the Lord's Supper. He had a great deal of support in the congregation and almost certainly could have worked out a compromise if he had wanted. He could even have continued to supervise the sacrament as a "symbolic" exercise, as he had been doing without complaining even to his journal. But instead he chose to insist on his position in a way that forced an end to his contract.

After he resigned, it did not take Emerson more than five years to become a professional man of letters. In fact, he eventually became one of the most famous and financially successful American writers and lecturers of his age. It is tempting to see his resignation from the Second Church as the liberation of a talented writer who had decided to free himself from the constraints of a clergyman's life and to take his chances in the literary marketplace. But in truth, he left the ministry without telling anyone what he planned to do. If he was going to "commence author," he did not confess it to his family or his journal. He defined his vocational crisis precisely, but only on one side: he was clear, publicly and privately, about what he would *not* do. But he carefully pictured himself, both to others and privately, as a man who had set himself adrift. His decision had been prompted in some measure by his very real grief for his dead wife. And he may have been lured on by the expectation that when her will was probated he would inherit enough money to equal twenty years of his starting salary at Second Church. But if he had definite plans, he only hinted at them, even to his brothers and his own journal.[18]

17. The cautions to William about lecturing and newspapers were in letters of April 3, 1828, and June 29, 1831, *Letters* 1:230, 326–27.

18. Emerson's journals and letters for this period hardly ever mention a "daily calling" or "practical vocation," except in a gallows-humor way. The sermon Emerson preached on the occasion of his resignation is in *The Complete Works of Ralph Waldo Emerson*, ed. Edward Waldo Emerson, 12 vols. (Boston: Houghton, Mifflin and Co.,

He did understand quite well that there was a literary career to be made. He knew he could try editing a journal, and he joked some with his brothers about founding one. He also knew he could try public lecturing, which had already become a well-paying career in New England for those who succeeded at it. But he was unwilling or unable simply to launch himself on the new career without some further step of preparation. In discussions with his family about his situation, he adopted a mixture of irony and self-deprecation: "Projects sprout and bloom in my head," he wrote to William a few weeks after quitting his pulpit, "of action, literature, philosophy."[19] He was at a marked vocational juncture, obviously, but he was unable (or perhaps just unwilling) to confront the problem directly. Instead, he let himself be peculiarly vulnerable to chance and impulse. He planned another trip south three months after his resignation, once more for his "health." When a vessel unexpectedly offered itself for Italy, however, he jumped at the chance with little or no explanation to anyone—not even to his own journal.

But what appeared to be chance and impulse developed a logic. He set out for Europe interested in literary—not physical—landscapes, monuments, and ruins. He did visit cathedrals and catacombs, but impatiently. It gradually became clear that the real purpose of his trip was to see men who had made triumphantly successful careers as writers. In England he visited Samuel Taylor Coleridge and William Wordsworth, and acted as though his only real purpose was to see that they were indeed ordinary men and not inimitable masters. When he met Carlyle, he was willing to regard him as a true monument precisely to the degree that Carlyle was willing to see *him* as a potential one. What he was looking for was a sense of assurance that he might indeed "commence author," and might do so without being either sheepish or ironic about it.[20]

1903–4), 11:8–25. It contains much more scriptural citation and close theological argument than usual for him. The episode can be followed in *Journals and Notebooks* 4:27, 29, 30, 32. See also *Letters* 1:352–53.

19. *Letters*, 1:356.

20. Warner Berthoff's introduction to *"Nature," with an Introduction, a Note on the Text, and a Bibliography Prepared by Warner Berthoff*, pp. vii–lxxxi, has some very intelligent observations about the relationship among Emerson's resignation, his trip to Europe, and the writing of *Nature*. Some similar arguments are well put in B. L. Packer, *Emerson's Fall: A Reinterpretation of the Major Essays* (New York: Continuum, 1982), p. 236 n. 26. See also Merton M. Sealts, "The Composition of *Nature*," in *Emerson's "Nature": Origin, Growth, Meaning*, ed. Merton M. Sealts and Alfred Ferguson (Carbondale: Southern Illinois University Press, 1979), pp. 175–93.

By the time he was ready to start home, in September 1833, Emerson was able to tell himself without confusion or embarrassment that his experiences with Wordsworth, Coleridge, and Carlyle had "comforted and confirmed me in my convictions." A few days later, aboard ship, he made clear what these "convictions" involved. "I like my book about nature," he said in his journal. Then he added, with only an ampersand to separate the thoughts, "& I wish I knew where and how I ought to live."[21] He seemed to be certain about the first thing, that he would write a book, and uncertain about the other, how he would live. But the two fell together easily in one sentence exactly because his conviction was that the first was part of the answer to the second. From this point onward, Emerson's experience would be organized almost entirely around the fact that he was a professional writer whose purpose was to get his living from his books, essays, lectures, and poems.

This change in profession was made easier, perhaps made possible, by Ellen Tucker Emerson's will. Her estate was settled in his favor, after being contested by some of the Tucker family, and the resulting capital of over eleven thousand dollars would yield a steady income. It was not quite enough to live on in good style, take a new wife, and give the kind of economic help he wanted to his family. He would have to continue for years to substitute in various Unitarian pulpits. But from September 1833 on, his central purpose was to make a career as a writer and lecturer. Over the next few decades, he would produce a great body of work, all of it in the hope that it would bring him a return. He himself could not only admit as much but joke about it with a charming candor. After the probation of his wife's will, he wrote a quite witty letter to his brother William, making a charming equation between having money and being able to live the life of Reason, as against being poor and subject to the demands of the Understanding, "that wrinkled calculator, the steward of our house, to whom is committed the support of our animal life."

> Reason is the highest faculty of the soul—what we mean often by the soul itself; it never *reasons*, never proves, it simply perceives; it is vision. The Understanding toils all the time, compares, contrives, adds, argues, near-sighted but strong-sighted, dwelling in the present, the expedient, the customary. . . . The Tucker estate is so far settled that I am made sure of an income of about $1200. wherewith the Reason of Mother and

21. Entry of Sept. 6, 1833, *Journals and Notebooks* 4:237.

you and I might defy the Understanding upon his own ground, for the
rest of the few years in which we shall be subject to his insults.

"I need not say," he pointedly added, "that when I speak in play I
speak in earnest."[22]

So Emerson's grief over his "loss of a dear friend" was bound to be a
complicated affair. He had lavished his "unmeasured affection" on
Ellen, but his marriage to her had been part of a vocational formula,
too. And her death surely contributed to his willingness to leave the
ministry, just as her will contributed to his material capacity to do so.
All these factors constituted a highly charged manifold of love, ambition, grief, and vocational risk. *Nature* itself—considered not as an
aesthetic practice or a collection of ideas and arguments but as a
published book—was not just a verbal outcome or token of this manifold, but also an element of it, another step in Emerson's painstaking
effort to fashion his new career. Most obviously, *Nature* was itself a
commodity, an object that even Emerson's "private poor man" might
find in one of the bookstores he frequented. But *Nature* was also an
effort to establish a reputation as a "fine thinker," the kind of reputation that might hasten success on the lecture platform. On the other
hand, the poet whose story Emerson tells in *Nature* is a figure whose
motives can scarcely include money. In pecuniary matters, Emerson's
poet is innocent, ready to deny the reality of "property." In one of the
most frequently noticed passages in this narrative of the quest for
Nature, Emerson takes the poet to a hillside and has him look over a
neat New England landscape with its fences and farms. The poet
figure knows the men who think they own the farms, but he also has
the subversive knowledge that their deeds register only illusions:

> The charming landscape which I saw this morning, is indubitably made
> up of some twenty or thirty farms. Miller owns this field, Locke that,
> and Manning the woodland beyond. But none of them owns the land-
> scape. There is a property in the horizon that no man has but he whose
> eye can integrate all the parts, that is the poet. This is the best part of
> these men's farms, yet to this their land-deeds give them no title. (p. 12)

The poet is seeing the landscape with the vision of Reason, of
course, and anyone who had read Emerson's letter about the way the

22. May 31, 1834, in *Letters* 1:411–12. A level-headed and even courageous discussion
of the significance of the inheritance is in Joel Porte, *Representative Man: Ralph Waldo
Emerson in His Age* (New York: Oxford University Press, 1979), pp. 55–63.

steady twelve hundred dollars a year from Ellen's estate would enable him to live the life of Reason and defy the "wrinkled calculator" might have been tempted to scoff at the poet's elevated disdain for property. In truth, many of the kinds of interpretations of art and literature that seem to be programatically materialist in the end do no more than expose such "hypocrisies." Such muckraking ("vulgar Marxism"?) is only slightly more difficult and no more productive than the most commonplace alternative: to accept and celebrate such pieties as Emerson's "vision" at face value ("vulgar idealism"?). Either way, not much has been learned. In Emerson's case, two facts are plain enough. First, he hoped to make money from his writing. Second, he presented in *Nature* and his other work an idealization of the poet and the scholar which lifted them to the highest moral and aesthetic ground his words could fashion, a ground on which the profit motive was unthinkable. He fed his figures of the poet and the Scholar on the currents of Universal Being and insisted on their "disgust at the principles on which business is managed."[23] The question is, what, if anything, do the two facts have to do with each other?

One obvious answer is, nothing, that *Nature*, like any work of art, so far transcends any particular set of motives Emerson had for writing it that even to discuss those motives is shoddy, beside the point, or both. Another equally obvious answer is that Emerson's hope for a profit from his work exposes his presentation of the figure of the true poet as little more than a confidence game. Both sorts of answers are reductionist. The first reduces cultural objects to forms, "expressions," or "texts," whose meanings are profoundly impoverished by being cut off from the experiences that gave rise to them, and the deliberate human purposes they serve. The second tends to reduce human practice to a set of mindless efforts to satisfy the material wants of an individual, group or class, and to treat works of art or intellect as somehow fraudulent or self-deceptive. The task of materialist criticism, surely, is to avoid both kinds of reductionism. To do so requires understanding the profound import of Marx's scandalous phrase "spiritual commodities," which leads far beyond the oxymoronic or the polemical. Objects are never commodities as such; they become so in history, and in highly specific ways. And spiritual commodities *are* spiritual, crafted to satisfy the emotional, intellectual, and aesthetic demands of

23. This remark is from "The American Scholar," the Phi Beta Kappa address Emerson gave at Harvard the year after *Nature* was published. It is in *The Collected Works of Ralph Waldo Emerson*, ed. Robert Spiller, Alfred Ferguson, et al. vol. 1 (Cambridge: Belknap Press of Harvard University Press, 1971), pp. 52–70.

both their producers and their consumers. These spiritual demands are no doubt shaped by the material needs and interests of individuals and classes, but once they are shaped, they do determine the sorts of things people write, paint, sing, or dance.

When Emerson wrote *Nature*, he was in a vocational crisis. He had provoked it himself, written its script, and was acting it out. Indeed, *Nature* was not just a book, not just a bundle of ideas presented in a carefully wrought style. It was also an act, a performance. Considered as action rather than merely as text, its purpose was plain enough. Emerson was presenting a portrait of the man of letters designed to make his own career decision appear not only legitimate but heroic. In leaving the pulpit of Boston's Second Church he had left much more than a job or even a calling. He had left behind the career that had been the center of his identity since childhood. He was relinquishing the vocation that had made his ancestral family into a local dynasty, that had made his first marriage possible, that had given him the "chamber" in which he read and wrote and provided him with the sermon as a secure literary form. The ministry, indeed, had defined the only conception of community that made any concrete sense to him. Now, like his poet, he was "retiring" from both chamber and society. The choice had little to do with ideas in any formal sense. The affirmations of his new "philosophy" were about as pale, really, as the "pale negations" he complained of in Unitarianism. Indeed, his decision would probably have been much easier if it had really been about theological or philosophical notions only. But he was surrendering much more than old ideas and was trying to lay claim to more than new notions. He was putting away the only conception of self and society he ever had had. If Ellen Tucker Emerson had not died, he probably would not have risked it, either in spiritual or material terms.

To be sure, Emerson's writing, like anyone else's, is full of ideas. And he also had some quite definite aesthetic commitments, which manifested themselves in a distinctive style and address. But his ideas and his aesthetic practices cannot be reduced to the level of mere intellectual belief. In his professional work, ideas and aesthetic practices were also instruments, the materials and tools of a trade that he prosecuted with extraordinary vigor and efficiency. If he declared himself on an almost limitless range of broad questions—God, nature, immortality, truth, beauty, goodness, and the like—it was partly because he was presenting himself as a "fine thinker," a man whose calling was exactly to traffic in such heady abstractions. And if he worked hard to develop a style that was peculiarly his, it was not for aesthetic purposes only but also to mark his prose as "original."

In the ministry Emerson's tools were a conventional body of doctrine and an equally conventional sermon form, which were employed through a settled understanding between him and the congregation about the particular *capacity* in which he spoke. He might have strained from time to time against the limits of doctrine, form, and capacity. But now, as a writer and lecturer on the open market, he had much more freedom—and need—to experiment with doctine and form to satisfy expectations that were not at all settled. He was also free to propose a new notion of the capacity in which he would speak and write. His primary task, in fact, was to develop a plausible (that is to say, publishable) conception of the career of the writer, a new figure of himself as an artist. And it was extremely important to him—and to his audiences, too—that this figure be one who was moved by purposes much more elevated than profit. The plain fact, as he knew, was that people would not pay to hear or read anyone who was publicly explicit about *wanting* to be paid. There could be little doubt, then, what Emerson's first subject would be. His book about nature would not be about Nature at all but about the figure of a man in nature: a man whose characteristic mode of experience is insight, whose medium is language, and whose purposes quite transcend any considerations of the marketplace—a man, indeed, for whom the "material" world exists only as "symbol."

Within the words of symbols, Emerson's poet is an extraordinarily greedy and selfish man: he wants to possess not just Miller's and Manning's farms but the horizon itself. It is this spiritual selfishness and greed that lends such energy to Emerson's obvious—and no doubt quite deliberate—gestures toward sex. There is much to suggest that the poet's purposes might not be entirely impeccable. After all, he comes to Nature like a bridegroom. He has put off his faded wardrobe. He is "bathed." He is the "lover of uncontained and immortal beauty." He "beholds somewhat as beautiful as his own nature." The narrative of the poet's experience is emphatically tinged with masturbatory fantasy. What the poet is seeking is "solitude." The euphemism for masturbation that had become conventional and widespread during Emerson's lifetime was "the solitary vice." Emerson chose language that hinted at the onanistic possibility. "In the woods," he says, "is perpetual youth." There the poet can become the "lover" of beauty, in touch with it with the heightened sensitivity of a snake that has just sloughed its skin. The transparent eyeball, the head bathed by the blithe air and uplifted into infinite space, and the flowing currents of universal being take on a concreteness and specificity (and perhaps, for some, an interest) they might not otherwise have. It is quite fitting that the poet, his fantasy tryst with nature completed, should suddenly feel a sense of loss, a tristesse, a nameless and elusive sadness implicit in "the heat of his own fire."

Emerson's narrative is also laced with hints of the oedipal family melodrama. He describes the tyranny of the past in patriarchal terms. Our age, he says, "builds the sepulchres of the fathers"; it "gropes" among their "dry bones"; it masquerades in their "faded wardrobe" (p. 1). And against this motif of patriarchal darkness, dessication, and deprivation, he sets a characterization of "Nature" as fulgent, liquid, and nourishing—in a word, maternal: "We are," he says, "embosomed for a season in nature, whose floods of life stream around and through us" (p. 1). The poet's task is precisely to triumph over the fathers' dry bones and to regain nature's nourishing bosom. To do so, he must become like a child in order to avoid the obvious pitfalls. At the climactic moment of his experience, the poet appears to devour the mother, attaining possession and union—"part and particle." "I am nothing," he says. But this very helplessness entitles him to repossess maternal Nature, at least with his voracious eye. "I see all," he exclaims in triumph, and "currents of Universal Being circulate through me." Fitting then, the drama accomplished, that his mind should turn to thoughts of death, grief, and "less worth in the population." Emerson was much too well-bred to force his poet to gouge out his eyes, but he does end his first chapter by momentarily depriving the poetic eye of its transforming powers.

The poet's incipient onanism and oedipal voraciousness is legitimated (and made harmless) by its perfect spirituality. Nature is an exercise in double-entry bookkeeping, in which the poet gains spiritual dimension precisely as he relinquishes material and social dimension. By 1838 this kind of aesthetic transaction was a Romantic convention, even a cliche, and if Emerson had been simply working away at his appropriation of it, then Nature would deserve the complaint of many readers that it is only an insipid Panglossian exercise. But he was doing more than honing Romantic conventions. He was trying to come to terms with what he had defined as the critical juncture of his own experience. On the surface of things, of course, Nature is mostly about the exhilarating prospect of a career as a poet, liberated from pulpit and chamber. But the contradiction between what Emerson says his poet is up to and what Emerson himself knew *he* was up to made the exhilarating prospect very precarious indeed. The poet scorned not only profit but "other men"; Emerson expected these other men to buy the book and attend his lectures. (There would soon be another mouth to feed, too; Lidia Emerson was seven months pregnant when *Nature* was published.) He was giving lectures, as many and as often as he could manage. During the winter season following the publication of *Nature*, he gave a series of twelve on "the philosophy of history" at the Masonic temple in Boston.[24] Then he repeated many of them in surrounding towns, including Plymouth and Salem. He wrote his own advertising, hired the hall, paid to have the tickets printed, and arranged to have them sold by a friendly bookseller—all with an eye to maximizing his net profit.[25]

If Emerson had merely ignored the disparity between the shopkeeping practicality of his purposes and the elevated spirituality of his poet's, kept it off his pages altogether, treating it as what Stuart Chase once called a "dirty little secret," the book would have suffered terri-

24. His average audience in Boston that winter was about 350 people. They paid $2 dollars for a ticket to the entire series, and his net profit after all his expenses was $350, far less than the interest he earned on Ellen Emerson's bequest but about 10 percent of the price of the house he had bought for himself and his new wife in Concord the year before. It would be two more years until he could afford to give up preaching altogether and earn enough from writing and speaking to make life comfortable. There is a good discussion of this lecture series in Allen, *Waldo Emerson*, pp. 287–92. On the cost of Emerson's house, see *Letters* 1:447. For an admirably careful history of the publishing life of *Nature*, see *Collected Works* 1:6.

25. On Emerson as a lecturer, see the very valuable work of William Charvat, *Emerson's American Lecture Engagements: A Chronological List* (New York: 1961); C. E. Schorer, "Emerson and the Wisconsin Lyceum," *American Literature* 24 (1953): 467. The standard work on the Lyceum is still Carl Bode, *American Lyceum: Town Meeting of the Mind* (Carbondale: University of Southern Illinois Press, 1968). An extremely useful discussion of the relationship between lecturing and publishing is Donald M. Scott, "Print and the Public Lecture System, 1840–1860," in *Print and Society in Early America*, ed. William Joyce et al. (Worcester, Mass.: American Antiquarian Society, 1983), pp. 278–99. Even more important are the same author's essays, "The Popular Lecture and the Creation of a Public in Mid-Nineteenth-Century America," *Journal of American History* 66 (March 1980), 791–809, and "The Profession That Vanished," in *Professions and Professional Ideologies in America*, ed. Daniel Calhoun (Chapel Hill, N.C.: University of North Carolina Press, 1983). An interesting contemporary comment, by a friend of Emily Dickinson's, is J. G. Holland, "The Popular Lecture," *Atlantic Monthly* 15 (March 1865), 187. Another friend of Dickinson's, her most important literary friend, described the lecturer as "moving to and fro, a living shuttle, to weave together this new web of national civilization," Thomas Wentworth Higginson, "The American Lecture-System," *Macmillan's Magazine* 18 (May 1868), 49.

bly. But he did not. Instead, he stretched the seams of *Nature* in quite ingenious ways to let in grief, shame, and dread, And it is this willingness to grapple with the materialistic nature of the writing enterprise that keeps the book from being a "happiness pill"—makes it, in fact, a fine piece of writing.[26] Nowhere in *Nature* does Emerson directly suggest that the figure of the poet masks the motives of a professional writer who is trying to get a start in the literary marketplace after quitting a most respectable ministry. What he does instead is to plant dark broodings at critical points in the book, enough to signal that there is something decidedly odd and unsteady about his poet's claims to Universal Being.

At the height of his ecstasy in Nature, the poet cries out, "Almost I fear to think how glad I am," and he has plenty of reason to fear his own gladness, for he is about to lose his adult manhood and become a perpetual child. He is also surrendering every capacity for social action, becoming a figure of no consequence whatever—very unlike the New England ministers who, traditionally at least, had been men of great consequence in their communities. Thus it is altogether fitting that the poet should fear, and even suddenly and without warning drop into mourning. The "dear friend" whose loss he mourns is almost surely the wife who had been so completely identified with the beginning and the end of his career as a minister. Little wonder that he should be reminded that he is risking a "calamity" and should feel a sadness in the heat of his own fire.

If Emerson had ample reason for fear and a sense of loss, he had perhaps even more reason to dread that the career choice he was announcing in *Nature* was plain silly. Almost everyone he had known would have told him that it was ridiculous to leave the Second Church to enter a still very fragile literary marketplace, writing and talking for strangers who might pay no attention, when he had a respectable congregation more than ready to pay not only attention but a very good and secure salary. Toward the end of *Nature* is a brief meditation on the possibility of ridicule which needs to be seen as rooted in these same vocational doubts. The setting has to do with work and production; the journal passage it modifies is about two Concord farmers who were Emerson's neighbors; the modifications are designed to increase the moral distance between the poet and men who do useful labor, to heighten the distinction between real work and the poet's enterprise,

26. "Happiness pill" is the phrase of Kenneth Burke, in "Eye, I, Aye—Emerson's Early Essay *Nature:* Thoughts on the Machinery of Transcendence," in *Emerson's "Nature,"* p. 150.

to point up the possibility that "other men" might find the poet ridiculous and that he might find himself equally so.

In the journal passage, Emerson observes as an evidence of "discord" between man and Nature that it is impossible to "admire a prospect" and at the same time "sympathize" with two Concord farmers, "Wyman and Tuttle who are digging in the field." In *Nature*, he uses this notion to end the chapter titled "Spirit" and also to set up a pun for the next chapter's title, "Prospects." In *Nature* the passage became: "For you cannot admire a noble landscape, if laborers are digging in the field hard by. The poet finds something ridiculous in his delight, until he is out of the sight of men." In rewriting the journal passage, Emerson made exactly the kinds of changes required by his definition of the poet's experience. He decided not to give the diggers names—even fictitious names—or to number them; they are but anonymous figures in a group of indeterminate number. He demoted them to the rank of "laborers," something any sturdy Wyman or Tuttle would have resented. Nor does he give the poet a choice between two *worthy* purposes—admiring the prospect or sympathizing with his neighbors. Instead, the other men become a mere obstacle to the poet's single purpose. He also insisted that the poet's landscape is "noble," making the distinction between the poet and the "laborers" much more telling than Emerson's own differences from Manning and Tuttle. Finally, he makes it plain that the poet must pursue his cosmic voyeurism in secret. He cannot have his delight in the presence of other men, cannot really *see* if he is seen. The laborers are a problem precisely because they are digging "hard by" (not because their digging is hard, like Manning's and Tuttle's, inviting sympathy). From an appropriate distance, they could have been part of a "charming landscape." But if they watch instead of being watched, they make the poet's "delight" seem "ridiculous." Earlier, just after the poet's ecstatic moment of being uplifted into infinite space and just before the mourning passage, Emerson had said that the greatest "delight" of the woods and fields was "the suggestion of an occult relation between man and vegetable" (p. 13). Now, near the end of his book, he sketches a different notion. The diggers' relationship to their vegetables is patent and instrumental, and very much at odds with the poet's occult and unproductive delight.[27]

Nature was not just a meditation, or only a manifesto about artists.

27. John Barrell, *The Dark Side of the Landscape: The Rural Poor in English Painting, 1730–1848* (New York: Cambridge University Press, 1980), is brilliant on the sorts of painterly conventions that Emerson may have had in mind as he worked over this passage.

Of course it was not *just* a commodity, either. It was an attempt to legitimate a particular kind of vocational enterprise that involved the
production of such commodities by men or women whose subject
matter was defined much more in the terms of his other chapter
titles—"Beauty," "Language," and "Spirit"—than by considerations
of "Commodity." But this meant, in turn, that the figure of the poet
might be suspected of having pecuniary purposes that needed to be
kept covert or translated into carefully controlled hints at shame, fear,
or grief. Emerson made a number of strategic choices in *Nature*,
choices that were designed to shield the poet from any visible sign of
ambition for fame, success, or profit. He took the poet into the woods,
far from his house and from other men, and gave him currents of
universal being for food and drink, as though a poet needs no other.
But still he hinted that the poet might be doing something slightly
illicit, something he could do only in private, something that made
him unexpectedly and unaccountably sad, or something that might
make him feel ridiculous in the sight of other men. The poet is simultaneously a figure of unmeasured ambition and a man of no social or
practical consequence whatever. On his own terms he is a perfect
success, but by what Emerson knew were the common standards of
the day, he is a solitary failure. Such a poet might well interrupt his
exultations from time to time to let the reader know that he is sometimes embarrassed, afraid, or mournful.

To speak in such terms is to adopt a convention of great age and
good standing—to suppose that a character in a fiction might have
"reasons" for doing or saying something. In its harmless form, this
conventional manner of speaking is only a shorthand way of saying
that Emerson attributed to his fictive figure of the poet certain characteristics and purposes that a reader might suspect would lead such a
person to certain kinds of acts or states. In its less harmless form, it
allows some kinds of critics and historians to talk about pieces of
writing under the charming illusion that they have what Richard
Ellman once called "auto-telic privacy," containing within themselves
all the intelligent answers to all the intelligent questions that might be
posed about them. Such critics and historians change their vocabularies from generation to generation, and sometimes more rapidly than
that. In one age, they insist that the only purpose of criticism is
"appreciation." In another, they insist that what make literature literary are its purely "formal" features. In another, they talk about reading

as a "closet" activity, which must never pay attention to anything but the piece of writing itself, as though it were a found object. Or they insist that writings are "texts" that are finally only about themselves or "other texts." But let the vocabularies change as they may, the general intention of such historians and critics does not seem to alter much. The underlying supposition seems always to be that it is either irrelevant or downright harmful to ask why an author might have turned out a particular piece of writing at a particular time in a particular way. And the harm comes, they suppose, in two forms: the question lets the author's intentions into the picture, and it threatens to reduce "great" literature to the status of "documents."[28]

The truth of the matter is that any piece of writing—or any made-up thing, for that matter—is both a text and a document. As text, it can be subjected to any amount of appreciation of its formal characteristics, any amount of closeted deconstruction, any degree of analysis of its place in some discourse. But the same object can be analyzed (without harm) as documentary evidence that its maker was up to something at a certain historical juncture. And like other documents, it can be made to reveal something of the intentions and purposes that lay behind the

28. In normal academic times documents are the stuff that historians use, and texts are what literary critics work with. But the times are not normal. The air is thick with conferences, symposia, and essays about literary scholars' "return to history." Or about "the return of literature" to the practice of historians. As the more intelligent of the essayists realize, such rumors are worse than premature, they are wrongheaded. There had been no time in this century when a lot of talented literary critics were not thinking of their work as a kind of history. And there has been no time when a good many practicing historians were not paying the closest kind of attention to literary and philosophical works. What such discussions of epistemological "turns" usually signal is not a change in practice so much as a heightening of our self-consciousness about our practice. For a particularly thoughtful essay, see David Simpson, "Literary Criticism and the Return to 'History,'" *Critical Inquiry* 14 (Summer 1988), 721–47. For a recent example from the side of the historians, see David Harlan, "Intellectual History and the Return of Literature," *American Historical Review* 94 (June 1989), 581–609. The essay is worth reading as an example of the way some historians fret rather fastidiously that if their colleagues really do begin to examine the monuments of literary and philosophical culture contextually, they are treating them "instrumentally," as "something other than themselves," and are in danger of a "tendency to reduce complex works to the status of documents" (p. 594). Unless we understand that all complex texts—perhaps most especially great texts—*are* documents and that all documents really are complex texts, writings really do become "something other than themselves." They become transcendental objects of admiration and "appreciation," not splendid human achievements wrought in time, out of the materials of experience, on its terms and for its purposes. They ossify and become "instrumental" in a perverted way, as elements of the "conversation with the dead about what we value" that is Harlan's idea of the end that "texts" ought to serve. (Harlan, "Reply to David Hollinger," ibid., p. 625.)

act of making it. But do these two ways of looking at the same object, as text and document, have anything to do with each other? I have meant to suggest that they do, and that a specifically materialist reading of *Nature*, taking it as a document that had much to do with Emerson's experience, not only leaves the book quite unscathed as a work of literature, a text, but actually improves our understanding of just how fine an effort it is. Emerson's artistry was not confined to his "works." While he was writing *Nature*, he was also recasting his own life, putting away a version of his self, his social world, and his career which he had polished and perfected since he was an undergraduate and substituting for it a version of himself as "author" which entailed new ideas and images of self and society. To this experiential effort he brought the same talents and skills—and the same potential deceptions, difficulties, and contradictions—that he deployed so artfully in his prose. With him, as with other artists, writers, and intellectuals, experience did not happen and then somehow find its way into his work. His experience, like his work, was a wrought affair, and his work was an important instrument in his effort to avoid having his "delight"—not his poet's but his own—seem "ridiculous" now that it was time to say openly to "other men" in the real world that he had indeed decided to "commence author." In a certain sense, though not the one they have in mind, the critics and historians who associate themselves with the likes of Jacques Derrida or Paul de Man are right when they say that "literature is everywhere." For all human and social experience is saturated with the formal and the textual. But it is equally true that "literature" is saturated with the quite concrete and material experience of the people who make it and read it. And any attempt to understand either art of experience apart from each other can hardly avoid some sort of vulgarity.

6

Keats and His Readers: A Question of Taste

Marjorie Levinson

There's no need, I think, to defend the statement that our commitment to a canonical Keats runs deep. Anyone who has thought critically about Keats in the past five years must appreciate the difference between the Keats commentary and the kinds of inquiries conducted on the poems of the other Romantics. This business of a canonical Keats is not a matter of explicitly idealizing or redemptive readings.[1] Rather, I'm talking about the assumptions that organize our working knowledge of the relations between Keats's life and writing and the social context in which they both materialized.

Keats, like Shakespeare, is a name for the figure of the capable poet.

This essay is a version of the Introduction to the author's *Keats's Life of Allegory: The Origins of a Style* (1988). Basil Blackwell's permission to reprint is gratefully acknowledged.

1. Alan Bewell's essay "The Political Implication of Keats's Classicist Aesthetics," *Studies in Romanticism* 25 (Summer 1986), 220–29, represents the beginning of a departure from the critical norm for Keats studies. Bewell's sensitivity to the special political discourse of the writer situated by the polis on its *under*side or *between* its categorical positions intimates a criticism beyond the margins of formalist, thematic, biographical, and metaphysical inquiry as these have developed in Romanticist scholarship over the past thirty years, *and also* beyond the "new historicism." This last observation is part of an argument about the new historicism in Romantic studies: see Marjorie Levinson, "The New Historicism: Back to the Future," in *Rethinking Historicism: Critical Readings in Romantic History*, ed. Levinson (Oxford: Basil Blackwell, 1989).

The best Keats criticism (Lionel Trilling, John Bayley, Christopher Ricks) and the smartest (the Harvard Keatsians) mark out the canonical extremes, and yet, these greatly disparate critiques emerge from a common premise, one that opposes *tout court* the governing thesis of the contemporary reading of Keats's poetry.[2] We all agree to know the man and his writing by their complete authenticity: Bayley's *gemeine*, Ricks's "unmisgiving" imagination, Helen Vendler's true craftsman. In order to produce this knowledge, we put what the contemporary reviewers called Keats's "vulgarity" under the sign of psychic, social, and textual unselfconsciousness: roughly, the sign of sensuous sincerity. Further, by the evolutionary tales we find coded in Keats's letters, we put the vulgarity that cannot be so sublimed in the very early verse and show its sea change into the richly inclusive seriousness that distinguishes the great work. Thus do we rescue Keats's deep meanings from his alluring surfaces, his poetic identity from his poetical identifications. Keats's writing is not, we say, an escape from the bitter reality of his life but a constructive operation whereby the truth of those sad circumstances stands revealed—and revealed as a new and deeply human beauty. We describe, in short, a transformation of experience by knowledge and by the aesthetic practice that knowledge promotes. The word that best describes this critical plot is *romance:* a march from alienation to identity. The governing figure of the narrative is the Coleridgean or Romantic symbol, and its rhetorical device the oxymoron, both irreducibly syncretic ideas. The hero of our critical history is a profoundly associated sensibility, and his gift to us is the exemplary humanism of his life and art.

Trilling, Bayley, and Ricks have discriminated a stylistic *badness* that occurs throughout Keats's poetry, a certain remove whereby Keats *signifies* his special interest in his representations. In so doing, these critics approximate the response of Keats's contemporaries, which I'll review later. By emphasizing the psychic investment rather than the social remove that prompts it, however, and by putting that excess in a dialectically progressive field, Bayley and Ricks rehearse the ro-

2. Walter Jackson Bate, *John Keats* (Cambridge: Harvard University Press, 1963); John Bayley, "Keats and Reality," *Proceedings of the British Academy* (1962), 91–125; Douglas Bush, *John Keats* (New York: Macmillan, 1966); David Perkins, *The Quest for Permanence* (Cambridge: Harvard University Press, 1959); Christopher Ricks, *Keats and Embarrassment* (Oxford: Clarendon Press, 1974); Lionel Trilling, "The Fate of Pleasure," in *Beyond Culture* (London: Secker and Warburg, 1955); Helen Vendler, *The Odes of John Keats* (Cambridge: Harvard University Press, 1983); Earl Wasserman, *The Finer Tone* (Baltimore: Johns Hopkins University Press, 1953).

mance.[3] Following these strong writers, we read Keats's lapses from the good taste of either an unmarked mimesis *or* transparent subjectivity as a determined consent to his own voluptuous inwardness and to the self-conscious recoil. By this willed abandon, Keats is said to transcend both enthrallments, thereby releasing the reader as well. In other words, those critics who register the stylistic vulgarity of Keats's writing set it under the sign of creaturely instinct and defense and not in the unredeemable category of externality, materiality, and ambitious reflexiveness. When Keats nods, they say, it is because he dares to "swoon," "sink," or "cease," not because he tries too hard.

The early reviews tell a different story. The most casual survey of this commentary reveals a response so violent and sustained, so promiscuous in its blending of social, sexual, and stylistic critique, and so sharply opposed to mainstream modern thought as to imply a determinate insight on the part of Keats's contemporaries and a determined oversight on the part of his belated admirers. While we're all familiar with *Blackwood*'s Cockney School attack ("so back to the shop Master John, back to 'plasters, pills, and ointment boxes'"), we haven't attended very closely to the sexual invective, and not at all to the relation between those two discourses. Time and again, the poetry is labeled "profligate," "puerile," "unclean," "recklessly luxuriant and wasteful," "unhealthy," "abstracted," and "insane." It is graphed as stylistically self-indulgent: prolix, repetitive, metrically and lexically licentious, overwrought. The diatribes culminate in the epithet "nonsense."[4]

---

3. John Bayley shrewdly divines that Keats's badness *is* his goodness. Had Bayley pushed his *aperçu* a little further, he would have come up against the meanings shadowed forth by the contemporary criticism. He would, perhaps, have associated the vulgarity of Keats's poetry with the situation, activities, and interests of the burgeoning middle class. As it is, Bayley's interpretative construct neatly registers this association by negation. *Das Gemeine*—a postulate of healthy, earthy Elizabethan (that is, sociologically and psychically nonstratified) consciousness—is the mirror image of the nineteenth-century Keats, or of a poetry experienced as sick, pretentious, horribly contemporary, and thoroughly mannered. To the early readers, Keats's poetry was the expression of a "folk" degraded by a bad eminence: the petty bourgeoisie.

4. All excerpts from contemporary notices are drawn from Donald Reiman, *The Romantics Reviewed: Contemporary Reviews of British Romantic Writers* (New York: Garland, 1972), C, I, 91–93, 95, 330–33, 339, 344–45, 385, 423–24, C, II, 470, 479, 531, 587–90, 614, 768–69, 807–8, 824–25, 829–30; and from *Keats: The Critical Heritage*, ed. G. M. Matthews (London: Routledge and Kegan Paul, 1971), pp. 35, 129–31, 150, 208–10, 248, 251. Some Byron materials are taken from *Byron's Letters and Journals*, ed. Leslie Marchand, vol. 7: *1820* (Cambridge, Mass.: Belknap Press, 1977), p. 217 (from letter to John Murray, Nov. 4, 1820; Matthews lists it as Sept. 4).

We have always related the savaging of the early poetry to the anomaly of Keats's social position and to the literary blunders that follow from it: generally, problems of diction, rhetoric, and subject matter, many of them reducible to the avoidable (and finally avoided) misfortune of Keats's coterie. Because we situate these blunders at a certain level and within a very contained biographical field and because we isolate them from the beauties of the great poetry, we haven't understood the deeper insult of Keats's writing, that which explains the intensity and displacements of the early response and the equal but opposite distortions of the twentieth-century view.

From the distance of today, one easily detects in those vituperative catalogs a governing model. Keats's poetry was branded as a form of masturbatory exhibitionism, an offensiveness further associated with the self-fashioning gestures of the petty bourgeoisie.[5] The erotic opprobrium pinpoints the self-consciousness of the verse: its end-stopped reflection on its own fine phrases, phrases stylistically objectified as acquired, and therefore *mis*acquired, property. Following Byron, the imagination Keats frigs is not even his own. The sexual language of the reviews was, naturally, an expedient way to isolate Keats without at the same time agonizing him, but it's also a telling index to the social and existential project outlined by Keats's style. In his overwrought inscription of canonical models the early readers sensed the violence of Keats's raids upon that empowering system, a violence driven by the strongest desire for the matter and means of authorial expressiveness and for the social legitimacy felt to go with it. In the overcharged reflexiveness of Keats's verse, the critics read the signature of a certain kind of life, itself the sign of a new social phenomenon. Byron's analysis of the style of the Cockney writers puts the matter plainly.

> The grand distinction of the under forms of the new school of poets is their *vulgarity*. By this I do not mean that they are *coarse*, but "shabby-genteel," as it is termed. A man may be *coarse* and yet not vulgar, and the reverse. . . . It is in their *finery* that the new under school are *most* vulgar, and they may be known by this at once; as what we called at

5. The association of masturbation with the individualism and materialism of the early middle class is something of an established literary theme. Swift's Master Bates, the physician to whom Gulliver is apprenticed, teaches his student more than a middle-class trade, he teaches him the principles of acquisition and display (in Gulliver's case anthropological), which constitute the middle class an *ideological* phenomenon over and above its economic being.

Harrow "a Sunday blood" might be easily distinguished from a gentleman. . . . In the present case, I speak of writing, not of persons.[6]

If we were not already convinced of Byron's ear for social nuance, we
would only have to recall this oft-quoted confession from Keats's
letters, "I look upon fine Phrases like a Lover."

Like our own criticism, the early reviews read in Keats's poetry "a
life of allegory," but the meaning they develop by that allegory lies in
the realm of social production, not aesthetics, metaphysics, or human-
istic psychology. To those early readers, "Keats" was the allegory of a
man belonging to a certain class and aspiring, as that whole class was
felt to do, to another—a man with particular but typical ambitions and
with particular but typical ways of realizing them. A world of difference separates this hermeneutic from Bate's "poignantly allegorical
life," an adventure in soul making, which has become today's John
Keats.[7] By respecting the social-sexual compounding evidenced by
those reviews, we recover the sense of danger underlying our formalist and performative readings of Keats's middling states: his adoles-
cence, his literariness, his stylistic suspensions, and his trick of turning his expressive means into his representational object. We focus
Keats's position—sandwiched between the truth of the working class
and the beauty of the leisure class—not as a healthy both/and but as
the monstrous neither/nor constructed in the reviews. We see that the
problem of Keats's early poetry is not its regressive escapism (its
instincts, so to speak) but its stylistic project: a social-ego enterprise.
The deep contemporary insult of Keats's poetry, and its deep appeal
(and long opacity) for the modern reader, is its idealized enactment of
the conflicts and solutions which defined the middle class at a certain
point in its development and which still to some extent obtain. We
remember that Keats's style can delineate that station so powerfully
precisely because of his marginal, longing relation to the legitimate
bourgeoisie of his day. In emulating the condition of the accomplished
middle class (the phrase is itself an oxymoron), Keats isolated the
constitutive contradictions of that class. The final fetish in Keats's
poetry is just that stationing tension.

Keats's most successful poems, it turns out, are those most elab-

6. Matthews, *Keats: Critical Heritage*, p. 130.
7. The much-quoted phrase "poignantly allegorical life" is Bate's allusion to Keats's
own observation that Shakespeare led "a life of Allegory." *Letters of John Keats*, ed. Robert
Gittings (1970; rpt. Oxford: Oxford University Press, 1979), p. 218.

orately estranged from their own materials and procedures and thus from both a writerly and readerly subjectivity. The poetics I describe, following the lead of Keats's contemporaries, is the very opposite of "unmisgiving."[8] The triumph of the great verse is not its capacious, virile, humane authenticity but its subversion of those authoritarian values, effects that it could not in any case, and for the strongest social reasons, realize. This is the triumph of the double negative. The awfulness of the very early work, by contrast, is explained as an expression of the *single* or suffered negative, a nondynamic reflection of Keats's multiple estrangements and of the longing they inspired. To describe Keats's accomplished verse as the negative knowledge of his actual life is not to consecrate him a precocious post-modernist. It is only to take seriously the social facts and meanings embedded in his representations and in the contemporary reception. It is to see in his style a parodic reproduction of the social restrictions that marked Keats as wanting—unequipped, ineffectual, and fundamentally fraudulent.

Keats did not, of course, realize by this stratagem the goodness he craved, that plenitude of being he worshiped in the great canonical models and which he images in autumn's breeding passiveness. What he *did* produce by what Shelley named "the bad sort of style" was a truly negative capability. I call this power "virtual" to bring out its parodic relation to authorized forms of power, "virtuoso" to suggest its professional, technically preoccupied nature, and "virtuous" by reference to its imposed and contrived limitations. To generate this verbal sequence is also to put as the ruling stylistic and social question the question of Keats's virility: to begin, that is, where the early commentary leaves off.

The story of Keats's life is much too familiar to bear recounting here. I would, though, like to recall those aspects of the tale that bear directly on Keats's stylistic development. To observe that Keats's circumstances put him at a remove from the canon is to remark not only his educational deficits but his lack of those skills prerequisite to a transparent mode of appropriation: guiltless on the one side, imperceptible on the other. He knew some French and Latin, little Italian, no Greek. His Homer was Chapman, his Dante was Cary, his Provençal ballads translations in an edition of Chaucer, his Boccaccio Englished.

8. "Unmisgiving" is Ricks's class term, taken from Keats, for the social, psychic, and rhetorical generosity of the poetry.

Keats's art education was largely by engravings and, occasionally, reproductions. His absorption of the accessible English writers was greatly constrained by his ignorance of the originals upon which they drew and by his nonsystematic self-education. To say all this is to observe Keats's literally corrupt relation to the languages of poetry, his means of production.

We might also consider a more mundane aspect of Keats's composition. Throughout his life, Keats felt compelled *physically* to escape his hard, London reality in order to write. A great deal of the poetry was conceived or composed at a number of modest, middle-class, and, as it were, ready-made resorts: Margate, Shanklin on the Isle of Wight, Burford Bridge (Surrey). Naturally, Keats could afford only the leanest accommodations, and often he adjourned to these spots alone and off-season. When even these small excursions were not possible, Keats sought his escape on Hampstead Heath or in the British Institution or a friend's well-furnished living room. In short, the graciously conformable gardens and dells enjoyed by Wordsworth and Coleridge were no more available to Keats than were the glory and grandeur of Greece and Rome, Byron's and Shelley's enabling resorts. "Romantic retirement" gains a whole new dimension with Keats. Imagine the solitude of a young man in a seaside rooming house in April, a borrowed picture of Shakespeare his only companion: a man with nothing to do for a set period of time but write the pastoral epic that would, literally, *make* him. Compare this privacy to the seclusion of a writer musing in a lime-tree bower, deserted by his wife and literary friends of an afternoon, or to the isolation of two highborn Englishmen, recognized poets both, galloping along the Lido and relishing their escape from Castlereagh's cant? Better yet, imagine a conversation poem, a social verse, or a lyrical ballad by Keats. Project from Keats's pen an ode on the order of Shelley's "Mont Blanc," or a *Defence of Poetry*, or a pamphlet on the Convention of Cintra. The experiment should point up the problematic nature, for Keats, of those elementary and, of course, normative literary effects: authority, authenticity, and ease.

Apropos that last and deeply Romantic effect, ease, we recall that Keats hadn't the luxury for a wise passiveness. His early detection of his disease, Tom's condition, the medical training, Keats's haste to make a name so he could marry Fanny—all these familiar facts precluded the meditative quiescence that supported in the other Romantics a rhetoric of consummate grace and sincerity. Wordsworth's compositional program was just not an option for a man who couldn't wait upon memory's slow digestive processes. Keats's writing trips were hasty and purposive; the work of this simulated leisure was the production of pleasure, precondition for the selfless and suspended exercise that was Keats's dream of art. The result of these sad, self-vexing outings is a poetry evincing the paradoxes by which it is made, a poetry too happy by far, too full by half. When Shelley disdainfully rejected Keats's advice, "load every rift with ore," he knew what he was about. He registered the class implications of Keats's plenitude and knew that he, for one, did not *have* to plump his poems to the core.

Before we can begin rereading Keats, we must really imagine what we know. We must see very clearly, as John Bayley saw, that Keats was a man whose almost complete lack of control over the social code kept him from living his life. He could not write his poetry in the manner he required, marry the woman he loved, claim his tiny legacy, hold his family together, or assist his friends. He could not, in short, seize any of the appurtenances of manhood. Keats was as helplessly and ignominiously a "boy" poet as Chatterton, and Byron's "Mankin" was a viciously knowing insult.

The range of paradoxes which Byron and others observed in Keats's poetry is ultimately referable to the fact that it was not given to Keats, a poet in Shelley's "general sense," to be a poet in the most pedestrian, professional "restricted" sense. Keats had to make for himself a life while writing a poetry that was, structurally, a denial of that life. At no time did Keats make any money from his writing. (One wonders *how,* exactly, Keats applied the title of "poet" to himself. How did he introduce himself in ordinary social interactions?) The oddly abstract materialism of the poetry—its overinvestment in its signs—takes on a new look when we remember Keats's remove from his representational objects and means, and also his want of those real things that help people live their lives. Is it any wonder that the poetry produced by this man should be so autotelic, autoerotic, so fetishistic and so stuck? Should it surprise us to find that his dearest fantasy—a picture of somebody reading, a window on the one side, a goldfish bowl on the other—takes the form of a multiply framed trompe l'oeil still life? "Find the subject," we might call it, or, what is the same thing, "Find the frame."

Keats's poetry was at once a tactical activity, or an escape route from an actual life, and a final construction: the concrete imaginary to that

apparitional actual. What was initially a substitute *for* a grim life became for Keats a substitute life: a real life of simulacra that, although
they do not nourish, neither do they waste. At the very end of his
career, Keats began, I believe, to position this parodic solution as part
of the problem. "Lamia" is Keats's attempt to frame the problematic of
his life and writing and thus to set it aside.

It is crucial to see, as John Bayley saw, that the deep desire in Keats's
poetry is not for aesthetic things or languages per se (that is, Byron's
"finery") but for the social code inscribed in them, a code that was, for
Keats, a human transformational grammar. The real perversion of
Keats's poetry is not its display of its cultural fetishes but its preoccupation with the system felt to organize those talismanic properties.
Keats could have had all the urns, Psyches, nightingales, Miltonisms,
Claudes, and Poussins he wanted; he was not, however, permitted
possession of the social grammar inscribed in that aesthetic array, and
this was just what he was after.

We illuminate Keats's legitimacy problem by way of the originality
anxiety that seems to have beset most of the Romantic and what used
to be called pre-Romantic poets. The past only lies like a weight on the
brain of those who inherit it. Or rather, the past imposes a special *kind*
of burden on those individual talents who feel themselves disinherited
by the tradition and thus, excluded from the dialectic of old and new,
identity and difference. Wordsworth's celebrated defense of his poetical innovations—"every author, as far as he is great and at the same
time *original*, has had the task of *creating* the taste by which he is to be
enjoyed"—must be understood as the statement of a man so assured
of his entitlement that he can trust his originality to be received as
intelligible and valuable. Keats, by contrast, could not begin to invent
an original voice without first and *throughout* establishing his legitimacy—roughly, his derivativeness.

Chatterton, the poet with whom Keats felt the strongest affinities,
developed a most economical solution to this problem. By his perfect
reproduction of "the medieval," Chatterton not only established that
epochal concept as a normative style, thereby sanctioning his persona
(Rowley) and that figure's verse; he produced as well and dialectically,
for the knowing reader, the originality of the entire oeuvre (that is,
poems, charts, maps, coins). Theoretically, Rowley's canon at once
created the taste, which it represented as already venerable and prestigious, and offered itself as the only artifact capable of satisfying it.

Practically speaking, however, Chatterton couldn't begin to fashion the readership he needed. Indeed, the logic of his enterprise compelled him to do all he might to malform—that is, *misinform*—his audience. The literariness of his poetry was strictly a function of its documentary, antiquarian presentation. The aesthetic dimension of the writing materialized only under the pressure of a historical interest, and in that case, of course, the literary credit went to Rowley. Chatterton's successful negotiation of the technical imperatives set him by his social facts required his entire self-effacement, as a man and a writer. A rare intuition of this paradox surfaces in the controversy prompted by the hoax poems. Those who defended the authenticity of the canon often argued that no right-minded writer would have preferred the inferior reputation of translator-editor to the glory of proper poetic genius, that is, originality. To us, of course, Chatterton's perversity indicates the illusoriness of his "choice." His election of the lesser fame, scholarly authority, was in fact an embrace of the bad originality of the counterfeiter. In that vexed ideal, we read the situation of the writer whose mastery consists exclusively in his self-violation.

Keats sidestepped Chatterton's suicidal solution. By the advertised *imperfection* of his canonical counterfeits (a parodic return upon his own derivativeness), Keats drew upon the licensing primacy of the code even as his *representation* of that total form changed the nature of its authority. The pronounced badness of Keats's writing figures the mythic goodness of the canon and, by figuring, at once exalts and delimits it. Thus did Keats plot for himself a scene of writing. By the double unnaturalness of his style, Keats projected the authority of an *anti*nature—stable by virtue of its continuous self-revolutionizing and secured by its contradictions. As a critical instance, a sort of proof of these claims, I'd like to offer a reading of "On First Looking into Chapman's Homer":

> *Much* have I travelled in the realms of gold,
>   And *many goodly* states and kingdoms seen;
>   Round *many* western islands have I been
> Which bards in fealty to Apollo hold.
> Oft of one wide expanse had I been told
>   That deep-browed Homer ruled as his demesne;
>   Yet did I never breathe its pure serene
> Till I heard Chapman speak out loud and bold.
> Then felt I like some watcher of the skies
>   When a new planet swims into his ken;

> Or like stout Cortez when with eagle eyes
> He stared at the Pacific, and all his men
> Looked at each other with a wild surmise—
> Silent, upon a peak in Darien.[9]

I have accented several words in the first three lines by way of amplifying the tone of Keats's address. Even if we were ignorant of Keats's social disadvantages, this fulsome claim to literary ease would give us pause. The very act of assertion, as well as its histrionically commanding and archly literary style, undermines the premise of natural authority and erudition. The contemporary reader might have noted as well some internal contradictions; not only *is* Homer the Golden Age, but not to "have" Greek and not to have encountered Homer before the age of twenty-three is (or was in 1817) to make one's claim to any portion of the literary empire suspect. (Keats's acquaintance with Pope's translation is suppressed by the sonnet.) Keats effectively assumes the role of the literary adventurer (with the commercial nuance of that word), as opposed to the mythic explorer: Odysseus, Cortes, Balboa. More concretely, he advertises his corrupt access to the literary system and to those social institutions that inscribe that system systematically in the hearts and minds of young men. To read Homer in translation and after having read Spenser, Coleridge, Cary, and whoever else is included in Keats's travelogue is to read Homer badly (in a heterodox and alienated way) and to subvert the system that installs Homer in a particular and originary place. Moreover, to "look into" Chapman's Homer is to confess—in this case, to *profess*—one's fetishistic relation to the great original. Keats does not *read* even the translation. To "look into" a book is to absorb it idiosyncratically at best, which is to say, with casual or conscious opportunism. Similarly, the substitution of "breathe" for the expected "read" in line 7 marks the rejection of a sanctioned mode of literary acquisition. To "breathe" a text is to take it in, take from it, and let it out, somewhat the worse for wear. It is, more critically, to miscategorize the object and in such a way as to proclaim one's intimacy with it. Both the claim and the title of Keats's sonnet are, in a word, vulgar.

One is reminded of Valéry's appraisal of museum pleasure: "For anyone who is close to works of art, they are no more objects of delight

9. Quotations from Keats's poetry are taken from *The Poems of John Keats*, Miriam Allott, ed. (New York: W. W. Norton, 1970).

than his own breathing."[10] Keats, we observe, rejoices in his respiration and goes so far as to fetishize the very air he admits. I single out the phrase "pure serene" because it is structurally foregrounded and because it reproduces in miniature the method—the working contradiction—of the sonnet. What Keats "breathes" is anything *but* pure and Homeric (since he reads in translation and perversely with respect to canon protocol), and the phrase formally exposes that fact. We cannot help but see that "pure serene," a primary reification, further calls attention to itself as a fine phrase, that Keats clearly looks upon as a lover. Not only is the phrase a Miltonic construction, but more recent usage would have characterized it as a sort of translator-ese. One thinks of Pope's "vast profound," of Cary's own "pure serene," a description of Dante's ether (1814), and of Coleridge's usage in the "Hymn before Sunrise in the Vale of Chamouni." Keats's reproduction of the phrase designates both his access to the literary system and his mode of access—that of translator to original. In effect, he intentionalizes the alienation he suffers by his social deficits. By signifying the restriction, he converts it into restraint, "might half-slumbering on its own right arm."

The thing to remark is the way Keats produces the virtues of his alienated access to the canon. The consummate image of the poem—that which accounts for its overall effect of "energetic . . . calmness"—is, obviously, that of Cortes/Balboa "star[ing] at the Pacific" while "all his men / Looked at each other with a wild surmise— / Silent, upon a peak in Darien." Cortes, we notice, is a "stout" and staring fellow: a solid citizen. *Stout* means, of course, "stout-hearted," but in the context, where Cortes's direct stare at the object of his desire is juxtaposed to the "surmise" of his men (and the alliteration reinforces these visual connections), one feels the energy of the men and the frozen state of their leader. By their surmise—a liminal, semidetached state—the men are "wild," a word that in the Romantic idiom means "free." We clearly see that the relation of the men to the punningly literal "pure serene," the Pacific, is indirect and perverse. Who in that situation would avert his gaze?

Claude Finney has reminded us that according to Keats's sources, Balboa's men were forbidden the prospect until their leader had had

10. Paul Valéry, quoted in Theodor Adorno, *Prisms,* trans. Samuel Weber and Shierry Weber (1967; rpt. Cambridge: MIT Press, 1983). The essay from which that quotation derives, "Valéry, Proust, Museum," deeply informs my discussion.

his full gaze.[11] It would seem, then, that the social discrepancy viv-idly sketched by Keats's original, William Robertson's *History of America* (1777), gets translated in the sonnet into an existential and self-imposed difference, and one that inverts the given power ratio by rendering the men, not the master, free and vital. One does not, I think, go too far in associating Keats with those capably disenfran-chised men.

It is the stillness and strangeness of the men—their peculiar *durée*—which stations Keats's sonnet, all the gregarious exploration meta-phors notwithstanding. Homer enters the poem as the Pacific enters the sensibilities of Cortes's men: through Chapman's/Cortes's more direct possession of/by the object of desire. Odysseus's extrovert en-ergy animates Keats's sonnet but, again, perversely. In the Keatsian space, that energy turns self-reflexive, reminding us perhaps of Ten-nyson's "Ulysses." The poem looks at itself as the men look at each other. The virtue of both looks is their impropriety; what they refuse by that gesture is the Gorgon stare, the direct embrace of and by the authorizing original. Keats's poem "speak[s] out loud and bold" by not speaking "out" at all. We finish the sonnet, which seems to be predi-cated on such a simple *donnée*, and we wonder where we have trav-eled. What happened to Homer, and to Keats for that matter? Why does Keats interpose between himself and his ostensible subject Chap-man, Cary, Coleridge, Gilbert, Robertson, Herschel, Balboa, Cortes, and Cortes's men? Why does Keats leave us with this off-center cameo, an image of turbulent stasis among the extras of the cast when what we expect is a "yonder lie the Azores" flourish by the principal? By the conventions the poem sets, it should strike us as a graceful display of literary inspiration and gratitude, but it seems other, and otherwise. How to explain the real power of its slant rhyme?

Let me recall Leigh Hunt's comment on the sonnet: "prematurely masculine." By emphasizing the adverb for a change, we begin to see that Keats's unnatural assumption of power, signified by the "poeti-cal" octet, does not *qualify* the "masculinity" of the sestet; it constitutes it. The direct and natural compression of the sestet is the stylistic effect

11. Claude Finney, *The Evolution of Keats's Poetry*, 2 vols. (New York: Russell and Russell, 1963), 1:126: "When with infinite toil, they had climbed up the greater part of that steep ascent, Balboa commanded his men to halt, and advanced alone to the summit, that he might be the first who should enjoy a spectacle which he had so long desired." From Robertson's *History of America*.

of the displayed disentitlement that is the functional representation of the opening eight lines. The pivot that constructs this before-and-after dynamic (the coordinates for a range of ratios—imitation: genuine, protest : power, struggle : ease) is, of course, the experience of reading Chapman. The experience takes place, significantly, in the breach between the two movements of the sonnet. Rather than imitate Chapman, Keats reproduces Chapman's necessarily parodic (that is, Elizabethan) inscription of Homer. The queerness of Chapman's "mighty line, loud-and-bold" version is rewritten in Keats's own parodic Elizabethan*ism* and through the queerness of the Cortes/Balboa image. It is the self-reflexive, fetishistic inscription of the canon—the display of bad access and misappropriation—that emancipates Keats's words. The sonnet breaks free of Homer and Chapman by mis-giving both. By the English he puts on Homer's serenity (he reifies it) and on Chapman's "masculine" extrovert energy, Keats produces the perpetual imminence that is the hero of his sonnet. In the Keatsian idiom, we could call that imminence a "stationing," with an ear for the full social resonance of Keats's aesthetic word.[12]

The instance of this poem would suggest that Keats's relation to the tradition is better conceived as dialogic (Bakhtin) than dialectic (Bloom). The poetry does not clear a space for itself by a phallic agon; it opens itself to the tradition, defining itself as a theater wherein such contests may be eternally and inconclusively staged. The authority of this poetry consists in its detachment from the styles or voices it entertains. By this detachment, these styles become *signatures:* not audible voices but visible, material signs of canonical voices. These signs—like all such marks, inauthentic and incomplete—are owned but they are not, ultimately, *mastered* by the master of ceremonies. And because they remain external to authorial consciousness, theirs is the empowering virtue of the supplement. In these magic supplements, "things semi-real," lies the terrific charm of Keats's poetry.

The contained badness of "Chapman's Homer" constitutes its goodness, which is to say, its rhetorical force. When Keats is great, it is because he *signifies* his alienation from his *materia poetica,* a fact that modern criticism and textual studies have suppressed.[13] This alien-

---

12. In his notes on Milton, Keats comments on "what may be called his stationing or statuary. He is not content with simple description, he must station." Quoted in Ian Jack, *Keats and the Mirror of Art* (Oxford: Clarendon Press, 1967), p. 142.

13. Jerome McGann, "Keats and the Historical Method in Literary Criticism," *MLN* 94 (1979), 988–1032. McGann's discussion of the textual history of "La Belle Dame" and of

ation—inevitable, given Keats's education, class, and opportunities—
was highly expedient. By it, Keats could consume the "stuff of creativity" without becoming consumed by it. Keats's poetry, inspired
by translations, engravings, reproductions, schoolroom mythologies,
and Tassie's gems, delivers itself through these double and triple
reproductions as the "true, the blushful Hippocrene." That phrase
describes, ironically, *precisely* a substitute truth. Again, Byron understood these things: "You know my opinion of *that second-hand* school of
poetry."

Let's return for a moment to Byron's attack on Keats's display of his
literary entitlement. "It is in their *finery* that the new under school are
most vulgar. . . . I speak of writing, not of persons." Byron's "finery"
designates those elements in the poetry which are perceptible *as* styles
because imperfectly appropriated, heaped heterogeneously together,
and reflected on by an "author" who is but the alter ego to those styles.
"I don't mean he is *indecent,* but viciously soliciting his own ideas into a
state, which is neither poetry nor any thing else but a Bedlam vision."[14] By his three-way equation, linking self-reflection, masturbation, and middle-class acquisition and display, Byron clarifies the
broad social offensiveness of Keats's poetry. As Byron well knew, a
good deal of his own poetry and that of his contemporaries solicits its
own ideas into a state. Byron had, of course, his quarrel with those
serious self-reflectors, the Lakers, and his attack on Keats is no doubt
part of that quarrel. *But* Keats was a figure from the "Mediterranean"
side of the great North-South, serious-sensuous divide: Byron's side,
that is. It would seem that Keats owes his rare achievement—to have
become at once Byron's and Wordsworth's whipping boy—to the
manifest *subject* disorders of his discourse.[15]

---

the Paolo and Francesca sonnet is an invaluable lesson in the ideological uses of textual
scholarship.

14. Matthews, *Keats: Critical Heritage,* p. 130; Byron to Murray, Nov. 9, 1820, *Byron's
Letters and Journals,* 7:225.

15. The poetry's lack of intrinsic reference, its deep insincerity, was its great and
largely unmet generic challenge. "But when the . . . arts have reached the period of
more refined cultivation, they cease to be considered as means through which to convey
to other minds the energies of thought and feeling: the productions of art become
themselves the ultimate objects of imitation, and the mind is acted upon by them instead
of acting through them from itself. . . . [W]hen imitative skill has brought an art the
nearest to perfection, it is then that its cultivation is the least allied to mind: its original
purpose, as a mode of expression, becomes wholly lost in the artificial object,—the
display of a skill" (Josiah Conder, *Eclectic Review,* Sept. 1817). On one level, Conder's criticism marks out the difference between a classically mimetic and a Romantic-

Byron is repelled by Keats's psychic fanes, first, because they are filled with false things, not human qualities or even authorial properties but *props*, or material signs of literary reality. Worse, everything acquired by the Keatsian consciousness, no matter how "good" originally, gets falsified within that precinct. Fine becomes "finery," cultivation becomes Culture, whole and living speech is rendered a quotation, and everything is like an artifact in an overwrought cabinet: framed, spotlighted, exhibited as possessions that are also signs *of* possession.[16] Keats's canonical "abstractions" (the word crops up throughout the reviews) exposed the canon as a construct, as authoritarian, and as subject to violation. This is to say, Keats's scavenging replaced the authority *of* Authority, a natural and internal quality, with that of a more literal and original authority: with the figure of the literary entrepreneur. No poetic style could have been more abhorrent to the respectively private and public transparencies of Wordsworth and Byron, or rather, to the class subject-forms projected by those good manners. Returning to Byron's "nonsense" verdict, when self-reflection is projected as reflection on other poets' selves, when "frigging [one's] *Imagination*" describes a dalliance with other men's surmises, when a signally autotelic poetry exposes the real interests served by its display of disinterest, and an autoerotic verse betrays the busyness—and business—of a working brain, then accusations of "nonsense" make perfect sense.

Keats's strangely alienated reflexiveness carried, I believe, an even stronger social charge than the one I've just identified. We get at this through another of Byron's colorful commentaries. Here is the strange little fable Byron produced for the purpose of characterizing Keats's poetry:

---

expressive mode. But this difference was, by 1817, a familiar one, and it doesn't cause Conder much distress.

What the review suggests is that the damaging fact of Keats's poetry was its expressive falseness. Where Wordsworth, for instance, offers himself in propria persona, Keats was felt to provide a tissue of received, heterogeneous, and often conflicting manners. That this was the source of the generic confusion is something Keats seems to have guessed. One feels in his penetrating characterization of Wordsworth's mode, "the egotistical sublime," an implicit reading of his own style, the egotistical bathetic. Or, where ego should be, there is alienated, interested reproduction.

16. This discussion is informed throughout by Jean Baudrillard, *For a Critique of the Political Economy of the Sign*, trans. Charles Levin (St. Louis: Telos Press, 1981); *The Mirror of Production*, trans. Mark Poster (St. Louis: Telos Press, 1975); and *Simulations*, trans. Paul Foss, Paul Patton, and Philip Beitchman (New York: Semiotext(e), 1983).

The *Edinburgh* praises Jack Keats or Ketch, or whatever his names are: why, his is the *Onanism* of Poetry—something like the pleasure an Italian fiddler extracted out of being suspended daily by a Street Walker in Drury Lane. This went on for some weeks: at last the Girl went to get a pint of Gin—met another, chatted too long, and Cornelli was *hanged outright before she returned.* Such like is the trash they praise, and such will be the end of the *outstretched* poesy of this miserable Self-polluter of the human mind.[17]

During the Regency, as before, Jack Ketch was a name for the common hangman, and both the name and character were linked to the puppet play of Punchinello. With this double dangling as his starting point, Byron goes on to explore, so to speak, the social and sexual resonance attaching to Keats's name. The fiction he unfolds describes a particularly laborious form of masturbation, *le coup de corde,* a trick that requires the technical assistance here of a prostitute. The "Italian fiddler's" busy contrivance is emphasized by his partner's fecklessness, and the comedy of the story (a "hoist with one's own petard" narrative) involves the exposure of a work : pleasure ratio where we least expect to find it, at the center of an autoerotic activity. The joke is perhaps more pointed yet; Byron involves a distinctly lower-class character in a perversion associated with aristocratic refinement, *ennui,* and unselfconsciousness—dare we say, *hauteur.* Presumably, one's valet wouldn't leave one hanging. The Italian fiddler is punished for his *social,* not his sexual aspirations, and Byron's word, *"outstretched,"* which maps Keats's verbal priapism onto a social figure, clinches the real perversion.

What Byron is driving at is the contradiction that organizes both masturbation and the reproductive habits of the middle class. We illuminate the connection by proposing that the dream or the concept of masturbation is one of knowing unconsciousness: "the feel of not to feel it," or, as in the "Ode to a Nightingale" sensible numbness. Inasmuch as one is both worker and pleasurer, giver and receiver, subject and object in masturbation, the act *should* produce a rare psychic unity. However, both the technical groundplot (a part of the body is fetishized and overworked) and the absence of a distracting other to absorb the purposiveness of the activity and naturalize the techne, install with unusual force the divided psyche, which must know itself busy for luxury.

17. Byron to Murray, Nov. 4, 1820, *Byron's Letters and Journals,* 7: 217.

We can, and Keats *did*, motivate that contradiction by suggesting that the deeper dream of masturbation is a fantasy of pleasure without the death of perfect gratification—or meaning/value without the loss of either reflexive consciousness or the object. The fantasized experience is one of energy *and* luxury, giving and receiving, high (cerebral) and low (genital), infinite metamorphosis contemplated by a center of consciousness keen to enjoy that lability. Ideally, or in imagination, masturbation establishes a psychic wholeness that *knows itself* to be dialectically contingent. Thus is it also vitally, *capably in*complete. The defensive virtue of masturbation, understood as a fantasy *of* (in place of/in addition to) proper sex, is its protection against the drive that, correctly enacted, must obliterate the consciousness that would *own* that pure pleasure, that death. "Now more than ever seems it rich to die, / To cease upon the midnight with no pain. . . . Still wouldst thou sing, and I have ears in vain— / To thy high requiem become a sod." Masturbation—the part for/in addition to the whole, the fantasy for/ plus the actual, the oblique for/with the direct, the sign for/alongside the thing—is a holding action: a way of holding on to a holding off. The formula could be recast in temporal terms. Masturbation, that unnaturally hasty act, dreams of a "slow time," a duration that neither wastes nor realizes, at once history's negation and its fulfillment. "Deathwards progressing / To no death was that visage" (or, for a categorical association, "purposiveness without purpose," Kant's definition of aesthetic experience). Many of our fondest moments in Keats's poetry describe this condition: "Their lips touched not, but had not bade adieu." Many describe a fantasy wherein the sign (let us say, the tradition—an empowering reproductive apparatus) and the thing (John Keats, an author-original) are simultaneous but distinct: a metonymic dream, or a fantasy of *being*, put under erasure by *having* and, thus, violated, idealized, effectuated, and *possessed*. Another way to frame this fantasy is as an instant(iation) wherein beauty (the sign of legitimacy: the signifying possession) and truth (the natural, unspeaking attribute) do not antithesize or succeed each other, neither do they coalesce. They exist, rather, side by side, as parallel, mutually delimiting total systems: value *and* "existences," symbolic *and* imaginary zones.

No one cared, of course, about Keats's exposure of the contradictions that inform masturbation. What did concern Wordsworth and Byron was the poetry's exposure of the relation between "working brain" and the "spontaneous overflow" or "rattling on exactly as I

talk" of Romantic poetry: that is, Keats's demystification of a prestigious idea of literary production. In the case of Wordsworth, we
might call this method "natural selection," a darkling deliberation
effected by memory and emerging as a spontaneous, strictly pro-
cessual value. Byron's worldliness, the counterpart to Wordsworth's
naturalness, establishes authorial purpose within a psyche so profoundly socialized (so *inherited*, one might say), and *accomplishes* those
purposes through audience reciprocities so exact, that calculation has
no place to surface. Both protocols are commonplaces of Romantic
criticism. Less obvious, perhaps, is that while these myths of production negate what the poets conceived as the age's dominant *material*
productive mode, the mechanical, they also *rehearse* a mode of social
and ideological production.

In order to constitute its structural betweenness (a neither-nor,
"nothing" state), an "existence," the middle class had to expose the
historicity of value, clearing the ground, as it were, for its own violation of inherited and naturalized values. At the same time, and so as to
sanction this originality and safeguard its middling position, threatened on the lower front by imitation and the upper by assimilation, the
class in the middle had to represent its own, invented values as either
ahistorical or as history's telos. The trick was to look valuably and essentially ambitious—history's coming class—and also eternal, a class
dreamed by Adam, who awoke and found it real. One logical solution
to this stylistic problem was the phenomenology of the *nunc stans*, or
the look of an *eternally coming* class, in motion/in place forever. The
display of ease, a contradiction in terms, was another device for con-
verting nothingness into prolific tension. By its self-identification as a
profitably consuming class, the bourgeoisie imitated the *ontologically*
productive condition of the aristocracy. At the same time, the rhetorical orientation of this mimesis, as well as its fetishism, marked it as an
ambitious gesture, literally, as *wanting*. The power of this mark, a
negative originality, was, of course, its determined negativity. A class
that is *self*-violating makes itself inviolable. That which has no center
cannot be seized; what has no character cannot be defamed; and what
is always and by definition moving is not easily removed.

I am describing a "bad" solution to an ideological bind: on the one
hand, the middle-class commitment to a program of social mobility
(Keats's "camelion poet," an ethic of becoming or, less Romantically, a
work ethic) and, on the other, its longing for the authority connected
with the generative passivity, stable identity, and "quiet being" that

were an influential fantasy of the leisure class. Keats motivates the contradiction in the style of the middle class but, because this was not "naturally" *his* solution and because it was, for him, greatly polyvalent, that style gets reified. Keats works at his pleasure and stations himself by that paradox. Wordsworth, we know, tends to suppress that conflictual figure which is no less the agency of his art than of Keats's. Wordsworth's genius is to operate a kind of double standard. Even as he identifies poet (for him, *speaker*) with reader-listener as both essential men, he splits apart production and consumption into respectively passive and active moments. The poet easily overflows with his own pre(*consciously*)meditated verse. The reader, however, is forbidden the spontaneous, inward delight that is the poet's prerequisite and prerogative. Indeed, the reader cannot emulate that noble ease without degrading it and himself, becoming but a seeker after "the pleasure of Frontiniac or sherry." Wordsworth's readers are instructed to *work* at their meanings, to "find" tales in the things the poet effortlessly makes available to them. By contrast, Keats's ambitiously masturbatory poetry correctly positions the work/pleasure contradiction in the act of production. Is it any wonder that Byron, a poet who reaped such profits by producing himself as an aristocrat for the delectation of the middle class, and Wordsworth, who did well enough by his "habits of meditation," should have been so shaken by Keats?

To conclude, let me say that Keats's poetry blushes more deeply and deliberately than we had thought. It blushes at the level of style. This is a discourse that "feeds upon" but does not assimilate its sources. It *engorges* itself—a transitive operation—in such a way as to make itself permanently, *intransitively* engorged—"stationed," in Keats's phrase. Keats's discursive procedures rehearse that protocol whereby the middle class of his day produced itself as a kind of collective, throbbing oxymoron: achieved by its ambitiousness, hardworking in its hedonism, a "being" that defined itself strictly by its properties, or ways of having. In the style of Keats's poetry, we read the dream of masturbation: the fantasy of "the perpetual cockstand," that solution to castration anxiety.[18] In both the dream and the anxiety, we, like Byron, discern the genetic code of the middle class.

18. Steven Marcus, *The Other Victorians* (1964; rpt. New York: Basic Books, 1974). My understanding of the early response to Keats's poetry and my argument for the complex purposes of that poetry began with a reading of Marcus's extraordinary book.

7

Public Virtues, Private Vices: Reading between the Lines of Wordsworth's "Anecdote for Fathers"

David Simpson

It is perhaps an overstatement to claim that the pursuit of literary criticism as an academic occupation institutionalized in British and American universities since the late nineteenth century has depended principally upon the teaching of poetry. British criticism has always built substantially on Shakespearean so-called foundations (although they are anything but that), and both bourgeois (F. R. Leavis) and socialist (Raymond Williams) cultural critics have privileged the novel. American criticism of American writing has mostly been dominated by interactions between various prose genres (sermons, novels, journals) and historical and material culture, perhaps the result of a working consensus denying (pace Whitman) the emergence of a distinctly "American" poetry much before the turn of the present century.

At the same time, those movements that have most consciously proclaimed themselves the property of a literary-critical elite, New Criticism and deconstruction, have tended to define themselves as committed to the close reading of poetry. It is in poetry that complex language has been held to be most complex, most likely to register polyphonously in the adverting mind (as for I. A. Richards), and to call forth our most sophisticated abilities to dissolve and dissipate in order to recreate. All too often, the reading of poetry has been articulated as a task beyond the sphere of ordinary language skills, even as therapy against the degradations of a popular culture. This tendency has only been exacerbated by a Marxist or leftist criticism that has historically identified the novel and the drama as emerging from and speaking to the people, while poetry is positioned as the lingua franca of an alienated bourgeoisie seeking to reinvent the aesthetic gratifications of bygone ages. Alternatively poetry has been seen as effectively hegemonic, as by Bakhtin, who sees in the history of poetic genres the influence of "the unifying, centralizing, centripetal forces of verbal-ideological life" doing the cultural work of the "higher official socio-ideological levels," and thus fundamentally at odds with the democratic heteroglossia instanced in the novel and in related prose genres. In poetry, for Bakhtin, the "internal dialogization of discourse" tends to be "extinguished." Poems may display conflicts and contradictions, but only at the level of content and subject matter: they "do not enter into the language itself."[1]

Bakhtin's is a sophisticated distinction and might go far toward an explanation of the absence of true "heteroglossia" from Wordsworth's avowed language of the ordinary person in a state of vivid sensation. In Wordsworth's poems, the exchanges between the educated speaker and the much-lampooned vagrants, bedlamites, and yeomen he encounters are transcribed in a decorous, subbiblical diction ("With something of a lofty utterance drest") that has always divided its readers according as they attribute different identities to ordinary language. They find the poet's reported speech to be either fraudulently euphemistic, and hence a concession to bourgeois taste, or plausibly dignified, and hence a reflection of the inherent respectability of working or homeless people. Clearly, one is here deciding for a politics rather than validating any factual evidence about what such people could or could not have said around 1800, and it is this crux that Wordsworth perhaps sought consciously to resolve in his retrospective insistence that Simon Lee's "I dearly love their voices" was "word for word from his own lips."[2]

This essay does not attempt to explore the question of the demographic credibility of Wordsworthian plain speaking, and I invoke

1. M. M. Bakhtin, "Discourse in the Novel," in *The Dialogic Imagination: Four Essays,* ed. Michael Holquist, trans. Caryl Emerson and Holquist (Austin: University of Texas Press, 1981), pp. 272–73, 284, 286.
2. *Lyrical Ballads: Wordsworth and Coleridge,* ed. R. L. Brett and A. R. Jones (London: Methuen, 1976), p. 284. This remark was recorded by Isabella Fenwick in conversations with the poet.

Bakhtin as merely one example (albeit an arguably fruitful one) of the prose/poetry dichotomy that runs, implicitly or explicitly, through much Marxist criticism. At the same time, much of the best criticism "after Marx"—as witnessed by Marjorie Levinson and Frank Lentricchia in this very volume—is turning to poetry as an exemplary object for attention. For the poets and poetic genres of the last two hundred years or so, such criticism is likely to constitute an account of the largely unsuccessful attempt to produce a socially consensual language (and hence a "living") or of the occasional reifications that enable "success." My reading of "Anecdote for Fathers" may be situated in this context as an account of the determinations and contradictions that legibly accompany the attempt to propose a shared language, a shared moral experience, a common sentence. Along the way and between the lines, there will be much to find of ideology, class, and gender, and I hope much to offer by way of alternative to the Bakhtinian and generically Marxist swerve away from poetry. If the poem does not loudly and clearly announce its participation in a complex social and historical register, neither does it conceal its placement. Indeed, all these words that we use to insinuate some deliberate referentiality to literary language—such words as *avow, declare, announce, explain*—are rather helpless when one takes seriously the problems of specifying an absolute borderline between the conscious and the unconscious conjunctions of subjectivity and language. Conversely, the notion of an efficient *repression* is hard to maintain when the mechanism of concealment is in fact educed from expressive language itself. Similarly, I shall argue against the usefulness of any distinction (other than of degree) between the private and public spheres of Wordsworth's life-in-language. Everything that we can recover of the poet's private life was known to somebody; one such person is already a public.

I begin by discussing the apparent "message" of the poem, the message that a reasonably prepared member of the poetry-reading public might have come away with in 1798. This reader is of course a purely heuristic construct, chiefly useful as a figure through which to describe the most likely highest common factors among Wordsworth's readers and hence to isolate those allusions as the ones about which the poet may be supposed least defensive. I then discuss the importance of other kinds of information, items the poet would not have supposed already available to a general reader but which certainly were known to some within the Alfoxden circle. These categories overlap, for the distinction is one of degree rather than kind—between a limited and a more general public. Finally, I explore the implications of these conjunctions for a prospectively theorized account of (this) language in history.

Here is the poem in its first printed version of 1798 (the only version I plan to discuss):

Anecdote for Fathers,

shewing how the art of lying may be taught

> *I have a boy of five years old,*
> *His face is fair and fresh to see;*
> *His limbs are cast in beauty's mould,*
> *And dearly he loves me.*
>
> *One morn we stroll'd on our dry walk,*
> *Our quiet house all full in view,*
> *And held such intermitted talk*
> *As we are wont to do.*
>
> *My thoughts on former pleasures ran;*
> *I thought of Kilve's delightful shore,*   10
> *My pleasant home, when spring began,*
> *A long, long year before.*
>
> *A day it was when I could bear*
> *To think, and think, and think again;*
> *With so much happiness to spare,*
> *I could not feel a pain.*
>
> *My boy was by my side, so slim*
> *And graceful in his rustic dress!*
> *And oftentimes I talked to him,*
> *In very idleness.*   20
>
> *The young lambs ran a pretty race;*
> *The morning sun shone bright and warm;*
> *"Kilve," said I, "was a pleasant place,*
> *"And so is Liswyn farm.*
>
> *"My little boy, which like you more,"*
> *I said and took him by the arm—*
> *"Our home by Kilve's delightful shore,*
> *"Or here at Liswyn farm?"*
>
> *"And tell me, had you rather be,"*
> *I said and held him by the arm,*   30

"At Kilve's smooth shore by the green sea,
"Or here at Liswyn farm?

In careless mood he looked at me,
While still I held him by the arm,
And said, "At Kilve I'd rather be
"Than here at Liswyn farm."

"Now, little Edward, say why so;
My little Edward, tell me why;"
"I cannot tell, I do not know."
"Why this is strange," said I.   40

"For, here are woods and green-hills warm;
"There surely must some reason be
"Why you would change sweet Liswyn farm
"For Kilve by the green sea."

At this, my boy, so fair and slim,
Hung down his head, nor made reply;
And five times did I say to him,
"Why? Edward, tell me why?"

His head he raised—there was in sight,
It caught his eye, he saw it plain—   50
Upon the house-top, glittering bright,
A broad and gilded vane.

Then did the boy his tongue unlock,
And thus to me he made reply;
"At Kilve there was no weather-cock,
"And that's the reason why."

Oh dearest, dearest boy! my heart
For better lore would seldom yearn,
Could I but teach the hundredth part
Of what from thee I learn.[3]   60

I first wrote about this poem more than ten years ago and well remember the self-esteeming pleasure with which I then understood it.[4] My reading neatly exemplified the overall paradigm I was then presenting for the reading of Romantic writings. I thought that I was reading more closely than any of the published critics, finding in the poem not only an example of the transference of authority from poet to reader (who has to decide what it is, after all, that the narrator has learned)

---

3. Ibid., pp. 64–66.
4. Simpson, *Irony and Authority in Romantic Poetry* (London: Macmillan, 1979), pp. 39–41.

but also an analysis of the place of transgression and even violence within the hermeneutic ambition ("While still I held him by the arm"). That ambition evolved within an improper mood, a mood of "idleness," which had already imprisoned the child within a sentimental-pastoral figuration of merely decorative attributes ("His limbs are cast in beauty's mould . . . And graceful in his rustic dress").

Looking again at the poem, I find that this reading still holds up and is indeed capable of further elaboration by looking again at the "words on the page." Note, for example, the exactness of the double bind that the adult imposes on the child. The first invitation to compare Kilve and Liswyn farm is made by positing them as equal: each is a "pleasant place" (l. 23). At the next mention, Liswyn farm is adjectively unqualified, while Kilve is given precise and desirable attributes: "a smooth shore, by the green sea" (l. 31).[5] This modification seems to persuade the child to decide on Kilve as the preferred place, to provide the answer he thinks is required. But as soon as the choice is articulated, the terms are reversed by the narrator. Now it is Liswyn that is "sweet," with "woods and green-hills warm," while Kilve has only a rather inhospitable and cold "green sea" (ll. 41–44). Having been thus completely trapped in a double bind, the child has recourse to an apparently inconsequential and purely contingent explanation: the other place did not have a weathercock.

This reading, with which I was previously so pleased, is really an elaboration of the manifest message of the poem, the function of which is indeed to put the "reader" into a position of ethical self-righteousness and interpretative capacity (or power). I will unravel this posture of self-command later in this essay. For now, I want to show that this message is not contradicted but in fact enforced by a recognition of the leading historical allusions registered in the poem. Most obviously it alludes to the contemporary debate about education and, in particular, to the question of the nature and origin of lying.

In response to the inherited puritanical assumptions about children as naturally deceitful until corrected by discipline, various radical theorists were extending Locke's arguments about the nonexistence of innate ideas to suggest that children were made corrupt, not born corrupt. Wordsworth's poem clearly endorses this second position and even suggests that the child has a natural inclination against

5. The same unconscious adjectival persuasion is applied by the old sea captain to the narrator (and reader) of "The Thorn."

falsehood. Forced to invent an excuse for declaring a preference that he does not even have, the boy is hesitant and uncomfortable. In this respect the poem's affiliation is to the doctrines of Godwin and Rousseau. In the *Enquiry concerning Political Justice*, Godwin noticed a general tendency among educators to project their own views rather than respect those of their charges: "We are wrapped up in ourselves, and do not observe, as we ought, step by step the sensations that pass in the mind of our hearer." Teachers continually fail "in wisdom of contrivance, or conciliation of manner, or both," so that "our labour is expended not in teaching truth, but in teaching falshood."[6] Godwin here anticipates the subtitle of Wordsworth's poem. And he developed his arguments further in *The Enquirer*, published the year before the first edition of *Lyrical Ballads*. Here, he endorses the general value of teaching the child "to discriminate, to remember and to enquire,"[7] but the account of how this is to be done confirms Wordsworth's narrator's final recognition that he has been making a mistake. Godwin specifies the primary motive in children's behavior as the desire for praise and approval (p. 57). This renders them particularly vulnerable to manipulation by adults: they will say whatever they think they are supposed to say to gain approval. And this asymmetry makes it all the more important that the adult develop the habit of critical self-reflection: "The first part that a skilful artificer would study, is the power of his tools, and the nature of his materials. Without a considerable degree of knowledge in this respect, nothing will be produced but abortive attempts, and specimens that disgrace the operator" (p. 120). The crucial element in this self-knowledge is "frankness," that quality which teaches us "to review our thoughts; to blush for their absurdity, their groundless singularities, and their exaggeration" (p. 149). This is what Wordsworth's narrator learns; and his child has done just what Godwin says children do: he has submitted the "turbulence" of his own passions to the turbulent passions of the preceptor (p. 61).

It is this tendency toward absolute power on the adult's part that leads Godwin to argue for the superiority of public over private education. In the company of other children, the child is less likely to feel the full weight of adult intimidation, apparent even when unintended: for

6. William Godwin, *Enquiry concerning Political Justice and Its Influence on Morals and Happiness*, ed. F. E. L. Priestley, 3 vols. (Toronto: University of Toronto Press, 1946), 1:44, 47, 48.

7. William Godwin, *The Enquirer: Reflections on Education, Manners, and Literature, in a Series of Essays* (London, 1797), p. 6.

"anxiety of individual affection watches the boy too narrowly" (p. 60).
Here Godwin takes issue with Rousseau's *Emile,* which had privileged
private over public education. Nonetheless, while Godwin explicitly
denounces Rousseau's methods in general, which he finds deceitful
and covertly authoritarian (pp. 120, 166), he is in substantial agreement with the findings of *Emile* on the matter of truth and falsehood.
Wordsworth's poem thus also echoes Rousseau perhaps even more
explicitly than it does Godwin. Rousseau is emphatic in the conviction
that childhood "has its own ways of seeing, thinking, and feeling;
nothing is more foolish than to try and substitute our ways."[8] He
claims that "the entrance of every vice can be traced" (p. 56). Early
education should thus be negative rather than positive: it should
preclude error rather than impose a truth that the child cannot understand as such for itself. Parts of the argument of the second book of
Emile constitute a near-exact anticipation of "Anecdote for Fathers."
Lying is not natural to children but is made so by the law of obedience.
A child's promises and assurances cannot be taken seriously, since no
child can "project into the future while he lives in the present." Thus
children's lies are "entirely the work of their teachers, and to teach
them to speak the truth is nothing less than to teach them the art of
lying" (p. 66).

Wordsworth's subtitle specifies that he too is describing "how the
art of lying may be taught," and his narrative endorses Rousseau's
argument that children do not possess memory and reason and cannot, therefore, generate adult-compatible moral judgments.[9] These
analogues in the writings of Godwin and Rousseau are not presented
as the last word on the "historicality" of "Anecdote for Fathers."
Others could surely be discovered. But the echoes in this poem of *The
Enquirer* and *Emile* do seem to me to argue that its "message" for that
already-imagined contemporary reader is composed by a coherent

8. Jean-Jacques Rousseau, *Emile,* trans. Barbara Foxley (New York: Dent and Dutton, 1911), p. 54.
9. This conjunction calls for a different account of Wordsworth's relation to Rousseau from that advanced by James K. Chandler in *Wordsworth's Second Nature: A Study of
the Poetry and Politics* (Chicago: University of Chicago Press, 1984), pp. 93–119. Arguing
(I think convincingly) for the identity of the 1798 five-book *Prelude* as an alternative
treatise on education to the five-book *Emile,* Chandler proposes a coherently anti-
Rousseauian Wordsworth. The desire to assimilate Wordsworth completely to Burke
pressures Chandler to reduce to negation the complex partly negative and partly positive relation between Wordsworth and Rousseau. On this relation, see also W. J. T.
Mitchell, "Influence, Autobiography, and Literary History: Rousseau's *Confessions* and
Wordsworth's *Prelude,*" ELH 57 (1990), 643–64.

relation between what can be inferred from a careful reading of the "words on the page" and what might have been known about the more famous contemporary debates about education and human nature. The poem's moral narrative takes some working out—it is never quite explicit—but it conforms to the Godwinian-Rousseauian account of the dynamics of dishonesty and to their common critique of bourgeois ethics. In this way Wordsworth positioned his poem within a general debate that seems to have remained important. To give only one example, Amelia Opie's later "Illustrations of Lying, in All Its Branches," first published in 1825, proposed a sophisticated taxonomy of various kinds and degrees of dishonesty (although it included no category of justifiable lying and no special exemptions for children).[10]

From here on things get more complicated. We know more about the poem than we can infer from a reading of the words on the page, and the words on the pages of Rousseau, Godwin, and perhaps other educational theorists of the time. Thanks to the survival of hundreds of documents—letters, recollections, rumors, even anecdotes—and to the efforts of generations of scholars in gathering and publishing them, we hardly ever find ourselves reading Wordsworth as we read, for example, Shakespeare, about whose biography so little is known in any detail. There is often a positive wealth of information whose relevance or irrelevance to the elucidation of the poems needs to be constantly reassessed. The case of Wordsworth thus presents itself as a very interesting example of the individual writing subject within the general historical-ideological sphere. We know enough about the individual to be unable to ignore the interesting difficulties we face in making him the paradigm of a representative generality, even as we are committed (as Marxist or materialist critics) to try to understand the operation of those general, intersubjective determinations.

I begin with three facts. First, the poem was written at Alfoxden House, in Somerset, between March and May (probably April) 1798, and based on an incident that occurred there.[11] Second, the actual child was not Wordsworth's, but a little boy named Basil Montagu. Third, the invented place, Liswyn Farm, is an adaptation of Llys Wen, in Brecknockshire, where radical John Thelwall had settled after fleeing the political harassment to which he had been subjected all over

10. *The Works of Mrs. Amelia Opie*, 3 vols. (Philadelphia, 1848), 3:414–98.
11. Mark L. Reed, *Wordsworth: The Chronology of the Early Years, 1770–1799* (Cambridge: Harvard University Press, 1967), p. 32.

England. All these details are mentioned by Wordsworth in his recollections as transcribed by Isabella Fenwick and edited by Ernest de
Selincourt.[12] Let us take the last of them first.

At the time of the poem's composition Wordsworth had never been
at Llys Wen, though he would visit it during the Welsh tour of August
1798, just before leaving the West Country for good, and a month or so
before the publication of *Lyrical Ballads*. Before coming to rest in Wales,
Thelwall had hoped to settle in the neighborhood of Alfoxden and
Stowey, with the Coleridges, the Pooles, and the Wordsworths. He
had visited in July 1797 to look over the situation but was informed by
Coleridge a few weeks after his visit that Somerset could not handle
any more radical democrats. The evidences for this conclusion are
quite convoluted. Thelwall was a notorious figure and had been fairly
steadily in the public eye since his acquittal in December 1794 at the
end of a famous treason trial. For two or three years afterward he
was hounded by "church and king" mobs every time he appeared
in public. Wordsworth and Coleridge reasonably thought that Thelwall's visit was what brought James Welsh, the government spy, who
showed up in August 1797 to report on the supposedly jacobinical
behavior of the men of letters.

Thelwall's two weeks with the poets seem to have passed cordially
enough on all sides. But Coleridge's letters to Thelwall, which date
from as early as April 1796, show themselves from the first suspicious
of his "impassioned confidence" and uneasily ironical about the contrast between Coleridge's own relative retirement and Thelwall's determination to "uplift the *torch* dreadlessly" in the arena of *"public
Life."*[13] After the 1797 visit, Thelwall recorded in one of his poems the
desire to share a "philosophic amity" with the Coleridge circle, which
he saw as an enlightened microsociety of kindred spirits.[14] But after
making earnest efforts on Thelwall's behalf, Coleridge informed him
in a letter of August 21 that the local landlord was inflexible in his

12. *The Poetical Works of William Wordsworth,* ed. Ernest de Selincourt, 5 vols. (Oxford:
Clarendon Press, 1940–49), 1:363.

13. *The Collected Letters of Samuel Taylor Coleridge,* ed. Earl Leslie Griggs, 6 vols.
(Oxford: Clarendon Press, 1966–71), 1:339, 277. For a useful account of the personal and
political atmosphere at Stowey in the summer of 1797, see Kelvin Everest, *Coleridge's
Secret Ministry: The Context of the Conversation Poems, 1795–1798* (New York: Barnes and
Noble, 1979), pp. 121–45.

14. John Thelwall, "Lines Written at Bridgewater, in Somersetshire, on the 27th of
July, 1797; during a long excursion, in quest of a peaceful retreat," in *Poems Written
Chiefly in Retirement* (Hereford: W. H. Parker, 1801), p. 129–30.

refusal to accept Thelwall as a tenant.[15] So Thelwall went to Wales, to a place that would appear in poeticized form as the present residence of Wordsworth's narrator, Liswyn farm.

Why is the poem set "here" at Liswyn farm? It is as if Wordsworth casts himself as Thelwall, albeit a Thelwall who is wondering about being elsewhere. The actual present place was, as I have said, Alfoxden House, and the previous residence, poeticized as Kilve, has usually been understood as Racedown.[16] (Even though there is a village called Kilve near Alfoxden, Wordsworth had never lived there.) Why did Wordsworth use two places he had not lived in, one of which was Thelwall's home, to represent two places he had lived in, but which go unmentioned?

More facts: the Wordsworths had been living rent-free at Racedown but were paying for Alfoxden the rather princely sum of twenty-three pounds a year—three times what they would pay for Grasmere two years later. And no wonder, for Alfoxden was quite simply the grandest place they would ever inhabit, as Dorothy made enthusiastically clear in her letters, describing a "large mansion with furniture enough for a dozen families like ours," along with spacious landscaped grounds and a deer park.[17] There must have been something uncomfortable in both the financial and symbolic dimensions of life at the house.[18] It was more than they could reasonably afford, and might well have seemed an odd place for a writer who was working on, of all things, "The Ruined Cottage" (February–March 1798) and who was surely thinking toward the ethic of frugality and simple subsistence which would constitute the implicit political economy of the 1800 preface to the second edition of *Lyrical Ballads*. They had signed the lease on July 14, 1797—Bastille Day.[19] And they appear to have given it up without having a real choice in the matter. Thelwall's visit seems to have alarmed the landlord, who let the house to other tenants without

15. Coleridge, *Letters* 1:343.
16. See Reed, *Chronology*, p. 221.
17. *The Letters of William and Dorothy Wordsworth: The Early Years, 1787–1805*, ed. Ernest de Selincourt, 2d ed. rev. Chester L. Shaver (Oxford: Clarendon Press, 1967), p. 190. Alfoxden House, with its gravel walk still extant, is illustrated in Berta Lawrence, *Coleridge and Wordsworth in Somerset* (Newton Abbot: David and Charles, 1970), facing page 124.
18. The same discomfort informs, I think, the narrative of "Simon Lee." See my *Wordsworth's Historical Imagination: The Poetry of Displacement* (London: Methuen, 1987), pp. 149–59.
19. Mary Moorman, *William Wordsworth, a Biography: The Early Years, 1770–1803*, corr. ed. (Oxford: Clarendon Press, 1969), p. 325.

consulting Wordsworth and in spite of Thomas Poole's letter on his
behalf, petitioning an extension.[20] The Wordsworths knew by March 5
or 6, 1798, that they were going to have to leave and by March 11 had
made up their minds to go to Germany with Coleridge.[21] So, by the
beginning of the period within which "Anecdote" was composed,
Wordsworth had some cause to wonder where he would rather be:
"here at Liswyn farm" was no longer an option.

It is hard not to suspect, then, that the child's choice of the weathercock as his explanation for preferring the other place might have been
as precisely motivated for the poet behind the text as it is apparently
unmotivated for the child in that text. Kilve (Racedown) had, he said,
no weathercock. And the one at Liswyn (Alfoxden) is more than just a
meteorological aid: it is a "broad and gilded vane," something, perhaps, one could hardly fail to notice. It thus suggests itself as a symbol
of the difference between the stately Alfoxden and the more modest
Racedown, as it is also perhaps an emblem of the mutability that was
so profoundly affecting the Wordworths' lives during these weeks in
the spring of 1798. William might well have wondered, of Alfoxden,
"whether vain"? And he might well have found his own ease of mind
in giving reason to evacuate a place offering the name and all the
addition of a country squire—a figure he could never be, or afford to
be, or wholeheartedly wish to be. Construed in this way, the poem
becomes an exercise in making virtue of necessity. If little Basil really
did pick on the weathercock, it might well have been as the result of an
intelligent five-year-old's sensitivity to adult concerns or conversations.

The renaming of Alfoxden as Liswyn may now be explained. There
is a teasing homophone latent in the real name of Thelwall's home:
"lease when"? And it is a complex overdetermination that implicates
Thelwall himself in a residence at Alfoxden, and identifies Wordsworth with Thelwall. By imagining radical John in a place with a broad
and gilded vane, Wordsworth eases his mind that he is not the only
democrat with a taste for grand houses. And that same grandeur
perhaps works as an imaginary compensation for the poets' own role
in obliging Thelwall to live elsewhere. Thelwall as narrator can be
located in a comfortable place, whereas the man himself was in fact
finding little peace in Brecknockshire.

20. See Mrs. Henry Sandford, *Thomas Poole and His Friends*, 2 vols. (London: Macmillan, 1888), 1:125, 240–43; and *Letters of William and Dorothy Wordsworth: The Early
Years*, pp. 209–10n, 220.
21. Reed, *Chronology*, pp. 222, 225.

So far, I have proposed that the (relatively) explicit message of the poem, as explained in the first section of this essay, goes along with a more private drama that has less to do with educational debates than with personal anxieties about home and shelter, about money, and about public images and political identities. What, then, is the point of the poeticizing of little Basil Montagu as "Edward," the narrator's own child? Young Basil was the son of Wordsworth's friend and contemporary Basil Montagu (1770–1851), whose wife had died in 1793 and who found himself unable to cope with the child of the marriage. Mary Moorman, Wordsworth's biographer, gives a good account of William's attempts to cure his friend's depressions and habits of wild living by means of an explicitly Godwinian discipline (pp. 260–66). As part of the plan, William and Dorothy took on the guardianship of young Basil, for whose upkeep and education his father would pay fifty pounds a year.

Young Basil was part of the Wordsworths' plans for financial security as well as for his father's well-being. At first they had planned to take in two children as paid charges. The income from this, together with the Calvert legacy, would have provided, according to Dorothy's calculations, an income of £170–180 a year.[22] As it happened, the guardianship of the other child, a girl, did not fall to them, and Montagu senior paid for only two years, after which the child was supported for a while at the Wordsworths' own expense (September 1797 through July 1798).

Well before the incident upon which "Anecdote" was based, Wordsworth had described Basil as a bit of a fibber. In fact, he wrote in March 1796, "he lies like a little devil."[23] In March 1797 Dorothy transcribed a detailed account of the plan on which his education was to be based: he was to attend chiefly to "the evidence of his senses," rather than to "*book learning*," and was to be led as far as possible toward a condition of happiness.[24] Theories of education were not just generally in the air, after Rousseau and Godwin; they were particularly so in the Wordsworth circle, owing to Basil's presence, to his observed habit of telling lies, and perhaps to the pedagogical discussions that accompanied Coleridge's plans for schoolmastering with Tom Wedgwood in September 1797.[25] The role reversal that the poem transcribes or invents must have come (or have been invented) as a powerful moment of

22. *Letters of William and Dorothy Wordsworth: Early Years*, p. 147.
23. Ibid., p. 168.
24. Ibid., p. 180–81.
25. Moorman, *William Wordsworth*, pp. 335–36.

illumination and self-accusation. The man who had accused Basil of being a compulsive liar comes to learn that he is himself teaching the art of lying.

William had other reasons for accusing himself, reasons that made him especially prone to think of himself as a guilty thing surprised. He was, as is now well known, the father of an illegitimate child, whom he had left behind with her mother in France in 1792. Caroline, Wordsworth's daughter by Annette Vallon, was born and baptized on December 15, 1792. Basil Montagu senior was also a natural son: his mother was Martha Ray, who found poetic immortality in "The Thorn." Little Basil was born on December 27, 1792, less than two weeks after Wordsworth's own daughter. And extraordinarily, Basil's middle name was Caroline! For a payment of fifty pounds a year, William and Dorothy had set themselves up as surrogate parents to a little boy almost exactly the same age as the poet's daughter and sharing even her name. They were being paid to care for one child, while the other would require them to assist in her support. Whatever incest fantasies might or might not have contributed to the setting up of the Alfoxden household, the companionship of a sister-spouse who was almost certainly conceived consciously as beyond the sexual pale might well have been something of a relief to William, as well as a pointed reminder of the sexual-familial relationship he had left behind forever in France, the place, indeed, of his actual "former pleasures" (l. 9). The poetic avowal of paternity—"I have a boy of five years old"—is a displacement of the paternity that goes unmentioned but could only have been constantly in mind in every exchange with Basil Caroline Montagu.

We now have two rather different accounts of "Anecdote for Fathers." The first, roughly, identifies its meanings in terms of a probably public reception, presuming, that is, a competent reader with no overpowering self-interest who might or might not have known the analogues to (or sources of) the poem in the writings of Rousseau and Godwin. This produces what I have been calling the explicit message. The second reading is rather different. It depends largely on information in the private sphere, shared only with a highly select group of the potential readers of 1798.

If these categories of private and public were absolute, then we might here be working with a clear distinction between the production of writing and its reception in the public sphere. We might say that the details of the poet's private life and personal relations illuminate only the coming-into-being of the poem and not its afterlife as a published text. But this distinction can be but one of degree, since some among the Alfoxden circle knew all the facts that have gone into my account of the "private" sphere, and all of them knew at least some of them. Moreover, we might extend the circle of informed readers into the general reading public on at least the matter of Thelwall's residence. Thelwall was a famous man, and as a favorite bogey of the right-wing press his doings were regularly reported. Indeed, in the very month of his visit to Somerset (July 1797) T. J. Mathias published a dialogue in which Thelwall was imaged as an "indefatigable incendiary and missionary of the French Propaganda" who "has now his *Schools of Reason* in country towns."[26] Readers of Wordsworth's poem, then, might well have picked up on Liswyn farm as an allusion to Llys Wen, even if they did not fully understand the motivations behind that allusion. In fact, given that *Lyrical Ballads* was published anonymously, they might even have taken Thelwall—also a poet—as its author.

We can only suppose that at some level Wordsworth "knew" full well that those who were most certain to read his poems—the Alfoxden circle—were exactly those in the best position to decipher most of the allusions and displacements. There is no truly "private" dimension to this poem. It is indeed hard to imagine even a reader from the Alfoxden circle coming up with all the shades of meaning for whose importance I have been arguing in this essay. But this unlikelihood is to be explained less as a matter of absolute than of relative necessity. A professional reader-critic in a post-Freudian culture and motivated by a special interest in the relations among language, subjectivity, and culture is going to overgo the limits of reader response in and around 1798. Thelwall himself could well have taken the poem as a gentle acknowledgment—for he too would have approved its explicit message about education—and looked no further. Perhaps these pre-Freudian and preprofessional conditions contributed not inconsiderably to Wordsworth's own ability to transcribe details that he had no preformulated incentive to perceive as incriminating or decisively self-revealing. In this way the public/private distinction might have been more effective for the competent reader of 1798 than it is for the professional literary critic of 1990. The published criticism of the times

26. [T. J. Mathias], *Pursuits of Literature: A Satirical Poem in Four Dialogues, with Notes,* 7th ed. (Philadelphia, 1800), p. 297.

suggests that contemporary readers were not primed to look closely at words and images for the sorts of displaced meanings that we now take rather more for granted as the stuff of poetic creativity. Indeed, some of the most urgent criticism by Wordsworth's peers takes issue with the poet's egotism, instead of finding in it detailed evidence of a historically exemplary subjectivity.

Despite these admissions of difference in the general conditions of reception governing the likely readers of poetry in 1798 and 1990, we still cannot deploy a model relying on the absolute difference between then and now. Wordsworth indeed seems to have written what was at one level and on occasions a coterie poetry, making deliberate reference to incidents or names (for instance that of Martha Ray, Basil Montagu Senior's actress mother) known to his immediate circle. These moments would seem to invite rather than to discourage connections between poetic fictions and known facts, especially when thematic parallels are as obvious as they are in the cases of "The Thorn" (illegitimacy) and "Anecdote for Fathers" (paternity, tenancy, and radicalism).[27] Because we have such generous records of many of the microcosmic moments in Wordsworth's life, we know that many of his "private experiences" were really not so: they were already oriented toward a circle of friends and acquaintances and already positioned within more general social-historical spheres. Thus Basil Montagu could not have impinged on Wordsworth's life as a son substitute without appearing also as a test case for the theories of education being discussed both at large and in the Wordsworth circle at that time. Nor could he, least of all as Basil Caroline Montagu, have failed to call up the specter of that other child whose actuality his own dependence on the Wordsworths must have both sharpened and softened. Further, the existence of Caroline Vallon was itself figured within and productive of the poet's evaluations of a "liberty" that was at once political-general and sexual-personal.[28] At the level of praxis,

27. This argues against the stronger thesis of Jerome McGann's important book *The Romantic Ideology: A Critical Investigation* (Chicago: University of Chicago Press, 1983), that Wordsworth's poetry is inclined and able to "annihilate" its history in the production of a "record of pure consciousness" (p. 90). But McGann is right to insist on the question of displacement and repression as central to that poetry.

28. Some of the important details are brought forward in Marjorie Levinson, *Wordsworth's Great Period Poems: Four Essays* (Cambridge: Cambridge University Press, 1986), pp. 80–100. See also my *Wordsworth's Historical Imagination*, pp. 22–55, and "Figuring Sex, Class and Gender: What Is the Subject of Wordsworth's 'Gipsies'?" *South Atlantic Quarterly* 88 (1989), 541–67.

the personal is not simply the political (this is indeed one of the major crises in Romantic self-perception); at the level of language and the constitution of experience, it certainly is.

The production of an exemplary class-historical formulation in "Anecdote for Fathers" may I think be explained by (mis)using Lukács's account of "the objective dialectic of accident and necessity." Lukács argues that whereas the "path of ideological development" is indeed "socially necessary," it is not so "in the fatalistic sense for every individual."[29] Lukács wants to use this model to identify the potential for an individual writer to transcend class existence, and thus to develop the idealist tendency in Marxist aesthetics. I propose that his phrase is useful to a different end: to suggest that class existence itself becomes fully expressive and exemplary only by way of the contingent determinations of the accidental. It is the urgency of the accidental (in this case, Wordsworth's actual paternity) that brings "Anecdote for Fathers" into fully representational focus. It is what Wordsworth does not share with every member of his class (or subculture) that brings to full articulation the common discourse of class identity. Necessity, in other words, requires contingency to express itself *as* necessity, the general-historical and idiosyncratic determinations reinforce each other and render each other critical. The avowed (albeit obscurely avowed) misunderstanding that generates the narrative of the poem is generated within other incriminating subject positions that are even more obscurely (but still "legibly") avowed even as they are purposively put to rest by the narrative's achieved knowledge. It is the "personal" motivations that render the politics most precisely. Thelwall, among the most famous of those who wanted to make Britain more like France, raised an image (for Wordsworth) that was inevitably personal and political, arguably personal *because* political (in that one has to imagine a scene within which sex outside marriage had some incipient subcultural sanction after 1789). Much of the poetry of Alfoxden inscribes a narrator who is *on edge* and poeticizes moments of release that are almost violent—chopping tangled roots and shaking little boys around. This verge of violence suggests a strong element of social-psychological insecurity and anxiety, one version of which is the refiguring of Alfoxden House, the place of genteel leisure, as Liswyn *farm*, the place of effort, industry, and ideally of self-subsistence. Thel-

29. Georg Lukács, "Marx and the Problem of Ideological Decay," in *Essays on Realism*, trans. David Fernbach (Cambridge: MIT Press, 1981), pp. 133, 132.

wall's appearance might have made the world, and its contradictions, seem too much with him. In *The Rights of Nature* (1796), Thelwall had accused Burke of the sort of political opportunism of which Words-worth might well have suspected himself (if only by his silence on Thelwall's own needs). Thelwall had written of Burke precisely that "change with him is no inconsistency. Mr. Burke and the weathercock, are only out of character, when they are fixed."[30] The image of vain-glory and luxury that was Alfoxden's weathercock ("a broad and gilded vane") was also Thelwall's image of Burkean unreliability (the negation of republican steadiness). Could this also have positioned Wordsworth farther across the fence from Thelwall than he cared to admit himself to be?

What are the implications for a Marxist-materialist literary criticism of this reading of "Anecdote for Fathers"? How does it situate the terms of this book's subtitle: ideology, class, gender? Certainly not as mutually exclusive or as hierarchically distinct—as if they could be arranged in order of effective determining power, one after the other. But if we cannot claim that any one of these categories causes the others, we can describe fairly clearly how they interact as parts of a whole. The schizophrenic subject position of the apprentice poet pe-ripheral to the middle class (as both a poet and a democrat) and further displaced from it both upward (by the social insignia of Alfoxden House) and downward (by the likely economic prospects of a hitherto largely unknown writer) marks almost every expressive moment in the poem. The regendering of Caroline as Basil Caroline (whence "Edward," the name of a number of truly *English* kings, and a "con-fessor" among them) and the account of the incident and its import register the dramas of both sex and gender.[31] The bald fact of Words-worth's paternity is mediated in a number of culturally decisive ways. In the poem, the boy's masculinity is oddly undercut from the start, as he is "cast in beauty's mould" (beauty was more usually a feminine attribute), made to "love" the narrator "dearly," and described as provoking a reaction whose intensity is at least as appropriate to lovers' quarrels as to parent-child interactions. The narrator's lie—"I

30. John Thelwall, *The Rights of Nature, against the Usurpations of Establishments. A Series of Letters to the People of Britain, on the State of Public Affairs, and the Recent Effusions of the Rt. Hon. Edmund Burke,* 2 vols. (London, 1796), 1:49.

31. I am grateful to Margaret Ferguson for helping me to focus and develop these remarks on the poem's genderings.

have a boy"—not only refigures the sex of his own actual child but places him in the position of having an *heir,* a firstborn son, one who might expect to inherit something. Wordsworth's early adulthood was constantly preoccupied with questions about inheritance. Here, while himself being supported by the Calvert bequest, he imagines himself with something to hand on, and someone to hand it on to: Wordsworth and Son(s).

This point becomes all the more apposite when we recall that the debate about education in the late eighteenth century usually relied upon making clear distinctions between boys and girls. Indeed, Rousseau's *Emile* was famous for its double standard in this respect, which Mary Wollstonecraft, among others, recognized and contested. Generally speaking, the kind of moral education and preparation for citizenship which "Anecdote for Fathers" images would have seemed more significant as an interaction between father and son than between either parent and a daughter. While a daughter might eventually amend manners by way of the domestic sphere, a son would be expected to operate in civic life. Although I am not in general discussing the revisions of this poem, it is worth at least pointing out that the replacement of the subtitle in 1845 by a Latin epigraph (and an obscure one at that) would have efficiently prevented most female and many male readers from getting any clue to the poem's "meaning," while it made that meaning a good deal *more* clear to anyone who could fathom the Latin, that is, to educated males. (It translates as "Cease this violence, for if you persist I will speak a lie.")

Another dimension to this refiguring of the poet's absent and unacknowledged daughter as a boy is constituted by the relocation from France to England and by implicitly observing the rhetoric of nationalism. The discomfort with things French which many Britons felt in the 1790s was not entirely determined by their attitudes to 1789 and its particular reinterpretation of political liberty. It was not just a matter of being for or against the rights of man, and the French constitution. For there had been in place, at least since the Restoration, a polemic against French foppery, frivolity, and moral corruption, qualities said to be destroying the English language, English manners, and most especially the civic capabilities of the English upper classes—those most vulnerable to foreign fashions as they were most committed to an intellectual and personal cosmopolitanism. The liberties that Wordsworth took in France with a French woman were in this way as much sexual and moral as political, or more so, and explicable less in terms of the direct effects of 1789 (whatever brief suspension of sexual conventions they included) than in relation to a long-standing suspicion of French culture and manners, especially sexual manners. In this context it would not have mattered much that Annette came from a royalist family; if anything, this origin might have made her even more emblematic of the French contagion, traditionally imaged as moving from aristocracy to aristocracy. In this respect, Wordsworth's trip to France becomes as much a parody of the grand tour as an original bourgeois alternative in search of a new cultural and political order that reflects itself.

What this aspect of the anti-French tradition afforded was, of course, a language for the English middle ranks to deploy against their social superiors. But Wordsworth's own experiences would not have allowed him to imagine that the threatening energies of French sexual freedoms were restricted to the aristocracy. For him, they impinged also upon bourgeois domesticity, whose ideal form is fictionally transcribed in "Anecdote"—the stable family group with a male heir and a choice of places to live. Hannah More in 1799 noted the "domestic mischief" emanating from France, which had little to do with the recent revolution: "This is not the place to descant on that levity of manners, that contempt of the sabbath, that fatal familiarity with loose principles, and those relaxed notions of conjugal fidelity, which have often been transplanted into this country by women of fashion, as a too common effect of a residence in a neighbouring country."[32] Wordsworth, already marginal (at best) to any bourgeois establishment (and self-establishment), would likely have felt more so for having transgressed the bourgeois nationalist ideal: he was too fashionable, as well as too democratic, for the middle-class consciousness.

And what of ideology? Perhaps no term is as frequently invoked in cultural criticism in such critically vague ways. Michel Foucault has called into question its implicit production of an antithetically defined notion of "truth" or "reality." Paul Smith has credibly observed that "orthodox Marxist theories about the hold that ideology seems to have over 'subjects' by and large neglect to specify the actual locus of that hold," so that their model remains "relatively mysterious." And Michèle Barrett has argued that the "analytic use" of a concept of ideol-

32. Hannah More, *Strictures on the Modern System of Female Education* (1799), in *The Works of Hannah More*, 2 vols. (New York, 1844), 1:328–29.

ogy requires that "it must be bounded" at once by reference to an economic condition and to a specific social experience in place and time.[33]

It has now become commonplace to describe ideology as everywhere, the emanation (as expression) of the interests of any social group or even individual. This habit has evolved as a truism from the rather technical work of Louis Althusser (especially) in criticizing the negative definition of ideology as a principally disabling concept. Ideology was once theorized as a single articulation representing the interests of the ruling class and negatively affecting all others. Now it is more common to describe every class or group as having its own ideology. The social whole is composed of the relations between them, so that the possibility of struggle and progressive contradiction is preserved *as a principle of consciousness* (it was always there at the level of general history). The older, more negative model of ideology had also preserved a space beyond false consciousness and thus "beyond" ideology—a space often occupied by art. Aesthetics, indeed, has a traditional interest in describing art as going beyond *something:* materiality, daily life, ordinary language, or consciousness, and so forth. How do these two definitions of ideology assist or inhibit the task of theorizing my reading of "Anecdote for Fathers"?

There is something to be said for reactivating the negative and limiting definition of ideology as false consciousness, as masking or refiguring into coherence a contradictory social-economic condition (often called "reality"). This is Theodor Adorno's model. In his view, art can continue to "grope for the truth" at the same time as it embodies the social antagonisms that render it expressive in the first place.[34] In his important essay on the lyric, Adorno maintains that works of art can "let those things be heard which ideology conceals," so that they go beyond or overgo (*übergehen*) mere false consciousness.[35] This model preserves a critical function for art, but it has tended to lead to a distinction between those works of art which are critical and those which are not—that is, between good and bad art and, all too often, high culture and popular culture. Analysis of the

33. Michel Foucault, *Power/Knowledge: Selected Interviews and Other Writings, 1972–77,* ed. Colin Gordon (New York: Pantheon, 1980), p. 118; Paul Smith, *Discerning the Subject* (Minneapolis: University of Minnesota Press, 1988), p. xxx; Michèle Barrett, *Women's Oppression Today: The Marxist/Feminist Encounter,* rev. ed. (London: Verso, 1988), p. 97.

34. Theodor W. Adorno, *Aesthetic Theory,* ed. Gretel Adorno and Rolf Tiedemann, trans. C. Lenhardt (1984; rpt. London: Verso, 1986), p. 113.

35. Theodor Adorno, "Lyric Poetry and Society," *Telos* 20 (1974), 58.

social condition of expressive forms has seldom been much assisted by definitional distinctions between "art" and "not art" or between good and bad art.

Nonetheless, a specific argument in Adorno's essay is useful for theorizing "Anecdote for Fathers." Adorno's opening finding is that the lyric articulates a voice "which defines itself as something opposed to the collective and the realm of objectivity" (p. 59), especially as that objectivity entails the hegemony of a commercial society. "Ideology" then expresses itself in the form of an avowed individualism, whether triumphant or despairing, so that the truth of a work of art becomes apparent when we read through its manifest content to its latent content, which is "grounded in a collective substratum" (p. 64). Looking at Wordsworth's poem, what do we see that is individual and what collective?

Clearly the narrator presents himself as a spontaneous individual: he does not explicitly signal the affiliations of his pedagogical lesson with the published doctrines of Godwin, Rousseau, or anybody else. But he can hardly be accused of complete concealment, since any reader familiar with those doctrines would have recognized their reappearance. The tactic of personalizing in poetry a truth that might otherwise remain at the level of abstract principle is very much in line with the consciously avowed purpose of *Lyrical Ballads*. But what is the poet-narrator's relation to the radical subculture that stands, as it were, as the collective behind the posture of individuality? In one sense, that subculture was indeed the voice of the emergent bourgeoisie, speaking out against aristocratic privilege and unrepresentative government. At the same time, its contempt for the decline in civic virtue which came with the commercial economy is a contempt for the very conditions that made possible the newly politicized middle class, that is, itself. We might then say that Godwin and Rousseau are at once expressive and critical of a bourgeois ideology or, alternatively, that they reproduce an incoherent or contradictory ideology, the emanation of a historically unstable class. Similarly we might say that Wordsworth either reproduces ideology in a *critical* manner (including various levels of self-critique) or reproduces an incoherent ideology.

At this point, it might be best to depart from the model of ideology as negatively determining, as false consciousness, both to avoid the implication that the poem "transcends" ideology and to decompose the otherwise incipiently monolithic identity of class consciousness (and thence class itself) into something more volatile, something as much structur*ing* as structur*ed*—that is, structuring itself as well as repeating residual conformations. This alternative is perhaps more compatible with the other (and now more common) model of ideology, which makes it the enabling expressive medium of any social class or subculture. We can now say that it is indeed *contradiction* that is most aptly expressive of the ideology of Wordsworth's poem, a contradiction between individual and collective at the level of what is avowed ("we" becomes "I") and a further contradiction governing the relation of the "we" (the radical subculture) to the larger social unit. In one way, Wordsworth disavows his relation to Godwin and Rousseau. The reader who did not already know them would not see the connection. In another way, he signals to those properly informed that such a relation exists (I do not imply an intentional "signaling"). The individuality of the lyric mode is thus uneasy, unstable. Wordsworth has an insecure relation to a subculture that is itself in a contestatory and divided relation to the rest of its culture. Without wishing to argue that the poet's class position is *prior to* other determinations (for how can we know this?), it would seem to be the case that the same experiences of gender and ideology would be different for, say, a Byron. Byron was born to the experience of places like Alfoxden House, rather habituated to the existence of illegitimate children, and immune by birth and breeding to the traumas of financial insecurity (though not to such insecurity itself). We do not find in Byron a poetry that works through these and other related anxieties, nor does he seem motivated toward a poetry of transgression or to that compulsively Wordsworthian concern about the imposition of one's views upon others. Byron's engagement with questions of gender was completely different: they were formulated within a quite different class position.

There is another dimension to Wordsworth's relatively covert allusion to Godwin and Rousseau and the radical subculture of the 1790s. It clearly has an opportunist function, whereby Wordsworth offers as uniquely his own what was in fact situated within a general debate. Theory is reinvented as original experience and accorded all the validation that "experience" acquires (most especially after 1789, when it became an alternative to the excesses of French theory). This reinvention positions the poem as offering a (partly) masked polemic, in a manner that bespeaks originality and hence marketability for its author. The allusions to Thelwall, Godwin, Rousseau (and even Caroline) serve as indications of community to the initiated but do not much disturb the impression of unique experience which a merely

"general" reader might derive. Wordsworth, and the poem, are having it both ways. Unsure which audience matters more, they gesture
at both. We seem to have a poem that registers the pressures of
different ideologies, that is, of different potentially generalized identities and affiliations. At this point, we may seem to be on the edge of
collapsing the very term *ideology* so fully into what is now often called
discourse that its usefulness threatens to expire. But ideology does
differ from discourse in that it preserves (in both of its common definitions) a determining relation to class, to subculture, rather than to
what often seems to be a hopelessly broad conglomeration of languages, practical-disciplinary systems, and prefigurations of all kinds.
Reference to the "discursive" most commonly avoids any exact specification either of the discursive itself or of the ways in which it impinges
upon experience (unless in the generalized and rather presumptive
form of "language"). By hanging onto "ideology" to do some of this
descriptive work, we may increase our chances of requiring at least
some complex attention to questions of mediation and totality, and to
an analysis of which language is taken as part rather than assumed to
be the whole.

This leads me, once again, to the Benjamin-Adorno exchange, discussed in the Introduction and by Colin MacCabe in his contribution
to this volume. In his analysis of Baudelaire's poetry Walter Benjamin
noted the "lack of mediation between his ideas," a syndrome he
related to the culture of the *bohème* in which each person was "in a
more or less obscure state of revolt against society and faced a more or
less precarious future."[36] Adorno accused Benjamin of reproducing
instead of analyzing this condition and thus stalling his own critique
"at the crossroads of magic and positivism," where "motifs are assembled but not elaborated." For Adorno, any properly Marxist criticism
must involve an account of "the mediation through the total social
process."[37]

The problem arises, then, that for a *literature* such as Baudelaire's
(and, I suggest, Wordsworth's), in which the transcription of individual alienation is also that of a class or subculture, the "total social
process" will be very hard to track down simply by *reading* that litera-

36. Walter Benjamin, *Charles Baudelaire: A Lyric Poet in the Era of High Capitalism*, trans.
Harry Zohn (London: New Left Books, 1973), pp. 71, 20.
37. Adorno to Benjamin, in Ernst Bloch, Georg Lukács, Bertolt Brecht, Walter Benjamin, Theodor Adorno, *Aesthetics and Politics*, trans. Ronald Taylor (London: Verso,
1980), pp. 129, 127, 130.

ture. The notorious problems attending this task have, after all, licensed generations of formalist critics in their exclusive focus on "the text." This is where Adorno calls in the need for "theory." But insofar as this is a move "off the page," that theory has always been resisted by literary critics who, if they are no longer traditional formalists, now frequently affirm that all explanatory contexts are subject to the same skepticisms required of textual-linguistic objects: either we read only the poem or we claim that everything we do read is poetic. Given the tendency of Adorno's "theory" to rely upon a priori totalizations, structural and teleological, its employment will inevitably raise very awkward questions about mediation and about the status of all evidence. All too often, literary critics have reacted to these questions by giving up or by affirming some other false solution that does not raise such apparently ineluctable methodological blockages. Hence we see a widespread inclination among literary critics for "Geertzian" models of total cultural saturation, wherein the putting together of any two items will produce significant meaning, with no need to address questions about mediation. This is one prominent feature of the "new historicism," when it is not wedded to a simple strong-determination model of established power producing a single discourse.

The rephrasing (certainly not a definition) of the syndrome of ideology I have proposed seems to go some way toward resolving the Scylla and Charybdis of literary-critical methodology: the Scylla of pure immediacy, of which Adorno accused Benjamin (though there is more to say here), and the Charybdis of abstract master narratives, at once a priori and extratextual and tending to produce reified models of class affiliation and class struggle. If we reimagine the entity called class as a structured mobility between sites and factor in a subjectivity that may be variously sensitive to various kinds and degrees of social determination according to its particular situations and desires, then we have done much to fine-tune the often unwieldy vocabularies of class and ideological analysis. Whereas "economism" is perhaps the most widely discredited motif in Marxist thought, we might project that for the literature produced by writers marginal to an already unstable bourgeoisie (such as Wordsworth), the determination of the *economic* is going to remain primary (if not uniquely primary) to a materialist criticism. While it is indeed language that remains the privileged site of interpretation for that criticism, that language must be explained in relation to a range of determinations that can be shown to have impinged on both its production and its original and subsequent receptions. This is why Marxism and psychoanalysis (rather than linguistics), with their traditionally general-historical and individual-subjective emphases, remain the two mutually correcting imperatives of materialist criticism, as they have been for a good twenty years. If language be understood as the site of common accountability of these two tendencies, in a manner that anticipates a likely (though not inevitable) *range* of resolutions, then both abstract totalities and the empiricism of contingency can be avoided. So too can the tendency to ignore the subject's idiosyncrasies (Wordsworth's abandoned daughter, for example) or to make them simply unique or to reinvent them as monolithically historical (as belonging to all people in 1798, rather than to one in particular) relations to ideologies and to economic and cultural opportunities.

This brings me back, and finally, to "Anecdote for Fathers." The poet as narrator purports to have realized how the art of lying may be taught, to have escaped from the prison house of adult consciousness and the either/or syndrome, behind which is an entire Protestant apparatus approving the habit of proper *choice*. By an act of learning, he has become again *as* a child, and in that it is lying that is now open for critical inspection, he seems to stand, at the end, beyond the lie. And yet, as we have seen, the entire poem is a lie, at almost every level. Wordsworth himself does not have "a boy of five years old," Liswyn is Alfoxden House (not farm), Thelwall looms throughout (with all he stood for), and the choice of residence is no choice—they have to leave. The posture of leisurely meditation, the "so much happiness to spare," could have emerged only as the fictive antitype of an acute anxiety that is perhaps fictively registered in the excessive violence of the questioning ("While still I held him by the arm"). The pain that the narrator learns to feel is a moderate one, containable by a gesture of self-correction; the pains that Wordsworth was likely to have been experiencing were not so open to self-administered resolution. I suggest that the word *anecdote* in the title is a striking claim for the validity of casual, private experience in published form. As recently as 1793, Isaac D'Israeli had defended the usefulness of anecdotes in the hands of a properly "philosophic historian": "A skilful writer of anecdotes, gratifies by suffering us to make something that looks like a discovery of our own; he gives a certain activity to the mind, and the reflections appear to arise from ourselves. He throws unperceivably seeds, and we see those flowers start up, which we believe to be of our own creation."[38] Is this not a perfect paraphrase of the strategy of Wordsworth's poem? The empowering of the narrator (who learns) is described in such a way that the reader must also (and this is formally demanded) perform an act of cocreation in deciphering what it is that the narrator might have learned. The reader then both acts *individually* and creates a microcommunity with that narrator, adding to the pleasure of self-esteem (shared with the narrator) that of achieved interpretation. This is the pleasure I myself experienced, quite uncritically, when I first worked with this poem more than ten years ago. As the child's tenaciously inconsequential answer startles the narrator into self-knowledge, so the narrator's unexplained assertion of that knowledge startles the reader into interpretative action. Both are invited to exercise (fictive) power, to achieve self-consolidation, to *find* a subject position for themselves. D'Israeli's pre-Freudian faith in the anecdotal as the true source of insight into human nature, which is "not to be understood by looking at its superficies, but by dwelling on its minute springs and little wheels" (p. 30), legitimates Wordsworth's bourgeois-individualist assertion of the grand moral effects of everyday interactions as potentially general and communal. We have seen that many of Wordsworth's own "springs and little wheels" are less visibly published in this poem: D'Israeli intriguingly mentions the Greek etymology of *anecdote*, "things not yet published" (p. v). But, as we have also seen, they are nevertheless available—to the Alfoxden coterie, to some members of the wider public, and hence to us now. Suppose then, that the urge to *reveal*, rather than (or as well as) to conceal, marks the production of Wordsworth's poem?

Here we come to the poem's utopian dimension, as it speaks for the potential conversion of radical subculture to cultural mainstream. The poem imagines that there really might be a world waiting to receive the sorts of lessons that the narrator learns from the child. At the same time, it suggests an explicit gap between the narrator and the community he might speak to, if he could: "*Could* I but teach the hundredth part / Of what from thee I learn." Adults are predisposed against learning these lessons, and having learned them, they are not sure how to teach them. The narrator's incapacity as generic adult may also include a specific limitation: "Could *I* but teach." The very expression

38. [Isaac D'Israeli], *A Dissertation on Anecdotes; by the Author of Curiosities of Literature* (London: Kearsley and Murray, 1793), p. 8.

of the utopian potential is embedded in the intimation of further alienation. The crisis in authority is a crisis in both self and society as here produced. To think of a world where Wordsworth might be able to teach is to think of a world where both subcultural and idiosyncratic inhibitions and traumas can be put to rest. It is to think of a world where the conditions of reception are sympathetic to these lessons. If they were so, then it would also be a world where Wordsworth's personal anxieties were assuaged. One function of Wordsworth's revelations, then, hesitant and obscurely coded as they are, is to imagine a world in which his errors might either be forgiven or never have been seen as such in the first place: a world in which there is no war (between Britain and France), no sexual misdemeanor, no guilt or shame, no class struggle or class consciousness—that is, no worrying over money (too much or too little) or about social visibility or over-visibility (living at, then leaving Alfoxden). It would be a world in which distribution had undone excess in all its varieties. We can, if we choose, find here a radical Wordsworth, a poet who creates from the very raw materials of his own conflicted life, in conjunction with the imagining of a few other natural hearts, a moment of hope, powerfully instanced in the sight of a child who has not yet formed a view of the world, or a world to be formed by. This is a child made fictionally innocent in order to stand in for one who cannot be innocently imagined. But the trenchantly hypothetical voice ("Could I but teach") and former incipient violence ("While still I held him by the arm") darken any predictive complacency about the likelihood of any innocent world. And here we can, if we choose, find a reactionary Wordsworth, one who mystifies social conditions as the consequences of universal maturation, child to adult (separated, need I say it, by the onset of sexuality). Finally, radical and reactionary do not seem the happiest terms for describing this poem, though they have their uses. For the questioning of the possibility of a nonrepressive individual as the basis of a nonrepressive society is the very form of the poem's social-historical determination, caught as it is not in a crystalline, synchronic paradigm of achieved bourgeois expressivity but in a dia-chronic and dichotomized struggle for both self and society. The fictive avowal of achieved knowledge avows also such a range of qualifications and negations as to seem a most unlikely but still desirable heaven in hell's despite.

8

Lyric in the
Culture of Capital

Frank Lentricchia

Writing in self-willed exile to a co-conspirator and ex-student from a cottage in Beaconsfield, England, which he called the Bung-Hole; still deep in literary obscurity, though not quite as deep as the obscurity he had experienced in America in the previous twenty years; writing in November 1913 with his first book out and warmly reviewed by the right sort of people, Ezra Pound among them, and with a second and maybe even a third book waiting in the wings, Robert Frost hatched the plot of his return to the United States as step one in his cunning pursuit of the fame that would eventually become the means of supporting himself and his family. And more: poetic fame would be courted because it would provide the material base for the realization of a desire he publicly announced in the 1930s and to which critics on the left might have responded sympathetically—but didn't. (Frost had come up through some pretty joyless working-class conditions.) That desire, at once induced and mainly prohibited in Frost's American culture, Yeats—who never earned Frost's right to it—called desire for "unity of being." Other high modernists would weigh in with other equally romantic phrases for a need that represented not only longing

Copyright © 1991 by Frank Lentricchia. An earlier version of this essay appeared in *American Literary History* 1 (1989), 63–88.

for another and better—because integrated—kind of life but also criticism of the social ground on which they stood. With crafted American homeliness Frost called it his "object in living" to unite "My avocation and my vocation / As my eyes make one in sight:" pleasure, play, doing whatever you want—in 1913, at thirty-nine years old, Frost had done little of the latter—fused with work, what you had to do if you were someone like Frost rather than someone like Yeats. The dream of Frost and many twentieth-century American poets (and fiction writers, too) was to sustain a commitment to their art with the daunting knowledge that their lives would be pressured by relentless economic need to which their art could bring no surcease.

So the definition of modern American poetry demanded by its economic circumstances is just this: the art of nonremunerative writing pursued by those who can ill afford to pursue the art of nonremunerative writing. The American literary dream in the twentieth century is to reconcile aesthetic commitment and economic necessity beyond the storied opposition that had more or less inescapably haunted writers ever since the eighteenth century, the more or less of nightmare depending on the more or less of cash a writer might lay easy claim to from an inheritance, say, or maybe a patron. But where was an American writer going to find a patron? And how many American writers in the twentieth century inherited leisure-class conditions?

Reflecting on the strong critical reception that his first book, *A Boy's Will*, had just won for him, Frost in November 1913 told his ex-student John Bartlett:

> You mus[t]n't take me too seriously if I now proceed to brag a bit about my exploits as a poet. There is one qualifying fact always to bear in mind: there is a kind of success called "of esteem" and it butters no parsnips. It means a success with the critical few who are supposed to know. But really to arrive where I can stand on my legs as a poet and nothing else I must get outside that circle to the general reader who buys books in their thousands. I may not be able to do that. I believe in doing it—don't you doubt me there. I want to be a poet for all sorts and kinds. I could never make a merit of being caviare to the crowd the way my quasi-friend Pound does. I want to reach out, and would if it were a thing I could do by taking thought.[1]

This ambition of Frost's to stand on his legs "as a poet and noth-

---

1. *Selected Letters of Robert Frost*, ed. Lawrance Thompson (New York: Holt, Rinehart, and Winston, 1964), p. 98.

ing else"—he had been barely standing as a teacher and reluctant farmer—by getting outside the critical circle of esteem to which his first book had admitted him that year in Pound's avant-garde London, is an outrageous ambition inside the emerging context of literary and social values that would be codified as "modernist" in the 1950s and that Pound was doing so much to help bring into existence in the year that Frost wrote his letter to Bartlett.

In 1913 Pound was defining his literary life as an intention to shape a career that would violate the tired literary inheritance incarnated in the guise of contemporary poetry which young American writers, who would become the important modern poets, were reading and despising while still youths in the first decade of this century. In so violating established literary culture, Pound would inaugurate another intention, not separable from his literary desire, to make social change: the transformation of the economic structure itself, which (Pound was convinced) had produced the literature he would displace, the very literature that was, Pound would argue, nothing less than his society's symptomatic expression in the realm of culture of its totalitarian direction. In 1913 Pound and his friends were imagining revolt against what another writer about thirty-five years later would call *1984*. In 1913 Frost was imagining turning the social system Pound hated to economic and literary advantage.

Inside Pound's context of avant-garde literary production and manifesto, Frost's desire—represented in his figure of economic sustenance (oh, for a parsnips-buttering poetry!)—can hardly help but be read as contemptible evidence of complicity. For by virtue of its deliberate strangeness of structure and discourse and its flaunted hostility to everyday life in capitalist culture, emerging high-modernist art was finding its honor precisely in its economic unviability, and in the distance that separated it both from the tradition of popular verse, which Frost had an eye on when he titled his first book in echo of Longfellow, and that tradition's square, mainstream audience—the "general reader who buys books in their thousands, " even books of poetry, a reader who is no figment of Frost's fame-hungry imagination but the material force that had made such as Longfellow and other Fireside poets, along with a number of women poets, best sellers (in the technical sense of the word) in nineteenth-century U.S.A.

Life at the edge of economic disaster in Greenwich Village, Kenneth Burke once explained in autobiographical reflection, was the choice of serious writers of his generation who hadn't already chosen the route of expatriation altogether, a social rejection out of *La Bohème:* Greenwich Village as expatriation from within.[2] In Pound's and Burke's avant-garde context, Frost's desire to make it economically as America's poet—he would choose neither form of expatriation—rules him outside the pale of modernist company, unless literary memory recalls that as the oldest of the American poets he is usually compared with— usually to the denigration of his reputation with university intellectuals who invented and sustained the official phenomenon called modernism—Frost was formed in the 1890s and early years of the twentieth century when, in the United States, no poetic company outside the mainstream existed. Frost's letter to Bartlett is therefore not the inauguration of an ambition against what would be called modernism or, finally, what it most immediately is, an expression of enmity born in his important and difficult relationship with Pound. The letter reiterates in the face of new opportunities for literary publication—the recently formed little magazines—an ambition generated in him by a poetry scene exclusively controlled by mass-circulation magazines (such as the *Atlantic, Harper's,* and *Century*), which were actually supporting the lives of a few genteel poets well known in the young manhood of Frost and Pound, though now passed from canonical memory; well known to Frost and models for poetic success after the examples of Bryant, Longfellow, and Whittier.

So for the young Robert Frost popular success in the mode of the Fireside poets did not represent the "mainstream" literary life (a term that presupposes an avant-garde margin of opposition) but the only "stream." In 1892, at eighteen years old, while contemplating marriage to Elinor White, Frost won his first kind of parsnips-buttering success when he was accepted by the New York *Independent,* a weekly in which the then well known Richard Hovey appeared frequently— Hovey a poetic celebrant, among other things, of red-blooded manhood and our imperialist move toward Cuba, whom the young Frost admired. For a single poem the *Independent* paid Frost nine dollars, a sum that bought considerable groceries in 1892, especially for those, like Frost, whose idea of groceries didn't include caviar. Those same mass-circulation magazines that Frost tried with virtually no success for the first twenty years of his career were also well known to Pound (and briefly tried by him, too): together with the writers they published Pound thought these magazines represented everything that was wrong with his country.

2. See Ben Yagoda, "Kenneth Burke," *Horizon* 23 (June 1980), 67.

But in spite of the resentment that tells us where he came from socially and literarily—he was the poet who faced the necessities of bitter parsnips, better buttered than plain—Frost wanted it both ways ("I want to be a poet for *all* sorts and kinds"). His literary identity was in some part shaped by the critical ideals of the emerging avant-garde. He wanted to get to those who read the *Atlantic* with pleasure, but he also wanted to get to Pound himself, whose approval he painfully sought, who reviewed Frost's first two volumes with guarded admiration, who pushed Frost to Harriet Monroe in Chicago and to editors of new-wave literary magazines in London, and who once punned the *Ladies' Home Journal* right into the *Ladies' Home Urinal.*

Frost returned to the United States in early 1915 in part because he thought he could work within its dominant commercial system of literary production. Making it at the level that Frost wanted to make it would, however, as he knew, require more than the ideal action of his intellect thinking its thoughts, writing its poems; he would have to do more on his behalf, as he implied, than "take thought." He would have to get practical in a way long forbidden by the anticapitalism of Romantic literary theory. He would have to become his own best public relations adviser and thereby become that commercial system's first broad-scale poetic media star, the ordinary man's modernist. And even better: if he could actually become a poet for all sorts and kinds, then he would succeed not only in making that system work on his economic behalf but also in having his literary way with it. Pound saw it otherwise: saw no way of living here and boring from within, no way of slyly subverting, much less seizing, the system of literary publication; so he expatriated himself to a space outside from which he propelled at his native country relentless charges of human betrayal, finally to return after World War II, against his will, as fascism's brightest modernist star.

In modernism's scene of emergence and triumph in America "Frost" and "Pound" may turn out to be not so much names of authors who quarreled over basic issues as signs of cultural forces in struggle, forces whose difference presented itself to Frost in 1913 as a choice between mass-circulation and avant-garde little magazines, forces whose persistent difference would constitute the scene of what would be called modernism. "Frost" against "Pound" as the American way of making it new against the socially stratified European avant-garde, those producers of aesthetic caviar culturally inaccessible to the American masses; "Frost," then, as bearer of a democratic rhetoric, suspicious of everything from the wrong side of the Atlantic, including and perhaps most especially the political radicalism of the aesthetic vanguard. Frost's compressed figure of simultaneous class and literary resentment is itself, in 1913, a prefiguring of an aesthetic and social argument within modernism that would shape the movement of the new poetry from its official date of birth, 1912, when the inaugural issue of *Poetry* appeared, to 1930, the close of its most fertile phase of literary innovation and negative political critique, when the major documents of modern American poetry—*North of Boston*, "The Love Song of J. Alfred Prufrock," "Hugh Selwyn Mauberley," *Spring and All*, *The Waste Land*, *Harmonium*, *A Draft of XXX Cantos*, and *The Bridge*— had not only all been published but also, with unpredictable speed, had become the textual conscience of our poetry and a controversial, internally conflicted core of social reimagination whose most radical question had to do with the political experiment called "America" and whether or not that experiment was even a qualified success or rather a sham and a failure. The aesthetic arguments within modernism were simultaneously arguments over what shape the American social future should take.

In 1929, with the literary revolution won, modernism fully in place, and Ezra Pound its widely hailed entrepreneur and guru, Pound told in the New York *Herald-Tribune* the story of his moment of awakening in London circa 1912. It would become the representative anecdote of his literary career, the substance of the larger tales that his poetry and his literary and social criticism would ceaselessly tell and retell of epiphanic revelation: the dawning upon him that aesthetic and economic production were insidiously related, that aesthetic production was the effect of an economic cause deadly to all individual identity (whether political or literary) and whose aesthetic products were not in kind different from those we conventionally know as commodities. Pound had had his definitive encounter with the culture of capitalism and had emerged a badly bruised romantic. Poetry, he learned, was an expression of the marketplace, not its critique as idealists since Kant had desired. Badly bruised, but more than ever a romantic whose will was now newly steeled for social change.

It struck him, he wrote, that if "the best history of painting in London was the National Gallery," then the best history of poetry "would be a twelve-volume anthology in which each poem was chosen not merely because it was a nice poem or a poem Aunt Hepsy liked, but because it contained an invention, a definite contribution to the art of verbal expression." With this idea in mind he approached a respected agent who was impressed by his plan for an anthology but apparently too indolent to recast Pound's "introductory letter into a form suited to commerce." The agent made contact with a "long-established publishing house;" two days later he summoned Pound in order to ask him, in astonishment, if he, Pound, knew what he had said about Palgrave, the editor of the most famous anthology of poetry in the English language. Pound: "It is time we had something to replace that doddard Palgrave." The agent: "But don't you know that the whole fortune of X & Co. is founded on Palgrave's *Golden Treasury?*" From that day on, Pound wrote, no book of his received a British imprimatur "until the appearance of Eliot's castrated edition of my poems. I perceived that there were thousands of pounds sterling invested in electro-plate, and the least change in the public taste, let alone swift, catastrophic changes, would depreciate the values of those electros. . . . against a so vast vested interest the lone odds were too heavy."[3]

Pound's anecdote clusters together at the site of literary production issues that shape the bigger story of his career as well as (they are not easy to separate) the career of modernism. If, as he thinks, a poetry anthology ought to function like the National Gallery—as a space of exhibits—then who or what will provide the economic wherewithal to sustain such space? Who or what will play the role of patron of the arts? And why should the patron, whether national agency or private agent, agree to underwrite a culture of invention ("swift catastrophic changes") implicitly at odds with an economic system so heavily invested in repetition, not change, precisely the system that sustains the would-be patron? A specific anthology of poetry, Pound learns—Francis Palgrave's *Golden Treasury of the Best Songs and Lyrical Poems in the English Language*—in fact functions not as the space for the exhibition of original literary talents and their inventions but as a commodity requiring heavy investment in electroplates, the sole purpose of which is to help make the fortune of those who control the means of its production, Macmillan Company, whose goal is realized by monopolizing the market and thereby avoiding the costly production of new plates.

Palgrave had hoped that his anthology, the poems themselves, not

3. *Literary Essays of Ezra Pound*, ed. with an introduction by T. S. Eliot (New York: New Directions, 1965), pp. 17–18.

(of course) the economic vehicle of their circulation, would assist in liberating the spiritual life of the capitalist subject (across the classes but most especially "labor and poverty" as he phrased it) from the everyday life of getting and spending. Instead, against his hopes, his anthology would actively reinforce the life of capital at the cultural level by normalizing (in this order) first taste (this is a poem), then taste's appetite (this is what I want more of), and finally taste's evalua-tive purpose (this is what a poem should be like). From out of its material economy—the mass-produced object, the system of its distri-bution—Palgrave's widely circulating text does the cultural work that is nothing but the civilizing work of capitalist culture. The cultural work that the anthology does—this is what Pound came to know—turns out to be not the negation of its editor's stated romantic cultural hope for liberating his readers from Mammon but its ironic fulfillment. For Palgrave's anthology inaugurates and sustains taste grounded upon itself as material text, taste immune to competitive versions of taste and therefore to other versions of what a poem might be. The major economic enemy of Palgrave's anthology, whether small or catastrophic, is therefore change, and not economic change but change of the cultural sort, aesthetic change of the kind indicated and longed for by those hallmark words of modernist critical vocabulary like "originality" and "creativity," what Pound calls "invention" and what Eliot, in a simple but telling phrase, calls "the individual talent."

Pound's idea of where he actually lives corresponds to Orwell's dystopian imagination of where we might live. We remember Julia, in *1984*, who works in the fiction-writing department, telling the senti-mental Winston that fiction is just another commodity, like "jam or shoe laces," a controlled substance of consumption produced for the better manipulation of its consumers, so that (Orwell's not Julia's point) they might become more like what they consume—normalized (pseudo) individuals, repetitions of one another, so much easier to dominate. For Pound social actuality has the feel of dystopian night-mare. And all of it, the culture and economics of capitalism, is mixed up for Pound and other modernists with the feminization of culture, himself unmanned. Poems that Aunt Hepsy might like, that symbolic reader and consumer of Palgrave—she is Pound's figure for a mass audience hostile to real invention—are uncomfortably close to the edition of Pound's poems that Eliot brought out under the aegis of Aunt Hepsy's cultural dominance, with Eliot her ironic agent: Eliot's edition an image of Pound castrated. Against such vast vested economic interests, he thought, the lone (male) odds were too heavy. What the time cried out for to make things right, in his vision, was not what his words about lone individuals might imply—a solidarity of individuals—but an epic hero to combat conspiracy, and Mussolini was just over the horizon.

Pound's revelation was double: Palgrave's anthology was transformed into a commodity by a publishing firm necessarily interested in dominating the cultural marketplace, and the literary contents of the book-as-commodity, thanks to Palgrave's perfectly deployed theory of the lyric, were similarly transformed, in their standardized literariness, into replications of each other, commodities of lyric sameness, literature reduced to the verbal sweetness you could get uncut onto a page or two of a collection simply filled with things you could get uncut onto a page or two. The unprecedented dominance of Palgrave's little book in the last four decades of the nineteenth and the first two decades of the twentieth century—it was the rarest of things poetic, an actual best seller in the United States—coupled with the rise in the United States of the popular magazine as an economic outlet for what those magazines demanded—little snippets of lyric grace, which magazine format virtually required as a condition for entry—had the effect of equating poetry in this period of the earliest stirrings of modernist literary activity with lyric itself in the traditional song mode as it was practiced from the mid–sixteenth century through Wordsworth and Shelley. In the scene of modernism's emergence, the poetry anthology, the mass-culture magazine, and the avant-garde little magazine share a single bias; they make a single demand: that poets write poems of traditional lyric size or not be published.

Palgrave's intention was to shape a lyric canon (a list embodying the rule or measure of literary value: a list for all seasons). So he refused chronological arrangment and he refused entry to living poets, including his inspiration and ghost editor, Tennyson, to whom his book is dedicated. He thought of all poems (he got this from Shelley) "as episodes to that great Poem which all poets, like the cooperating thoughts of one great mind, have built up since the beginning of the world." If a canon is by definition for all seasons it is similarly by definition for all audiences (readers of "all kinds and sorts," as Frost would say). Palgrave's intention was partly to teach those who already love the poets "to love them more," but predominantly it was popular, class-crossing, with a bias toward the working class: to provide "a storehouse of delight to labour and to Poverty," to provide "bet-

ter reading" than what usually fills the "scanty hours" that most
men (who mainly work and do not have time for it) "spend for self-
improvement." As if in the world of capital a "self" were exactly the
sort of thing that one attended to only in leisure time, as if one had no
"self," or held it in abeyance, when one worked the jobs that one
worked if one were one of those referred to under Palgrave's rubric of
"labour and Poverty." Palgrave's aim was to turn such men away from
an exclusive preoccupation with the self-precluding grind of work,
turn them toward the ideal plane of poetry and the "one great mind"
that knows no time—toward poetry's special treasure of selfhood.
Hating the economic, Palgrave yet draws his title metaphor from it—
treasures "more golden than gold" which lead us in "higher and
healthier ways than the world."[4] In so many words, lyric provides
consolation for those scanty hours when we are released from our
unhappy "work." Not insight, then, and not intervention but therapy
for all those impoverished who labor because they must, who inhabit a
world they never made and believe they can never change, and whose
belief is tacitly bolstered by lyric disengagement.

In a passage in his preface which represents considerable antithetical motivation for emergent high-modernist thinking on the lyric,
Palgrave defended his choices by defining lyric as writing by exclusion. No narrative allowed, no intellect at meditation, no description
of local reference, no didacticism, no personal, occasional, or religious
material, no humor (the very antithesis of the "poetical"), no dramatic
textures of blank verse because the speaking voice is alien to song lyric
(a redundancy: Palgrave recognized no dramatic lyric, no Donne, no
Blake); certainly nothing that might show up in a realist novel. No
details of faint smells of beer or of steaks cooking or of cats licking
rancid butter or of dirty fingernails or yellow soles of feet—no details,
in other words, drawn, as T. S. Eliot draws those I've just cited, from
naturalist fiction. Palgrave's effort to define lyric is representative of
mainline Kantian aesthetic and nineteenth-century literary commonplaces about poetry's noble social role. Like Kant's aesthetic mode of
attention, lyric is defined by what it is not, even by its emptiness, by
poems that do not—this is why Palgrave selected them—touch down
on determinate historical terrain, a poetry, in other words, benignly
neglectful of the social space, late nineteenth-century England and

4. Francis Turner Palgrave, Preface to *The Golden Treasury of the Best Songs and Lyrical
Poems in the English Language,* selected and arranged with notes by Palgrave (London:
Macmillan, 1861), n.p.

America, in which it was received. As negative poetic being emptied of the world's interest, lyric discourse turns on the homogeneity of the *isolate,* unmixed feeling: no ironists need apply. So in a very few paragraphs Pound's enemy had managed not only to set forth an idea of lyric sensibility as dissociated sensibility, an idea that virtually every modernist would combat, and in virtually the same terms, but at the same time sounded some of the key notes of the romantic anticapitalism that is worked so deeply through the modernist aesthetic: poetry as an alternative, special kind of discourse whose values are a would-be repudiation and transcendence of Mammon at a powerful moment in the late Victorian life of capital.

Young poets growing up in the United States at the end of the nineteenth century (Pound, Frost, Eliot, and Stevens all fall into the category), in search of models of literary change and innovation, found instead literary models of continuity and repetition. The best-seller power of Palgrave (in the 1860s alone it sold almost 300,000 copies in the United States) must have felt repressive, overwhelmingly so. Palgrave wanted to promote the continuance of the old lyric tradition and had obviously succeeded by reaching exactly the audience he had posited as his aesthetic target—a popular readership eager for the lyric pause that refreshes the long work week: Shakespeare and Herrick at once as escape from labor and labor's worldly gold and as civilizing contact with a transcendent culture, above time, "more golden than gold," which Americans feared they'd never produce. Worse, Palgrave spawned even more continuity by provoking economic competitors and therefore aesthetic imitators in the American scene. F. L. Knowles's *Golden Treasury of American Songs and Lyrics* (1898) saw seven editions in about fifteen years and Jessie Belle Rittenhouse's *Little Book of Modern Verse*—a book Frost hated, featuring a table of contents in 1912 of American poets almost all now unknown—sold a hundred thousand copies in its first edition.

E. C. Stedman's *American Anthology, 1787–1900,* published in 1900, reflects in its title (this is an *American* anthology) and in the first sentence of its introduction ("The reader will comprehend at once that this book was not designed as a Treasury of imperishable American poems") economic and cultural anxiety over the presence of what Stedman calls in the third sentence of his introduction "Palgrave's little classic." And anxiety over Palgrave is just the tip of the iceberg of Stedman's anxiety for American poetry in its capitalist American setting. His introduction is a compendium of issues just barely under the control of expository procedure, a legacy of problems that modern poets would spend careers working at but never through. The books of the popular Fireside poets in their "homiletic mood," as Stedman phrased it, "lay on the center-tables of our households" as tangible manifestation of the success with which they had conceived and played out their roles as cultural ministers of a new society, in moral mediation of English romantic forms: literary counterparts and enforcers of America's most powerful engine of cultural ministration in the nineteenth century, the Protestant clergy. But now, in Stedman's America, the Fireside poets were fast becoming cultural dinosaurs, and their roles of cultural ministry were being usurped by realist writers whose values seemed, in genteel perspective, to be infected by what their narratives were representing—the materialist values of the Gilded Age. The ever-increasing cultural centrality of the realist novel was pushing poetry into a cultural "twilight"; in response to its marginalization poetry should renounce the world of Howells, Twain, and the capitalist devils by resisting all temptations of history (the Civil War, after all, had motivated no "little classics of absolute song"). So the pure aesthetic note needed to be recovered and sounded fullthroatedly; the lyric voice in its vernacular-free universal cast, its origin a world elsewhere, was to be sought, and the historicizing voice in local color, the new voice of prose fiction, with its temporal and regional contamination, was to be negated.[5]

But with the (realist) novelization of literature virtually achieved, could poetry of lyric grace and feeling make any difference, or could it function only as a haven in a dirty world? Was poetry, as Howells argued to Stedman's horror, a dead genre?[6] Could a lyric poet become a professional, lyric letters a means of subsistence? The Fireside elders of the genteel group had made it in the literary marketplace. Moreover, the growth "of American journals, magazines, and the booktrade" clearly coincided, Stedman understood, "with a wider extension of readers than we had before." Fiction writers could now cash in, but could poets do so without compromising their social rejection of Howells's America? "Poets, in spite of the proverb," Stedman wrote, "sing best when fed by wage or inheritance." But poetry was only rarely paying wages, and he, a representative American man of no

5. Edmund Clarence Stedman, Introduction to *An American Anthology, 1787–1900,* ed. Stedman (Boston: Houghton, Mifflin and Co., 1900), pp. xv, xxv, xxvi, xxxi.
6. See Robert J. Scholnick, *Edmund Clarence Stedman* (Boston: Twayne, 1977), p. 105.

inheritance, had turned to Wall Street. Was Stedman the poet, by the terms of a cruel logic, less of a man? His rhetoric tells us that he was uneasy about the answer: "It cannot yet be said of the Parnassian temple, as of the Church," he wrote in response to the phenomenon of the popular American women poets, "that it would have no parishioners, and the service no participants, if it were not for women. The work of their brother poets is not emasculate, and will not be while grace and tenderness fail to make men cowards, and beauty remains the flower of strength." The question that Stedman posed in all but words is: What profits it a man to write a history-free autonomous lyric if he thereby lose his economic viability and so his manhood and his historically honored role in America of cultural ministry—a role that encourages nothing if not acts of social intervention?[7]

POET

Out of a Job

Specialties: incisive speech, sarcasm, meditation, irony, (at special rates), ze grande manair (to order). Will do to travel, or stand unhitched while being fed. Price 1 E per hour. Special rates for steady customers.

In February 1908, after a brief and comically disastrous teaching stint in middle America, Ezra Pound essentially left the United States for good. In February 1910, however, with his first volume of poems, *A Lume Spento*, behind him, and his first American volume, *Provença*, about to be published by a Boston house, he responded to the pressures of his parents to return to Philadelphia, where he might be able to get on without periodically having to hit up his father for loans, where he might get himself located again in the university context for which his graduate training in romance languages and literatures had so well prepared him. Pound was sending his poems to magazines like *Harper's* because in America in 1910 there were no other kinds of magazines to send them to, and they were sending them back. Like Frost, though in somewhat easier financial circumstances—his background was comfortably middle class; his father had indulged his requests to support his literary life—he needed to find a way to sustain himself while pursuing his economically unresponsive first love. Like Frost, he tried to write fiction in the hope of securing his material base. And again like Frost, he was not successful. The advertisement that he had written in Italy and then sent to his father with instructions that he

7. Stedman, Introduction, pp. xxvii, xxviii.

actually place it in a major Philadelphia daily would suggest, in the words of his most recent biographer, "a certain crisis of confidence," with the socially sarcastic tone of the young aesthete's advertisement for himself compromised by the necessities that impinge even on an aesthetic radical as uncompromising as Ezra Pound, whose pun on his own name betrays what was constraining his hopes for a life in art, while forecasting what would become a lifelong obsession with what he imagined as the conspiracies of money: "Price 1 E per hour."[8]

Pound stayed home for about a year, during which time he witnessed the publication of what he regarded as the unethically overpriced American edition of *The Spirit of Romance* and spent much time in New York, where he gathered his thoughts for one of the most decisive pieces of social and literary criticism he would compose, the monograph-length essay whose Italian title, "Patria Mia," reflects at once his attachment and longing and—in his refusal to say it in English—his distance, his alienation.

Pound's divided feelings are expressed in "Patria Mia" in his hopes for what he called an "American *Risorgimento*" and in his savaging of our foremost literary disease, that "appalling fungus" which is the commercial system of magazine publishing and circulation, "dry rot, magazitis." But the stakes in Pound's criticism of America were not primarily literary, because they did not involve only the suppression of all potentially "original" and—Pound's synonym for "original"—all potentially "free" artistic talent. The suppression of idiosyncratic artistic impulse was for him symptomatic of a more general extinguishment in America of all possibilities of human "individuality" (yet another and perhaps Pound's key synonym, via Emerson, for freedom). The tyrant was an economy whose ends were even then, as Pound wrote "Patria Mia," being assured by the chief theorist and technician of capitalist discipline in the early century, Frederic Taylor, and by the process baptized in honor of his time-and-motion studies, "Taylorization," a term that named the method of transforming the factory into a space of maximum efficiency by the manipulation of laborers into mindless mechanisms of repetition, so much the better for producing the standardized products called commodities. This process was reflected in a kind of cultural Taylorization, the planned cultural economy of the big commercial magazines. Laboring subjects so productive at the economic and cultural levels—whether factory

8. John Tytell, *Ezra Pound: The Solitary Volcano* (New York: Doubleday, 1987), p. 58.

workers or writers—are themselves produced, Pound thought (and Charlie Chaplin would concur in *Modern Times*), standardized mediums for the standardized expression of a larger political process whose economic end was necessarily totalitarian—an ironic and unintended conclusion of democracy in capitalist context, in "patria mia."[9]

Writing out of his deepest antiimperialist mood in 1917, Pound saw modern democratic society drifting toward totalitarianism and the violation, as he phrased it in Blakean reminiscence, of "all outlines of personality" and "all human variety" (p. 192). The most shocking evidence he found was culturally ingrained in the Germanic ideal of higher education that unwittingly turned students into "impotent" and "pliable" tools of the state by keeping them ignorant of all connections between the minute particulars of their philological research and the larger process of the social whole within which they carried on their scholarship (p. 193). What is encouraged is a dangerous provincialism, which he thought could lead only to hatred of those outside the province and to the desire to control them. In 1910 in "Patria Mia" Pound believed he could see the drift to political slavery vividly on display in what passed for poetry in the mass-circulation magazines. For if Germanic scholarly ideals, as he came to think, are an educational forerunner of economic Taylorization, then the genteel magazines are its aesthetic realization, the perfection of the cultural division of labor and the poem as commodity: "As the factory owner wants one man to make screws and one man to make wheels and each man in his employ to do some one mechanical thing that he can do almost without the expenditure of thought, so the magazine producer wants one man to provide one element, let us say one sort of story and another articles on Italian cities and above all, nothing personal" (p. 111).

Pound's extended comparison insists on the equivalence of cultural and economic production not in order to make some roughly Marxist point about the determined relations of culture to the economic base of American society (though he does make that point in effect) but in order to decry the economic condition that transforms cultural agents into mindless and selfless producers who turn out poems, articles, and stories as their factory counterparts turn out screws and wheels, virtually without thought, certainly without personality, all in the service

9. Ezra Pound, "Patria Mia," in *Selected Prose, 1909–1965*, ed. with an introduction by William Cookson (New York: New Directions, 1973), pp. 109, 110, 115, 130, hereafter cited in the text.

of the magazine-factory's finished product. The economic setting of capitalist culture, according to Pound, is the index of culture's degradation under capitalism and our severely diminished capacity under such conditions—here Pound's idealism comes ringingly through—to be human. And by "human" Pound means something other than an economic being. The insistent economic profile of culture in capitalist society is the implicit self-condemnation of capitalist society (in Pound's romantic perspective), but the condemnation of capitalism is not, in Pound, issued nostalgically on behalf of some other social context, historically now out of reach, in which it was once presumably easier to be human ("individual") rather than some cog in a machine. It is a criticism of capitalism for what subversion it had done to the promises of democracy in his country.

All who choose to write within the American system of literary circulation, and Pound knew from personal experience that it was hard to choose otherwise, become "part of the system of circulation," its faceless expression, its faceless productive agents. All urges to invention are shut off, he believed, because when writers discover the formulas that pay, they produce those repetitions in the normalized style demanded by the literary system of publication (p. 111). As agents of a mode of literary production Pound thought unimaginable outside capitalism, these poets write the poems of capitalism not by didactically singing its praises but by shaping the discourse of lyric according to the productive ideals of its cultural economy and the captains of lyric industry—Palgrave, Stedman, Knowles, Rittenhouse, and especially R. W. Gilder, R. U. Johnson, and Henry Van Dyke, genteel cultural powers whose names Pound liked to name in 1910, men, as he liked to say, who if not born base were made so by the literary system they worked in. In a capitalist cultural setting, repetition is a permissible and encouraged sort of literary forgery, with no authentic original standing in silent accusation, the mechanical reproductive technique of choice for those editors ultimately responsible for getting out the commodified lyric of the mass-culture magazine.

But in " 'San Zeno' at Verona, one finds columns with the artisan's signature at the base. Thus: *'Me Mateus fecit.'* That is what we have not and can not have where columns are ordered by the gross. And this is a matter of industrial conditions" (p. 107). The signed column at San Zeno bears the artisan's guarantee of social responsibility: his name tells us whom to blame should the column collapse; the signed column is the mark of the artisan's ability to retain his name and face in a society where his desire for creative freedom and personality has a chance to be nurtured. But in the modern economic order, the names and faces of artists are obliterated by the logic of mass production—to standardize, to repeat, and so remove the accidents of personality, so much the better to produce art in its commodity form: not to repress the "unique" personality—Pound was no believer in mute and inglorious Miltons—but to so establish and saturate the conditions of creativity as to eliminate all social spaces that might be hospitable to personality of idiosyncratic imagination.

The commodity form of art is the death of what Pound thought literature essentially to be, the essence of real literature a nonessence, historical contingency itself, always surprising and unpredictable, "something living, something capable of constant transformation and rebirth" (p. 136). A true literary event—Eliot would codify the point in a famous essay—is both a radically original moment and a memory of the history of original moments and their authors: the past that has been transformed and reborn lingering, haunting the new, so forming the central paradox of literary history, the tradition of the modern. What the commodity form of art threatens to remove from the historical stage for the first time—this belief is the source of all critical urgency in Pound—is the avant-garde author himself, who is no contemporary phenomenon but a perpetual possibility, the creative traces of whom Pound spent a lifetime recording and preserving in his essays and in *The Cantos*. The avant-garde author (the exemplary "individual"): not God's gift to society, but a recurring historical phenomenon, motivated by various tyrannizing social contexts, and his best paradoxical example may be Pound himself, whose sensibility is born with specific historical density, or so "Patria Mia" would indicate, as an emerging counterstatement to the society and culture of the commodity which he excoriates.

At its hottest Poundian pitch, literary modernism was and still is (in the guise of postmodernism) *desire for* authentic individuality in literary style and voice—a necessarily harsh critical impulse, directed against the proliferated methods and ideals of mass culture. Literature is "constant transformation," or else. Even yesterday's transformations, when they become hardened—the style of 1880 become a school—are the agents of aesthetic death, the collective loss of memory for readers and writers both. And it was precisely the (Pre-Raphaelite) style of 1880, Pound argued in 1910, that the magazines were beginning to crystallize as a "contemporary" product (pp. 112–

13). The poetic commodification of literary styles of recent origin is a relentless attack on the historical sense, with the history of literary invention relegated to the junk heap of antiquarian interest (that is, an outmoded product). Pound's attack on American magazines with mass circulation is an attack on the packaging of poetic manners and the circulation of literature a la mode. Because of the mass-cultural circumstances of its birth, then, Pound's avant-garde sensibility demands escape from the fashionably contemporary, demands historical quest, research, and preservation.

"Patria Mia" forecasts Pound the poet as patron of poetic styles (the troubadors, the seafarer poet) and of forgotten social heroes (Sigismundo Malatesta) whose values contemporary magazine editors and anthologists cannot peddle as "new." Pound's poetry will become a sort of vocal gallery, a hospitable space for the exhibition of often unsung and always original talents, and Pound himself a tissue of masks. But what he does not become, despite his celebratory reference to what was possible in " 'San Zeno' at Verona," is an escapist longing to recapture some lost golden world. One meaning of Pound's directive to "make it new" is "make it old." Modernism in Pound (a word he never used) is the desire for radical originality, not in order to wipe out history but to recover and join it as a tradition of individual talents now blocked from our contact by the totalitarian present of the commodity.

It is the function of the American millionaire businessman, he wrote in "Patria Mia," to die and leave gifts for the support of artists, so that artists might exempt themselves from "the system of circulation," so that they might, Pound means this literally, be free to experiment (pp. 126–27). The hope for America, as he saw it in 1910, lay not in a revolution against capital but in a utilization of capital which would release writers from the marketplace and the temptation to commodify their art—sell out—by setting alongside the logic of mass production and mass culture an alternative logic of patronage that would nurture the expression of *virtu*, Pound's name for the quality in authorship and writing most absent in the heavily academicized American poetry of 1910: *virtu* as the goal of experiment; *virtu* as the literary expression of individuality (in no two writers is it the same), the basis of an original ("self-reliant") writing and the reason of its persistence; *virtu* as bravery, courage, strength, in a word, the *manliness* that has been obliterated by a feminized culture; that manliness the absence of which explains why literature in America "is left to the care of ladies' societies, and of 'current events' clubs, and is numbered among the 'cultural influences' "—and Pound's quotation marks (a favorite satiric device) around "current events" and "cultural influences" set the contemporary culture business in a perspective of acid (p. 109). *Virtu* as the virtuosity of individual performance, the only virtue Pound would ever recognize until, in his later writing, more than aesthetic virtuosity, *virtu* becomes the basis of a social model (pp. 28–31).

What he did not question in 1910—how much potential virtue would have to be crushed as those American Medicis gathered the financial means to become generous patrons of the virtuous artists—he implicitly questions in his late political writings, where in his new model for society not only artists and powerful capitalists are given the space to find their virtuoso selves. Pound's idea of *The Cantos*—a literary curriculum all by itself, a literary National Gallery in one volume—and his idea of the humane state will become strictly homologous: "A thousand candles together blaze with intense brightness. No one candle's light damages another. So is the liberty of the individual in the ideal and Emersonian state."[10] Except that these sentences were written in Italian in 1942 under the heading "Fascio" and the phrase is actually "ideal and fascist state," the place, Pound imagined, for the better safekeeping of the American dream and the avant-garde writer.

Less than a month after writing John Bartlett from England in November 1913 about his ambition to be a best-selling writer, Frost expressed doubt about his own capacity to bring it off and doubt about the generic suitability of poetry for such a task. In a letter to another old American friend, in which he said, "At most poetry can pave the way for prose and prose may or may not make money," he admitted not having much stomach for the money-making side of writing and that he wasn't, at any rate, all that inclined to prose. In his bad old American days, he told Ernest Silver, he would try prose for two or three days at a time, "having resolved it was the thing for a man with a family to do. But just when I bade fair to produce a novel, right in the middle of chapter three or four I would bring up in another consequential poem. . . . It remains to be seen whether I shall take hold and earn a living as a writer."[11]

Frost's novelistic energies in fact came to some consequence as they

10. Pound, "Fascio," ibid., p. 306.
11. *Selected Letters of Robert Frost*, pp. 102–3, hereafter cited in the text.

got rechanneled into poetic narratives, dialogues, and monlogues, into those longer poems, outside his lyric mode, which dominate his second volume, *North of Boston*, published in 1914, or about a year after uttering his true confessions of econo-poetic need to Bartlett and other friends. Frost returned home in 1915 to find himself famous, still poor, and wondering in a letter written in April of that year what he might have earned, had he freshly in hand, in the moment of his newfound poetic notoriety, those longish *North of Boston* poems ready to be sent off to the very magazines that had routinely rejected him before. "The thought that gets me," he writes, "is that at magazine rates there is about a thousand dollars worth of poetry in N. O. B. that I might have had last winter if the people who love me now had loved me then. Never you doubt that I gave them the chance to love me" (p. 168). Just a few days later in another letter, in more expansively embittered mood, he writes: "These people once my enemies in the editorial offices are trying hard to be my generous friends. Some of them are making hard work of it. Some are making very hard work. . . . Twenty years ago I gave some of these people a chance. I wish I were rich and independent enough to tell them to go to Hell" (p. 171).

Now that he was home, however, and being made such a fuss over "in a country where I had not one [friend] three years ago," he found that he really could get up some stomach for the money-making part of writing: "While the excitement lasts you will see that it would be affectation for me to pretend not to be interested in it. It means nothing or next to nothing to my future poetry" (p. 171). He then adds an after-thought that would predict the scornful highbrow modernist reaction to him, from Pound to the present, while showing how even he, the ordinary man's modern poet, had internalized Pound's avant-garde perspective on the necessary antagonism of mass-cultural values and authentic aesthetic value, the idea of the modern being perhaps unintelligible outside that antagonism of commercial and aesthetic which Pound's critique of the commodifying media of mass culture had brought into such sharp focus. Frost himself would never forget that his first two volumes were brought out by a small London publisher; Frost also had his thoughts about "patria mia." So the new (me too) American excitement over his English success coupled with his interest in his own fame, the pursuit of which would shortly become virtually his vocation as he assumed the role of a tireless and frequent subject of newspaper interviews, as he became the champion if not quite the inventor of the poetry-reading circuit, maybe our first poet in university residence, and most certainly the grand master of the poetry business: all of this, he writes with startling prescience, "means nothing or next to nothing to my future poetry; *it may even hurt that*" (p. 171).

But by June of 1915 all has changed. He tells another correspondent that his "rage has gathered considerable headway," that Ellery Sedgwick, editor of the *Atlantic Monthly,* "has just written me a beautiful letter and sent me fifty-five beautiful dollars for poetry" (p. 179). In August 1915 Frost would make the first of his many appearances in the *Atlantic* with a group of short poems that included "The Road Not Taken," likely his most anthologized poem and therefore, given Frost's broader audience, the most anthologized poem of the important modern American poets. "The Road Not Taken" would become, soon, the lead-off poem of his first American volume, *Mountain Interval* (1916), and would eventually lend its title to all manner of books and articles, including a biography of Frost, a study of U.S. race relations, at least one work of feminist scholarship, a study of U.S. social conditions, an essay that excoriates American literary theorists for not going the way of the Italian Marxist Antonio Gramsci, a proposal for alternatives to prison for nonviolent felons, a biography of an eighteenth-century Jesuit, and an analysis of a crisis in highway repairs and maintenance in Connecticut. The poem is also a chestnut of high school teachers of American literature and a frequent citation on greeting cards of rugged American sentiment. All in all, a veritable American adage, a pithy concentration of our proudest wisdom of self-reliance from Emerson to John Wayne: the very idiom of American desire. Ellery Sedgwick apparently knew what he was doing when he welcomed Frost into the pages of the *Atlantic.* Frost was well on his way to selling books "in their thousands," to standing on his legs "as a poet and nothing else," but not, apparently, to being "a poet for all sorts and kinds."

Frost once said about his basic strategy as a poet in search of mass cultural impact that he would "like to be so subtle at this game as to seem to the casual person altogether obvious,"[12] a remark that decisively clarifies the split between mass and modernist cultural desire which marked the difference of Frost (and Robinson, Lindsay, Masters, and Sandberg) from the company of the high modernists, Ste-

12. Quoted in the Introduction to *Selected Letters,* p. xv.

vens, Pound, and Eliot. For who could ever imagine for Stevens, Pound, and Eliot a "casual" reader who could respond to *The Cantos, Notes toward a Supreme Fiction,* and *The Waste Land* as if they were "altogether obvious"? Frost's desire to reach a mass audience by becoming, among other things, acceptable to mass-circulation magazines like the *Atlantic* shaped his rhetorical literary relations to his imagined ordinary reader. He could become a poet for all kinds but only by favoring the ordinary reader, by fashioning an accessible and seductively inviting literary surface that would welcome the casual reader of poetry (as opposed to the intellectually armed scholar of modernism) while burying very deep the sorts of subtleties that might please those accustomed to Pound's aesthetic caviar. And judging by the reaction to him from high-modernist quarters, Frost buried his subtleties right out of sight. For by choosing to fashion a transparent instead of a forbidding surface he succeeded in telling his highbrow critics that his writing was undergirded by no challenging substance. If obscurity of surface in high-modernist writing has typically been received in standard accounts of modernism as an index to complexity of social analysis, then the fact that the easy Frost *looked* like no modernist poet meant, in modernist context, that he required no effort of engaged reading.

The stylistic difference of Frost and Pound may in some part be a difference in temperment (style is the man), but it is also a historical difference, one conditioned and driven by alternative means of literary production, the difference say of the *Atlantic* and the *Little Review,* an engendering sort of difference, moreover, which conditions and drives alternative means of literary reception—a popular as well as an elite academic canon—and, therefore, alternative accounts of the history of modern American poetry. In 1920 the arguments within modernism in the United States were fully engaged and unresolved, with Conrad Aiken taking the side of Pound, Eliot, and the avant-garde, and Louis Untermeyer taking the side of Frost and the native tradition, the low modernists out of Dickinson and Whitman. Frost's side lost. Our recent chief accounts of modernist poetic history find him anomalous, a poet of the twentieth century but not a truly "modern" poet. Yet if modernism out of Pound means an attack on official genteel poetic culture, then the poet who wickedly links the beautiful with money rather than with poetry (as in "fifty-five beautiful dollars") may be making not only a comment that no modern American (male) poet could be out of sympathy with, since no modern American (male) poet could not but worry about securing the means of his and his family's subsistence; he might also be launching a sneak attack on the airy ideals of conventional accounts of poetry (with a capital letter) and "the beautiful" which had descended to Frost through Stedman and his Victorian forebears.

"The Road Not Taken" might actually be the best example in all of American poetry of a wolf in sheep's clothing, a hard-to-detect subversion of both the principal American myth—that of autonomous selfhood—and the deeply abiding Fireside poetic form within which in this poem Frost chooses to embody his dramatization of cardinal liberal principle and his reflections thereon.

> Two roads diverged in a yellow wood,
> And sorry I could not travel both
> And be one traveler, long I stood
> And looked down one as far as I could
> To where it bent in the undergrowth;
>
> Then took the other, as just as fair,
> And having perhaps the better claim,
> Because it was grassy and wanted wear;
> Though as for that the passing there
> Had worn them really about the same,
>
> And both that morning equally lay
> In leaves no step had trodden black.
> Oh, I kept the first for another day!
> Yet knowing how way leads on to way,
> I doubted if I should ever come back.
>
> I shall be telling this with a sign
> Somewhere ages and ages hence:
> Two roads diverged in a wood, and I—
> I took the one less traveled by,
> And that has made all the difference.[13]

Self-reliance in "The Road Not Taken" is alluringly embodied as the outcome of a story presumably representative of all stories of selfhood, whose central episode is that moment of the turning-point decision, the crisis from which a self springs: a critical decision consolingly, for Frost's American readers, grounded in a rational act when a self and

13. Robert Frost, "The Road Not Taken," from *The Poetry of Robert Frost*, ed. Edward Connery Latham. Copyright 1916, © 1969 by Holt, Rinehart and Winston. Copyright 1944 by Robert Frost. Reprinted by permission of Henry Holt and Company, Inc., Jonathan Cape, and the Estate of Robert Frost.

therefore an entire course of life are autonomously and irreversibly *chosen*. The particular Fireside poetic structure in which Frost incarnates this myth of selfhood is the analogical landscape poem, perhaps most famously executed by William Cullen Bryant in "To a Waterfowl," a poem that Matthew Arnold praised as the finest lyric of the nineteenth century and that Frost had by heart as a child thanks to his mother's enthusiasm.

The analogical landscape poem draws its force from the culturally ancient and pervasive idea of nature as allegorical book, in its American poetic setting a book out of which to draw explicit lessons for the conduct of life (nature as self-help text). In its classic Fireside expression the details of landscape and all natural events are cagily set up for moral summary as they are marched up to the poem's conclusion, like little imagistic lambs to slaughter, for their payoff in uplifting message. Frost appears to recapitulate the tradition in his sketching of the yellow wood and the two roads and in his channeling of the poem's course of events right up to the portentous colon ("Somewhere ages and ages hence:") beyond which lies the wisdom that we jot down and take home:

> Two roads diverged in a wood, and I—
> I took the one less traveled by,
> And that has made all the difference.

If we couple such tradition-bound thematic structure with Frost's more or less conventional handling of metric, stanzaic form and rhyme scheme, then we have reason enough for Ellery Sedgwick's acceptance of this poem for the *Atlantic:* no "caviare to the crowd" here.

And yet Frost has played a subtle game in an effort to have it both ways. In order to satisfy the *Atlantic* and its readers he hews closely to the requirements of popular genre writing and its mode of poetic production, the mass-circulation magazine, but at the same time he has more than a little undermined what that mode facilitates in the realm of American poetic and political ideals. There must be two roads and they must, of course, be different if the choice of one over the other is to make a rational difference ("And that has made all the difference"). But the key fact, that on that particular morning when the choice was made the two roads looked "about the same," makes it difficult to understand how the choice could be rationally grounded on (the poem's key word) perceptible, objective "difference." The allegorical "way" has been chosen, a self has been forever made, but not because a text has been "read" and the "way" of nonconformity courageously, ruggedly chosen. The fact is that there is no text to be read because reading requires a differentiation of signs and on that morning clear signifying differences were obliterated. Frost's delivery of this unpleasant news has long been difficult for his readers to hear because he cunningly throws it away in a syntax of subordination that drifts out of thematic focus. The unpleasant news is hard to hear, in addition, because Fireside form demands, and therefore creates the expectation of, readable textual differences in the book of nature. Frost's heavy investment in traditional structure virtually assures that Fireside literary form will override and cover its mischievous handling in this poem.

For a self to be reliant, decisive, nonconformist, there must *already* be an autonomous self out of which to propel decision. But what was choice propelled out of on that fateful morning? Frost's speaker does not choose out of some rational capacity; he prefers, in fact, not to choose at all. That is why he can admit to what no self-respecting self-reliant self can admit to: that he is "sorry" he "could not travel both / And be one traveler." The good American ending, the last three lines of the poem, is prefaced by two lines of storytelling self-consciousness in which the speaker, speaking in the *present* to a listener (reader) to whom he has just conveyed "this," his story of the *past*—everything preceding the last stanza—in effect tells his auditor that in some unspecified *future* he will tell it otherwise, to some gullible audience, tell it the way they want to hear it, as a fiction of autonomous intention.

The strongly sententious, yet ironic last stanza in effect predicts the happy American construction "The Road Not Taken" has been traditionally understood to endorse, predicts, in other words, what the poem will be sentimentally made into, but from a place in the poem that its *Atlantic Monthly* reading, as it were, will never touch. The power of the last stanza within the Fireside teleology of analogical landscape assures Frost his popular audience while, for those who get his game—some member, say, of a different audience, versed in the avant-garde little magazines and in the treacheries of irony and the impulse of the individual talent trying, as Pound urged, to "make it new" against the literary and social American grain—for *that* reader, this poem tells a different tale: that our life-shaping choices are irrational, that we are fundamentally out of control. This is the fabled "wisdom" of Frost which he hides in a moralizing statement asserting the consoling contrary of what he knows.

In the American situation for poetry in 1915, when "The Road Not Taken" was published, Frost's poem is a critical expression (that manages for a few readers to have it both ways) from out of the very production quarters (the mass-circulation magazine) that Pound condemned, and in so condemning launched modern poetry. The poem is an instance, famous at that, of what mass-cultural media demanded from American poets and simultaneously what Frost, like Pound, wanted to say against that mode (its editors, after all, were also his enemies as he struggled to be heard through his twenties and thirties), a savage little undoing of our mainline literary and political sentiments. So "The Road Not Taken" is an internalization of the very opposition within the mode of poetic production—mass or avant-garde little magazine?—which was, in 1915, becoming the sign of the modern.

But over the years "The Road Not Taken" has attested to the power of convention to withstand those who would subvert from within. It remains a famous poem, one of the "best loved of the American people," not for its irony but for the sentiments that make its irony hard to see. Frost wanted to be a poet for all kinds, but he mainly failed. He is the least respected of the moderns. Pound wanted a few fit readers, and he got them. Thus far, the alternative means of literary publication in American culture prohibit in either direction crossover poetic careers because they engender two different and mutually hostile readerships.

Contributors

John Barrell is Professor of English at the University of Sussex. His most recent books are *The Birth of Pandora and Other Essays* (1991) and *The Infection of Thomas De Quincey* (1991).

Catherine Gallagher is Professor of English at the University of California, Berkeley. She is author of *The Industrial Reformation of English Fiction* (1985), and is currently writing a book on British women authors and the literary marketplace from the Restoration through the eighteenth century.

Frank Lentricchia is Katherine Everett Gilbert Professor of English at Duke University. He is best known for *After the New Criticism, Criticism and Social Change*, and *Ariel and the Police*. He is also the editor of The Wisconsin Project on American Writers, and of *Introducing Don DeLillo*.

Marjorie Levinson, Professor of English at the University of Pennsylvania, is the author of *The Romantic Fragment Poem* (1986), *Wordsworth's Great Period Poems* (1986), and *Keats's Life of Allegory* (1988). The collection *Rethinking Historicism* (Levinson et al.) appeared in 1989. She is currently studying Hardy's poetry and practices of negation in Romantic, modern, and postmodern writing. During the period 1991–94, she will be visiting Professor at the University of Michigan.

Colin MacCabe is Director of Education at the British Film Institute and Professor of English at the University of Pittsburgh. His books include

James Joyce and the Revolution of the Word (1978) and *Theoretical Essays: Film, Linguistics, Literature* (1985).

Mary Poovey is Professor of English at The Johns Hopkins University. She is the author of *The Proper Lady and the Woman Writer: Ideology as Style in the Works of Mary Wollstonecraft, Mary Shelley and Jane Austen* (1984) and *Uneven Developments: The Ideological Work of Gender in Mid-Victorian England* (1988).

David Simpson is Professor of English at the University of Colorado, Boulder. He is currently finishing a book titled *Romanticism, Nationalism, and the Revolt Against Theory.*

R. Jackson Wilson is the author of *In Quest of Community: Social Philosophy in the United States, 1820–1860,* and *Figures of Speech: American Writers and the Literary Marketplace from Benjamin Franklin to Emily Dickinson.* He has taught at Arizona and Wisconsin, and is presently Professor of History at Smith College.

Index

Adorno, Theodor, 8, 14–16, 31, 44–46, 154, 183–84, 186–87
Agency. *See* Subjectivity
Alison, Archibald, 93
Allen, Gay Wilson, 126–27, 137
Althusser, Louis, 8–9, 16, 19–22, 26, 183
Anderson, Perry, 19
Austen, Jane, 12
Author: concept of, 23–24, 34–46

Bakhtin, Mikhail, 156, 164–65
Barrell, John, 28, 94, 139
Barrett, Michèle, 182–83
Barthes, Roland, 24, 34–35, 37–39, 43
Bate, Walter J., 144, 147
Baudelaire, Charles, 43–46, 186
Baudrillard, Jean, 158
Bayley, John, 144, 150–51
Beckett, Samuel, 38
Benjamin, Walter, 14–17, 22, 26, 28, 31, 43–46, 186–87
Bentham, Jeremy, 91–92
Berthoff, Warner, 130
Bewell, Alan, 143
Braudel, Fernand, 23
Bryant, William Cullen, 194, 214

Burke, Kenneth, 138, 193–94
Byron, George Gordon, Lord, 145–47, 149–50, 157–62, 185

Cabot, James Elliot, 124, 126
Cahiers du cinéma, 38–40, 42
Callinicos, Alex, 4, 26
Career: topic of, 25–27, 30, 124–62, 191–216
Carlyle, Thomas, 67, 130–31
Chadwick, Edwin, 28, 65–83
Chandler, James, 170
Chartism, 78–79
Chase, Stuart, 137–38
Chatterton, Thomas, 150–52
Class: paradigm of, 1–3, 5, 68–83, 143–62, 179–96
Cohen, Walter, 13
Coleridge, Samuel Taylor, 130–31, 149, 154, 172, 174–75
Colquhoun, Patrick, 86, 110, 112
Commodification, 62–64
Copyright, 36
Corrigan, Philip, 65
Cullen, Michael, 68, 71

Davidoff, Leonore, 77

Deconstruction, 5, 163
de Lauretis, Teresa, 3
De Man, Paul, 142
Derrida, Jacques, 25, 35–36, 38, 142
Dews, Peter, 5
Dickens, Charles, 27–28, 47–64, 67
Discourse: paradigm of, 4, 92–118, 186
D'Israeli, Isaac, 188–89
Division of labor, 84–118, 204–5
Document: and 'text,' 141–42
Domesticity, 68–83

Eagleton, Terry, 14, 21
Economic determination, 119–42, 187–
    88, 191–216
Eliot, T. S., 197–98, 200, 207, 212
Elwin, Rev. Whitwell, 70–71
Emerson, Ralph Waldo, 26–27, 119–42
Encyclopedias: eighteenth-century il-
    lustrations in, 98, 109
Engels, Friedrich, 6

Feltes, N. N., 29
Feminist criticism, 6, 8, 25
Film: authoring of, 34–46
Finer, S. E., 66–68
Finney, Claude Lee, 154–55
Flinn, M. W., 66–67, 70
Foucault, Michel, 4–5, 13–14, 22–24,
    38, 182–83
Frost, Robert, 26–27, 191–96, 209–16

Gallagher, Catherine, 27–28, 51
Gavin, Hector, 71–72, 74
Geertz, Clifford, 12–14, 187
Gender, 1–3, 25, 69–70, 76–83, 155–62,
    180–81, 202–3, 208–9
Gilpin, William, 92–95, 97, 99, 101,
    112–13
Godard, Jean-Luc, 37, 39
Godwin, William, 169–71, 175–76,
    184–85
Goldmann, Lucien, 8
Greenblatt, Stephen, 13
Guillory, John, 26
Gypsies: in painting, 113–14

Hall, Catherine, 77
Hamlin, Christopher, 59
Haraway, Donna, 20

Harlan, David, 141
Hawks, Howard, 39
Heath, Stephen, 40
Hovey, Richard, 194
Howard, Dr. Baron, 74–75
Hunt, Leigh, 155
Hunt, Lynn, 2

Ideology, 1–3, 182–90

Jameson, Fredric, 11, 20
Jung, Carl, 45

Kant, Immanuel, 200–201
Keats, John, 26–27, 143–62
Kingsley, Charles, 60
Knight, Richard Payne, 92
Kramer, Lloyd, 2

Lentricchia, Frank, 23, 26, 165
Levinson, Marjorie, 26, 143, 165, 178
Locke, John, 168–69
Lukács, Georg, 8, 16, 18, 22, 179

MacCabe, Colin, 28–29, 31, 42, 186
McGann, Jerome, 156–57, 178
Macherey, Pierre, 21–23
Macmillan Company, 197
Malthus, Thomas, 49–52
Mandeville, Bernard, 89–90
Mann, Horace, 71
Marcus, Steven, 162
Marx, Karl, 22–23, 25, 43, 84–85
Marxism, 7–12, 22–26, 32, 163–65,
    179–90
Materialism, 5–33, 43–46, 116–18, 133–
    34, 180–90
Mayhew, Henry, 72, 75
Mill, John Stuart, 8, 67
Milton, John, 36
Modernism, 191–216
Montagu, Basil, 175–76, 178, 180
Moorman, Mary, 173, 175
More, Hannah, 182
Morland, George, 95, 104, 109, 112

Nietzsche, Friedrich, 22–23, 25, 29, 37

Opie, Amelia, 171

Palgrave, Francis Turner, 197–201, 206
Pecora, Vincent, 12
Picturesque, the, 92–118
Poovey, Mary, 28, 76
Postmodernism, 10–12
Poststructuralism, 9
Pound, Ezra, 26–27, 191–216
Pyne, William, 28, 84–118

Reader reception, 177–78
Ricardo, David, 52
Ricks, Christopher, 144, 148
Ross, Andrew, 10
Rousseau, Jean Jacques, 169–71, 175–
    76, 181, 184–85
Rusk, Ralph, 126–27
Ruskin, John, 47–56

Said, Edward, 12, 31
Sayer, Derek, 65
Screen magazine, 40–41
Sedgwick, Ellery, 211, 214
Shakespeare, William, 36, 171
Shelley, Percy Bysshe, 148–49, 199
Simmel, Georg, 45
Simpson, David, 17–18, 24, 113, 117–
    18, 141, 167, 178
Situationists, 37
Slaney, Robert A., 68
Smith, Adam, 51–52, 86–87, 89–90
Smith, Paul, 182–83

Spivak, Gayatri, 12
Stallybrass, Peter, 77–78
Stedman, E. C., 201–3, 206, 213
Stedman Jones, Gareth, 2, 79
Subjectivity, 3–4, 23–30, 34–46, 171,
    177, 180–90, 195–96, 213–16

Taylorization, 204–5
Thelwall, John, 171–74, 177, 179–80,
    185
Totality, 10–12, 18–20, 31–33, 43–46,
    117–18
Truffaut, François, 39

Valéry, Paul, 153–54
Veeser, H. Aram, 13
Vendler, Helen, 144

Watercolor: status of in the eighteenth
    century, 96–99
Welles, Orson, 40
Welsh, Alexander, 70
White, Allon, 77–78
Widdowson, Peter, 29
Williams, Raymond, 8, 33, 36, 163
Wilson, R. Jackson, 26, 123
Wordsworth, William, 16–18, 27, 130–
    31, 149, 151, 157–58, 160–90, 199

Yeats, W. B., 191–92

Library of Congress Cataloging-in-Publication Data

Subject to history: ideology, class, gender / edited by David
    Simpson.
        p.   cm.
Based on papers presented at a conference held at the University
    of Colorado, Boulder, in March–April 1988,
        Includes bibliographical references and index.
        ISBN 0-8014-2561-1 (alk. paper).—ISBN 0-8014-9791-4 (pbk.:
    alk. paper)
        1. English literature—History and criticism—Congresses.
    2. American literature—History and criticism—Congresses.
    3. Literature and history—Congresses.   4. Historical materialism—
    Congresses.   I. Simpson, David, 1951– .
    PR7.S83 1991
    809—dc20   91-13592